This highly readable handbook is the clearest and most up-to-date analysis of the American population available. It provides for the first time *in one book* information on the American population that is absolutely essential for those interested in all aspects of the social sciences as they apply to American life.

Unless we can accurately forecast the many features of our population, and thus plan some degree of prevention or cure, we face the prospect of crucial social problems becoming more and more threatening because of the numbers and kinds of people we are. *Population and People* clarifies the major elements and trends of our population, and offers indispensable information and analysis.

Using the science of demography and the world population situation as a framework, Mr. Stockwell describes the six key elements of population: mortality, fertility, and migration (the basic processes of population change), and population size, composition, and distribution (the major variables which affect our political and economic realities). In each area, the author discusses major trends and the "causes" of these trends, with major attention to such problems as poverty, race, birth control, urban congestion, and air pollution, all of which are directly connected to our population patterns.

PROBLEMS OF AMERICAN SOCIETY
Bernard Rosenberg, General Editor

Population and People

Population and People

EDWARD G. STOCKWELL

Quadrangle Books | *Chicago*

For JANET, *and our own more immediate "population problems":* TED, CHRIS, *and* SUSIE . . .

Preface

This is a book about the population of the United States. Its purpose is to describe the more basic facts about that population today (what it is, how it got that way, what factors are influencing current trends, what problems it has created or is creating, and so on). My firm conviction is that a knowledge of the objective demographic status of any population—its size, the characteristics of its members, its distribution in space, and its patterns of growth and change—is a fundamental prerequisite to understanding the various social problems confronting that population. Limitations of space have naturally precluded a discussion of all relevant topics. Moreover, it has not been possible to give more than brief consideration to those few topics that have been covered. Nevertheless, I hope there is enough here to accomplish three objectives: (1) to acquaint the reader with the most significant population trends in the United States; (2) to give him an appreciation of the very close relationship between population trends and a wide variety of problems which the society must face; and (3), most important, to stimulate the reader to pursue the various topics more thoroughly on his own. To this end, suggestions for further reading will be found at the end of each chapter.

As with any undertaking of this sort, the ultimate product reflects the contributions of many more persons than the one listed on the title page. Indirectly, I owe an immeasurable debt to my many teachers (most notably to Professors Vincent H. Whitney and Sidney Goldstein) and to numerous other scholars and scientists whose earlier works helped prepare me to write this book. Although it is not possible to cite every article or book I have read on the broad subject of population, I have tried, when appropriate, to acknowledge specifically those references on which I have relied most heavily.

More direct assistance has been rendered by several of my colleagues who were kind enough to read and comment on all or parts of earlier drafts of the manuscript. Although I did not always follow their suggestions, I do want to express my sincere appreciation to the following persons: Robert G. Burnight, Lincoln H. Day, Harold F. Goldsmith, H. Theodore Groat, Walter C. McKain, and Charles B. Nam. A special acknowledgment is due Dr. D. Y. Yuan, who was not only instrumental in getting me to undertake the writing of this book but who also contributed many helpful suggestions of content—notably in Chapters 4 and 7. Needless to add, final responsibility for any errors or inadequacies in the text rests solely with the author.

I am also indebted to the College of Agriculture Experiment Station of the University of Connecticut for providing an atmosphere particularly favorable to the pursuit of academic achievement—and for providing the time with which much of the book was written.

Finally, my thanks to Miss Carol McBurney, who bore the largest burden of typing and retyping the many drafts of the manuscript.

EDWARD G. STOCKWELL

Storrs, Connecticut, 1967

Contents

Population and People

1

Introduction

RECENT WORLD POPULATION TRENDS

During the years since the end of the Second World War, population problems have increasingly become a matter for public debate and discussion. The reason for this lies in the sharp rise in the rate of population growth and the concomitant tremendous increase in the number of people living in the world. In 1965 there were half again as many people living on this planet as there had been before World War II, and the population was increasing at a rate of 2 per cent a year—a rate that would lead to a doubling of numbers in about thirty-five years.

The causes of the current world "population explosion" are not difficult to comprehend. Two or three decades ago human survival was an extremely touch-and-go affair in many parts of the world. Hunger and disease were widespread throughout most of Asia, Africa, and Latin America, and death rates were very high. In many cases, the average length of life for a man was only thirty-five or forty years—in some cases even less. It was not at all uncommon to find situations in these areas of the world where from 20 to 30 per cent of all newborn infants died before they were a year old. In the face of such high death rates, and especially because of the low probability of surviving infancy, it was "necessary" to have a very high birth rate. If the high death rate was not balanced by a high birth rate, the population in question would quickly have passed out of existence. As a consequence, many aspects of society in Asia, Africa, and Latin America have traditionally been structured so as to encourage maximum fertility (women were accorded status only by virtue of their being mothers; a man's prestige among his peers was often determined by the number of sons he had sired; in primitive familistic societies, economic and political strength was determined by the size of the family; religious doctrines extolled the virtues of childbearing and tended to condemn any form of birth control; economic security in one's old age could be insured only by having children to provide support; and so on). But the worldwide war on poverty, hunger, and disease during the postwar years has done much to alter this situation. Efforts of the Food and Agricultural Organization and the World Health Organization of the United Nations—not to mention the variety of programs sponsored by individual national governments and a myriad of private organizations—have been most successful in curbing famine and disease throughout the world. By so doing, they have helped to bring about drastic reductions in the death rate.

The widespread reductions in the death rate in recent years have not been accompanied by any semblance of a decline in birth rates. Although people have generally been receptive to health improvement programs and have been eager to adopt practices that would enable them to postpone dying, they have been much more reluctant to alter the many structural features of the society that might encourage a reduction in the birth rate. In contrast to death, which has always been more or less regarded as a necessary "evil," birth has been fairly universally regarded as a "good." Whereas people are anxious to avoid evil, they will go out of their way to achieve what society regards as good. Thus birth rates have tended to remain at the same high levels that have historically been functionally necessary for the survival of the species. This means that where once there were three to four deaths for every four to five births, there are now, in the postwar period, one to two deaths for every four to five births. As a result, world population is today undergoing an unprecedented rate of increase.

Regardless of whether or not the "population bomb" represents a greater threat to the peace and security of mankind than the hydrogen bomb (and more and more writers and scholars are beginning to regard this assertion as valid), the inescapable fact is that the rapid and accelerating rate of population growth in recent years has created an extremely dangerous situation in many parts of the world. Ironic as it may seem, the greatest numerical growth in the world today is taking place in those poverty-stricken underdeveloped countries that can least afford it. These nations have only recently emerged from an economically primitive stage and are just now starting out on the long, hard road to modernization. To the extent that population growth continues to be rapid, it will act as a major obstacle to economic development. Where population is growing rapidly, it means that a larger share of the national income must be diverted away from productive investment and directed toward the support of the added numbers; and in this way, too rapid population growth retards efforts to improve the lot of the underprivileged millions now living in Asia, Africa, and Latin America. In other words, we face a situation in which the poorer nations of the world are struggling valiantly to raise their standards of living, but in many cases their efforts are being frustrated by continued rapid population growth which offsets potential economic gains.

The question we must now face is, what will happen during the years to come if the underdeveloped nations of the world continue to encounter such frustrations in their efforts to improve their lot? While the future cannot be predicted with any certainty, it is hard to visualize continued failure in this struggle leading to anything but even greater international tensions than those which already exist in the world. It is the growing awareness of the seriousness of this population problem that lies behind the now heightened public discussion of causes and consequences of, and possible solutions to, the world population explosion. Whether or not this discussion will bear fruit in terms of workable and acceptable solutions to the many problems associated with world population growth trends, however, is something that remains to be seen. In the meantime, we can only hope—and draw some encouragement from the fact that more and more people (and nations) are at last becoming aware of the problems that exist and are working toward their solution.

POPULATION AS A PROBLEM IN THE UNITED STATES

While the magnitude of the current world population crisis cannot be overemphasized, it should not obscure the fact that one of the greatest population explosions during the past two or three decades has taken place right here in the United States. When the first federal census was taken in 1790, the population of the United States numbered less than 4 million. It was nearly 180 million in 1960, and by the middle of the decade there were roughly 195 million people living in this country. In the relatively short time since its formation as a nation, the United States has grown from a population of a few million to one of several hundred million, and has come to be the fourth most populous nation in the world (exceeded only by China, India, and the Soviet Union). Moreover, as of 1965 the United States was characterized by an annual growth rate of approximately 1.2 per cent and was adding close to 2.5 million persons each year. The entire history of mankind records no other population having grown to such a size and at such a rate over such a relatively short period of time.

Population is never stationary but is always in a continuous state of change. The extent and direction of population change are in large part determined by other social, economic, or political aspects of society. In primitive agrarian societies, for example, a poor crop year will lead to population decline either because some people will move away to seek greener pastures, or because the resulting food shortage will influence a rise in the death rate. Conversely, a good crop year will lead to a population increase both because people are more likely to marry and have children, and because those children that are born will be less likely to succumb to an early death because of malnutrition or some related disease. On a higher cultural level, the social, economic, and political determinants of population trends and changes can be illustrated by such things as (a) the vast numbers of people who have left Europe and come to the United States in search of freedom of thought and expression; (b) the rapid populating of the American West after the discovery of gold in the middle of the nineteenth century; (c) the historical decline of the birth rate in the Western world as cultural values shifted from an emphasis on the group to an emphasis on the welfare and development of the individual; and (d) the particularly sharp reduction of the birth rate in the United States (and in many countries of western Europe as well) during the depression years immediately preceding the Second World War. More recently, one can see in the United States such things as (e) the tendency for migration to flow from areas of low employment opportunities (for example, farm areas) to areas where jobs are more plentiful (such as urban industrial centers); (f) the existence of an inverse relationship between economic status and death rates; and (g) the tendency for birth rates to vary among religious groups according to doctrinal differences regarding the moral rightness or wrongness of deliberately limiting fertility through the use of contraceptive devices.

Of more importance, perhaps (certainly not lesser), is the converse of the preceding—the fact that population trends are often a major factor influencing changes in these other aspects of society. For example, it has long been a recognized *sociological* fact that the need for laws and other formalized mechanisms of social control increases in direct proportion to population size. Similarly, it has long been a recognized *economic* fact that, in a given environment with a given level of technology, population increase will result in an increase in per capita productivity until an optimum point is reached, after which the "law of diminishing returns" begins to operate. Finally, a good example of the extent to which population trends may have a *political* influence is provided by developments in Japan following her defeat in World War II: in this case high birth rates, rapid population growth, and an intensification of the pressure of numbers on a limited land space all combined to bring about the legalization of abortion as a method of birth control in this traditionally strong familistic society. Still other illustrations of how population trends may influence national policy are provided by such post–World War II developments as (a) the erection of the Berlin Wall in an effort to stem the tide of refugees fleeing from East to West Germany; (b) the conclusion of an agreement between the government of the overpopulated Netherlands and underpopulated Canada to effect an exchange of population between the two countries; and (c) the recent extension of federal programs for the elderly in the United States as a response to growing numbers and proportion of older persons in the population.

The implication of the preceding examples is that as long as the changes being influenced by population trends are compatible with the basic values, organization, and goals of a society, then population will not be viewed as a problem. Population becomes a "problem" only when it is regarded as a threat to the established order or the overall well-being of a people. In this regard, then, it may strike some people as absurd to talk about "population problems" in the United States. After all, was it not the rapid growth of the population during the nineteenth century that greatly facilitated our industrial development and led to the emergence of the United States as one of the richest and most powerful nations in the world? Moreover, was not the population of the United States at mid-century living at a level of comfort and well-being unknown anywhere else in the world (in spite of a rapid rate of population growth)? And has not one of our major problems long been how to handle and dispose of vast surpluses of food? Yes, but such questions fail to consider that America today is vastly different from the America of the nineteenth century. Moreover, food does not and should not represent the only criterion in evaluating the well-being of a population. There are also such concerns as the adequacy of school and college facilities, housing, public utilities, employment opportunities, hospitals, and a myriad of other services; and the present rapid rate of population growth is daily putting more and more pressure on the ability of such services to meet the needs of the people.

Those who question the existence of a population "problem" in the United States also ignore the question of aesthetics. Given that the land area of our country is finite, long-range prognosticators point out that the increase in leisure time resulting from technological progress creates a greater need and demand for parks, wilderness areas, beaches, and other open spaces for recreational purposes. Then they ask how such open spaces can be provided where the amount of land remains constant but where population continues to increase. Instead of city parks they foresee city parking lots; instead of acres of meadow and rolling hills, acres of high-rise apartments; and instead of quiet stretches of sandy beach, bustling desalinization and seaweed conversion plants. Considerations such as these justify looking at population growth in the United States with a somewhat more critical eye: maybe it does not represent as serious a problem as some people think, but it is certainly not necessarily such a "good thing" as the traditional view would hold.

While the rate of growth and the increase in numbers generally represent the most dramatic aspects of the population problem, they do not encompass all of them. On the contrary, many problems of population are entirely unrelated to size or rate of growth. Populations consist of much more than specified numbers of people. Rather, they consist of numbers of people who are dispersed over a varied land area and who possess very different characteristics; who must contend with a variety of different problems, many of which are determined by the nature of the area in which they live or the particular characteristics that they possess. People who live in large urban centers along the eastern seaboard face vastly different problems than the farmers of the plains states; Negroes face certain problems simply because they are Negroes, regardless of where they live; problems of youth differ from problems of old age, and so on. It follows that as the proportion of the population living in particular areas or possessing particular characteristics changes, then their unique problems become recognized as more general problems of the society as a whole. To take a recent illustration, the continued rapid increase in the number and proportion of the United States population living in cities has intensified national awareness of the problems of urban life to such an extent that the mid-1960's saw the creation of a cabinet position in the executive branch of the government (Housing and Urban Development) to concentrate on solving the problems of contemporary urban society. Other recent developments that illustrate this phenomenon include the creation of Medicare legislation as a response to the increase in the number and proportion of older persons in the population; the establishment of the Job Corps and other programs to retrain persons who have been displaced from their traditional occupation through increased automation; and the passage of more and stronger civil rights legislation as a growing Negro population (championed by a sizable, voluble, action-oriented youth group that has come to represent a major portion of the national population) has let it be known that a substantial segment of the society does not have an equal share in the general affluence characterizing mid-century America.

But even adding distribution and composition to the major variable of size will not indicate all of the dimensions of the population problem. Population size, distribution, and composition are not constant. On the contrary, they are in a continuous state of change; and the *processes* through which population change is brought about (fertility, mortality, and migration) are another side of the population issue. For example, although the United States as a whole has one of the lowest death rates in the world today, several groups within the population have death rates substantially higher than those of other groups. Similarly, although modern techniques of contraception today make it possible for married couples to determine with reasonable success how many children they will have and when they will have them, many groups in the society do not have access to these techniques (in some cases are not even aware of their existence). Year after year these people continue to have many more children than they want to have or are capable of supporting at a decent level of living.

On the basis of the preceding discussion, there are at least two ways in which population can be viewed as a "problem" in the United States today. First, many of the major social issues and problems that we face today (or will face tomorrow) have been directly influenced by trends in the size, composition, and distribution of the population. Second, although the United States as a whole may be one of the "healthiest, wealthiest, and wisest" nations in the world, there are marked differences throughout our population in the extent to which the good things of our society are shared equally by all members. Such inequalities within a nation that has for so long stood as a champion of freedom, justice, and equality for all men certainly indicates the existence of a problem.

A fundamental prerequisite for adequately understanding contemporary American society and the problems with which it must contend, both now and in the future, is a thorough knowledge of the population situation. This knowledge can best be imparted within the general framework of the science of *demography*. Although some idea as to what this discipline is all about may be gained from the preceding discussion, a more detailed statement is desirable. Hence the following section is concerned with the nature of demography and the general demographic frame of reference.

THE FRAMEWORK OF DEMOGRAPHY

The word "demography" comes from the Greek words *demos,* meaning people or populace, and *graphy,* a combining form meaning "the writing of" and used to denote either the art of writing and describing, or a branch of learning descriptively treated. In the broadest sense, then, demography may be defined as the science that deals with the description of human populations. More specifically, when he looks at the population of any given area, the objectives of the *demographer* (one whose vocation is the study of population) consist essentially of finding answers to three basic questions:

(1) How many people are there in the area? (*Population Size*)
(2) What traits and characteristics do the people in the area possess? (*Population Composition*)
(3) Where are the people located within the area? (*Population Distribution*)

These three aspects of population—size, composition, and distribution—are the *major demographic variables,* and they constitute the fundamental subject matter of the science of demography. On this basis, then, one can formulate an initial definition of demography as *the science that is concerned with ascertaining the size, composition, and distribution of the population in any given area of human habitation.*

Although this definition indicates in rough outline the basic dimensions of the science of demography, it is far from complete and adequate. The interests of the demographer go beyond the mere description of specific facts about a population at one point in time (*population statics*): he is also interested in seeing whether or not these three basic demographic variables are changing, and if so, the nature and extent of the changes taking place (*population dynamics*). Is the number of people in the population increasing, remaining relatively stable, or decreasing? If the population is increasing or decreasing in size, how rapidly is this change taking place? Is the population becoming younger, or is the average age of the inhabitants rising? Is the number of men relative to the number of women at the marriageable ages changing, and if so, in what direction is it changing? What is the trend with regard to the proportion of the population that resides in large urban centers as opposed to the proportion living on scattered farms, and how rapidly is this trend progressing? These and many other similar questions are in the back of his mind when the demographer undertakes a study of the population in any given area.

In addition to observing and measuring the nature and extent of any changes that may be taking place in the major demographic variables of population size, composition, and distribution, the demographer is also interested in the means by which such changes are being achieved. When he observes, for example, that a population is increasing in size or that the pattern of its distribution in space is changing, he is interested in knowing what factors are operating to produce these changes. Demographically speaking, there are only three ways in which any population can change: (1) people can be born into it (*fertility*); (2) people can leave it by dying (*mortality*); and (3) people can move into or out of the area of habitation (*migration*). These three variables—fertility, mortality, and migration—are known as the *basic demographic processes,* and it is through the operation of these processes that changes in population size, composition, and distribution take place. Thus, when the demographer observes, for example, that the size of the population in a given area is increasing, he is interested in knowing if this increase is due to an excess of births over deaths, to a greater number of people moving in than out of the area, or to some combination of these two processes. Similarly, if he sees that the population is becoming younger, he is interested in knowing if this is because there has been an increase in the number of births, or because large numbers of young people have moved into the area (or older people have moved out). Finally, if he notes that the spatial arrangement of the population within the area is shifting, the demographer seeks to determine whether this is being caused by people moving into or out of different regions within the area, or if it is due to significant differences among the various parts of the area with respect to levels of fertility and mortality.

We can now elaborate on the initial definition of demography as the science that is concerned with describing the size, composition, and distribution of human populations. Based on the preceding paragraphs, demography may now be defined more completely as the science that is concerned with ascertaining (1) the size, composition, and distribution of the population in any given area of human habitation; (2) changes that have occurred or are occurring in these three major demographic variables; and (3) the processes—or the trends with regard to fertility, mortality, and migration—by means of which such changes have been or are being achieved.

Conceived in the narrow sense, demography is largely a methodological science that deals with the statistical description of population phenomena. In the broader sense, however, it also involves the explanation and analysis of observed population facts. In this respect, it is convenient to distinguish between the narrow realm of pure or formal demography and the broader area of general population study. In general, the term *formal demography* is reserved for the purely *quantitative* aspects of population study, and is used primarily to refer to the *statistical* description of population trends and characteristics. *General population study,* on the other hand, is largely *interpretive* and is concerned with understanding the underlying determinants and consequences of these trends and characteristics.

Formal demography entails such things as the computation of birth, death, and migration rates and the statistical description of how these processes, and changes in these processes over time, affect the major demographic variables of population size, composition, and distribution. What are the current trends with respect to levels of fertility and mortality, and what influences will these trends have (or have they had) on the rate of population growth? What are the characteristics of persons moving into or out of an area, and how is this pattern of migration affecting the composition of the population in that area? What differences exist among various parts of an area with respect to the balance between births and deaths (or with respect to the balance between in- and out-migration), and to what extent are such differences operating to bring about a redistribution of the population within the area? Answering such questions requires the statistical manipulation of population data, and such statistical manipulation is the core of formal demography.

As already noted, however, the demographer is not solely interested in statistical description. He is not interested, for example, in noting merely that a sudden rise in the birth rate has caused an increase of such-and-such magnitude in the rate of population growth in one area, or that the out-migration of young people has contributed to a decline of such-and-such magnitude in the size of the population in another area. Rather, the student of population is also interested in the various underlying social, psychological, and economic forces that have influenced such changes; and he is interested in the possible implications that such changes have for the established order of the society. For example, if the number of births should increase while the number of deaths stays the same, or nearly so, as it did in the United States during the late 1940's, the demographer is not only interested in how much fertility has risen or in how much of an increase in the population this increase in births has brought about. He is also interested in knowing what forces in the larger society prompted births to increase in the first place. Have new attitudes and values with regard to the "ideal" number of children or desirable family size emerged? Have there been any changes in marriage customs or in the structure of the family that could explain the increase in births (such as a younger age at marriage, or a decline in the importance of economic self-sufficiency of young people as a prerequisite to marriage and childbearing)? Or has the general economic and political climate altered in such a way as to create an atmosphere conducive to a higher level of fertility?

As well as asking "why?" about the increase in births, the demographer is also interested in the consequences for society of the fertility increase and resulting population growth. What are its implications for the adequacy of available school facilities? Will the increased number of consumers have any effect on the rate of saving and investment, and thereby on the rate of economic growth? What effect will the growing number and proportion of young people in the population have on such things as juvenile delinquency, the demand for housing and recreation areas, styles of dress, tastes in entertainment, and the general attitudes and values of the society as a whole?

To take another example, consider the process of "urbanization." Urbanization is a demographic phenomenon that consists essentially of a change in the pattern of population distribution, a change characterized by a decline in the size of the rural population, an increase in the number and size of urban places, and an ever-increasing concentration of the population in these urban places. Taking the formal demographic point of view, a more or less complete explanation of urbanization can be arrived at through the observation, measurement, and description of such things as streams of migration from rural to urban areas, differences between rural and urban areas with respect to levels of fertility and mortality, and the settlement of a disproportionate number of immigrants in urban areas. But such an explanation does not really tell us much about the phenomenon of urbanization. It does not tell us why a population that had been predominantly rural should suddenly start undergoing a transformation to an urban society. It does not tell us what conditions had to be met in order for the process of urbanization to take place, nor does it tell us what changes urbanization implies for social life. A more complete explanation for urbanization would have to go beyond the mere statistical description and analysis of the phenomenon and note such things as the creation of an agricultural surplus that freed part of the labor force from the necessity of engaging in food-producing activities, and the development of alternative employment opportunities through the emergence and growth of urban industries. It would also have to consider some of the consequences of urbanization—a need to increase housing facilities, to enlarge and expand local governments and administrative agencies to handle the growing urban population, to develop more efficient transportation and communication networks, to increase the number and size of schools, to expand the amount and kind of public services offered (for example, police and fire protection, hospitals, welfare programs), and so forth. What is more, attention should be given to the possible consequences of urbanization for the basic demographic processes, particularly to how it is likely to effect levels of fertility and mortality, and through them the rate of growth and the composition of the population.

In short, given a specific population fact or trend, the demographer is not content with a mere quantitative analysis of what this fact or trend is or how it came into being. While such "what?" and "how?" analyses form an integral part of all demographic research (and of research in other branches of learning as well), they do not lead to a complete knowledge and understanding of the population fact or trend in question. To gain a fully adequate knowledge and understanding of a specific population phenomenon, the demographer has to push a step further and ask "why?" and "what does it mean?" In the very broadest sense, then, the science of demography may be conceived as having *four* major objectives: (1) ascertaining the size, composition, and distribution of the population in any given area of human habitation; (2) observing, measuring, and describing changes in size, composition, and distribution over time; (3) observing, measuring, and describing the processes (the interaction between fertility, mortality, and migration) through which such changes are being effected; and (4) analyzing the underlying determinants and consequences of such changes. The first three objectives constitute the core of pure or formal demography, whereas the analysis of the determinants and consequences of population trends forms the subject matter of general population study.

At this last point, where the underlying determinants and consequences of population trends and changes are sought, the demographer must leave the narrow confines of his own specialty and enter the broad area of interdisciplinary study. That is, when the demographer moves beyond the realm of simple observation and description, when he seeks to interpret and explain his data, he turns to a variety of theoretical sciences for help. He turns to *geography* for aid in explaining the spatial distribution of population over the world's land surface; to *medicine* and *public health* for help in analyzing mortality trends and differentials, and in explaining the changing importance of specific causes of death; and to *economics* for an understanding of the effects of population change on such things as the size and productive capacity of the labor force, the adequacy of available resources, and the implications these changes have for the rate of economic development. The demographer looks to *biology* for knowledge and understanding of the workings of the human reproductive system; to *political science* for help in understanding the effects of population change on the balance of world power and on the trend in international relations; and he looks to *sociology* and *anthropology* to help him understand and analyze the intricate relationships between demographic phenomena and the sociocultural environment. In short, the study of population calls upon a wide variety of scientific disciplines, all of which aid the demographer in broadening his knowledge and gaining a better understanding of the underlying causes and implications of changes in human populations.

Although demography, defined in its broadest sense, is truly an interdisciplinary science, and although the demographer calls on scholars in a wide variety of fields for help in explaining and interpreting his data, it must be emphasized that the main causes of population trends are *social,* and that demography is essentially and basically a social science. In the well-chosen words of one author: population trends are both *socially determined* and *socially determining.*[1] The demographic processes take place within the *man-made environment* of human society; the size, composition, and distribution of population are partly influenced by this environment, and they in turn exert an influence on it. The extent to which this man-made environment can influence population phenomena is easily seen by a consideration of the reproductive capacity of the human female. During her reproductive span (roughly between the ages of fifteen and fifty years) the average woman is biologically capable of bearing anywhere from fifteen to twenty children; yet very few women actually ever realize this potential. A whole complex of social factors prevents a woman from doing so and helps to keep human fertility on a level far below that which it is biologically capable of attaining. Among these factors, to name only a few, are laws governing the age of consent at marriage; social attitudes concerning the appropriate age at which a person should marry (very few marriages actually take place immediately upon attainment of the legal age of consent); legal obligations to feed and clothe children; the economic handicap of a large family; and moral obligations to provide one's children with more than the minimum requirements for survival (such as a college education).

It is likewise easy to demonstrate the influence of population phenomena on the society. To begin with, population *size* and the rate of growth are an indication of a nation's military strength, and may have a profound effect on national policy (for example, the United States concept of Manifest Destiny, and Hitler's quest for more *lebensraum*). Furthermore, changes in population size affect the needs of the society with regard to schools and recreation areas, housing, transportation facilities, public and professional services, and welfare programs, to name just a few.

Second, the *composition* of a population is significant, not only because it is closely related to many other differences that characterize various segments of the population, but also because the specific needs of a given population are determined to a great extent by the composition of its members (as well as their number). A population with a high proportion of older persons is likely to be more conservative in outlook than one composed predominantly of young people, and it is apt to be less productive economically. Similarly, the educational level of a population will determine not only the technical skills and productive capacity of the labor force, but will also be reflected in such things as levels of fertility, consumption habits, and tastes in entertainment. Also, levels of fertility and mortality will affect the age composition, and this in turn will have an influence on the burden of economic dependency, problems of aging, the adequacy of available school facilities, the general outlook or philosophy of life of the population, and so forth.

Finally, the influence of population *distribution* on society can be seen in such things as the increasing concentration of the population in large urban clusters (which was itself influenced by the transformation from an agrarian to an industrial society), leading to a greater freedom for the individual, the decline of local community solidarity, the emergence of a more blasé outlook on life, and the development of a more liberal philosophy concerning man's relation to other men. This urbanization trend has also led to the emergence of a wide range of problems—housing shortages, the growth of slums and ethnic ghettos, daily traffic jams, air and water pollution, overcrowded schools, shortages of public health and welfare personnel, and so forth. More recently, the growing popularity of suburban living—encouraged by the emergence of the automobile and the development of a large, interconnected system of highways—has created a need for expansion of local services, such as education, offered by the rapidly growing suburban communities. It has also been influential in generating vast urban renewal programs in many of our larger cities in an attempt to make them more attractive places in which to live and thereby, it is hoped, slow down the current exodus to "suburbia."

SCOPE AND ORGANIZATION OF THE BOOK

The overall purpose of this book is to describe the major population trends in the United States (past and present) and to indicate briefly the nature of the various problems that can be generated by particular demographic developments. Hopefully, the background provided by this book will give the reader a better understanding of the relationship between population change and social change, and this in turn will make him better prepared to comprehend the society in which he lives and thus able to cope more efficiently with its many and varied problems. The attempt to accomplish this purpose will consist of describing the more significant population trends in the United States with regard to questions such as: "What is the current status of a particular trend?" "How did it get that way?" and "What are its implications for the general well-being of the society?" Given the demographic framework, we shall describe the determinants and consequences of trends in the three basic processes of population change (mortality, fertility, migration), and the determinants and consequences of changes in the three major demographic variables (size, composition, distribution). In each instance, some attention will be given to a few of the broader problems relating to particular demographic developments, and to some of the things that might be done to facilitate solutions to these many "population problems" that currently exist in American society.

The rest of the book is divided into seven chapters. Chapters 2, 3, and 4 discuss each of the three basic demographic processes and the particular problems associated with each. Chapter 2 (*Mortality*) describes the trend in the United States death rate as it relates to the overall world picture; it focuses particularly on the various factors that influence the level of mortality, in so far as these factors indicate particular health problems in the United States today. Chapter 3 (*Fertility*) will be concerned with the causes and effects of changing birth rates in the United States, and with the implications of the increasing role of family planning techniques in controlling the level of human fertility. In Chapter 4 (*Migration and Mobility*) attention is focused on the past and present role of foreign immigration on the development of the national population, and on the nature and implications of residential mobility patterns within the United States. In all three of these chapters, our attention will not be limited to general overall trends but will also focus on the causes and implications of *differential* birth, death, and migration patterns that exist within the society.

Chapters 5, 6, and 7 are concerned with each of the three major demographic variables. In Chapter 5 (*Population Size and Growth*) population growth trends in the United States are discussed in terms of their relation to the current worldwide population explosion, and in terms of the problems they are creating within the United States today. Chapter 6 (*Population Composition*) is concerned with major developments in the composition of the population in the United States, and with the various problems associated with these features. Finally, Chapter 7 (*Population Distribution*) discusses the causes and consequences of the major shifts in the distribution of the population, with particular emphasis on the shift from rural to urban areas and the many problems that have been generated by the rapid metropolitanization of the society in the postwar period. Once again attention will be focused on differential patterns of growth, composition, and distribution within the United States, as well as on a general discussion of the determinants and consequences of overall national trends. Finally, Chapter 8

(*Conclusions*) presents a few concluding remarks on the socio-logical significance of the "demographic variable" in the United States today.

REFERENCES AND SUGGESTIONS FOR FURTHER READING

Kingsley Davis, "The Sociology of Demographic Behavior," in Merton, Broom and Cottrell, eds., *Sociology Today,* New York, 1959.

Philip M. Hauser and Otis Dudley Duncan, eds., *The Study of Popula-lation,* Chicago, 1959, Chapters 1–6.

2

Mortality

There are several reasons for beginning the discussion of the three basic demographic processes with a discussion of mortality, or death. For one thing, mortality is basically a very simple concept. Death is a decidedly unambiguous condition, and there are no problems of definition associated with it (as there may be in the case of birth or especially migration). Similarly, the problem of individual motivation hardly needs to be considered when it comes to analyzing the question as to why people die; whereas motivation is a crucial issue with regard to the questions, "Why do people move?" and, albeit to a lesser extent, "Why do women have babies?" For another thing, there are many aspects of both fertility and migration that cannot be considered adequately without having some knowledge of the associated mortality experience. For example, it is not possible to know to what extent a given level of fertility is contributing to population growth unless one also knows the mortality level that is found in conjunction with it.

Perhaps the most significant reason for starting out with mortality, however, is that the changes in this vital process have had the most profound impact on the human population. As will be discussed more fully in a subsequent chapter, the most significant demographic development characterizing mankind is the tremendous increase in his numbers over the past two or three centuries; and a decline in the death rate has played the major role in bringing about this unprecedented numerical increase that is today referred to as the "population explosion."

Before proceeding any further with this discussion of mortality, it might be well to define more specifically a few of the more common technical terms that will be used. In particular, there are two specific concepts with which the reader should be familiar: "death rate" and "average life expectancy." Unless otherwise specified, the term "death rate" refers to the *crude death rate,* which is defined as the number of deaths occurring in a given population during a calendar year per 1,000 people in the population. To illustrate: there were 1,711,982 deaths in the United States during 1960. The average number of people living in the country during the year (i.e., the midpoint population, or the population as of July 1, 1960) was estimated at 180,684,000. The crude death rate can then be computed as 1,711,982 ÷ 180,684,000 x 1,000 = 9.48. This means that in 1960, there were roughly 9.5 deaths for every 1,000 people in the United States. Compared with an overall world death rate of approximately 18 per 1,000 population, this clearly emphasizes the relatively favorable mortality experience generally characteristic of the American population.

The other term with which the reader should be familiar is *average life expectancy,* by which is meant the number of years lived, on the average, by each member of a given population. Looked at from a slightly different perspective, average life expectancy may be defined as the average age at death prevailing in a given population. The relatively favorable mortality situation in the United States is again revealed by an average life expectancy in 1960 on the order of seventy years, compared with less than thirty-five years in many countries of the world.

HISTORICAL MORTALITY CONDITIONS

Although precise statistical evidence is lacking, the little that scientists have been able to compile from various anthropological and archaeological sources indicates that throughout most of his existence man has had to contend with an extremely high death rate. The brutally harsh conditions of life in the pre-industrial world made human survival very much a touch-and-go affair. A newborn infant had no more than a fifty-fifty chance of surviving to adulthood; the average life expectancy of primitive man was probably not much in excess of twenty-five or thirty years. Even more significant, the survival situation was not a great deal better as recently as the middle of the eighteenth century. Early records for the state of Massachusetts, for example, indicate that average life expectancy in colonial America was still somewhat less than forty years.

The situation today in the modern, urban-industrial nations of the Western world is substantially different than it was in the pre-industrial era; and in many countries the average length of life actually approximates the biblical three score years and ten. In the United States, for example, life expectancy in the mid-1960's was approximately sixty-seven years for men and was as high as seventy-three years for women. As just indicated, this situation represents a radical departure from the situation that has prevailed throughout most of human history, and it is obvious there must have been some very startling changes in the nature of the social and physical world in order to bring about this marked increase in average life expectancy. These changes and the impact they have had on man's chances for survival can best be appreciated by considering first some of the factors that combined to promote such high death rates in the past. Broadly speaking, there were two: (1) an unstable food supply, and (2) an extremely unsanitary environment.

A major cause of high death rates in the past (and in some parts of the world even today) can be traced to an inadequate food supply. The impact of famine or acute food shortages on the death rate is obvious and does not require much elaboration: if man does not have any food to eat, he will very soon starve to death. Famines were recorded in Europe as late as the middle of the nineteenth century. Probably the most famous of these is the great Irish potato famine of the 1840's, during which the death rate rose to three times its normal level. In connection with this relationship between mortality and the food supply, it must also be noted that a high death rate is promoted by chronic food shortages which result in high levels of undernourishment and malnutrition in the population. While less spectacular than outright famine and starvation, malnutrition, which lowers one's resistance to even the mildest diseases, is a major factor behind the high death rates that still exist in many parts of the world. In a recent report issued by the Food and Agricultural Organization of the United Nations, for example, it was noted that more than half of the people in the world do not get enough food for a healthy existence.[1] Not only do they get too little food, but their diets consist mainly of cereals and starchy foods and are lacking in foods such as meat, eggs, and milk. This lack of good-quality protein in the diet is a serious deficiency, and it has been said that protein malnutrition is the greatest single source of death in children between the ages of one and five. Large numbers of adults also die each year of deficiency diseases such as beriberi; and those who do not die often show the results of undernutrition in their stunted growth, lack of energy, and low resistance to disease. In these parts of the world the average life expectancy even today is only about thirty to thirty-five years.

Although an unstable and nutritionally inadequate food supply has always been a major contributing cause to high mortality, by far the most important cause has been extremely poor sanitary conditions. Throughout most of his history, man has somehow managed to keep himself and his environment unbelievably filthy. Until well into the nineteenth century, sewage and refuse disposal were virtually non-existent, and the street was the accepted place to dispose of garbage and other household refuse. Housing conditions were deplorable, especially in the cities. People lived crowded together in grimy, unlighted, rat-infested tenements where bathing and toilet facilities were, if they existed at all, extremely inadequate. It has been reported that in mid-nineteenth-century America from 3 to 5 per cent of the population in larger cities such as New York and Boston lived in damp, vermin-ridden, underground rooms. "Narrow crooked streets, lack of proper sewage and ventilation, absence of open spaces for recreation, inadequate and unprotected water supplies, intramural burials, and fetid nuisances (such as slaughter houses and manufactories of offensive stuffs) made pestilential enclosures of some cities both in North America and Europe." [2] And if sordid living conditions were not enough, personal cleanliness was virtually unheard of: people seldom bothered to wash (perspiration was looked upon as nature's way of cleansing the body), and more often than not cleaning one's clothes consisted of little more than an occasional shaking-out to get rid of a few clinging lice.

The unspeakable filth in which man lived served as an ideal breeding ground for a wide variety of infectious disease germs, and when man was not fighting hunger he was likely to be fighting one of the periodic epidemics of plague, cholera, smallpox, and typhus that were commonplace throughout the pre-industrial world. The most infamous of these virulent killers was plague—or the Black Death as it was more popularly called—and outbreaks of this dread disease periodically decimated large segments of the population. It is estimated that plague in one form or another killed from 20 to 25 per cent of the population in Europe between 1348 and 1350, and that outbreaks of bubonic plague killed one-fifth of the population of London in 1603 and another sixth in 1625. Epidemics of plague with accompanying tremendous increases in mortality were reported in Europe as late as the middle of the eighteenth century.

Although perhaps the most dramatic, the Black Death was not the only disease to assume epidemic proportions and contribute to excessively high mortality. Cholera also frequently caused heavy mortality, as did periodic outbreaks of typhus; and smallpox was a particularly deadly scourge before Jenner's introduction of a vaccine in 1798. During the seventeenth and eighteenth centuries, smallpox accounted for nearly one-tenth of all deaths in Europe. Between 1780 and 1800 it is estimated that as many as one-fifth of all deaths in the city of Glasgow were caused by smallpox; and roughly one-fourth of the population of France during the eighteenth century were either killed, crippled, or severely disfigured by this dread disease. Epidemics have not been entirely unknown in the present century; the influenza epidemic of 1918, for example, resulted in a 50 per cent increase in the United States death rate for that year.

Throughout most of human history, then, the periodic recurrence of acute and chronic food shortages, as well as the periodic outbreak of virulent epidemics as a result of extremely unsanitary conditions, served to promote very high death rates among human populations—death rates that were frequently on the order of 40 to 50 per 1,000, compared with the 8 to 10 characterizing many countries in the Western world today. The decline in the death rate to these relatively low levels was of course due to a general improvement in the everyday conditions of life: the creation of a more regular and varied food supply, and increasing control over epidemic diseases through advances in medical science and environmental sanitation.

MORTALITY DECLINE IN THE MODERN WORLD

To cite a more abundant food supply and a "cleaner" environment as the factors responsible for the historical decline of the death rate in the modern world is in a sense far too general, and does not take into account the many specific changes in human society during the past two or three hundred years. On the other hand, to try and list all of the significant developments of the past three centuries would be far beyond the scope of this book. It is possible, however, and also desirable, to cite a few of the more important changes that have taken place and that have contributed substantially to a reduction of the death rate in the Western world. To facilitate this discussion, the various developments may be considered in terms of whether they represent (1) a change in the *material* aspects of culture, (2) a change in the *non-material* aspects of culture, or (3) advances in the broad areas of *medicine, public health,* and *sanitation control.*

(1) *Changes in material culture.* A substantial part of the mortality reduction during the modern era can be traced to changes in the material aspects of culture. By changes in "material culture" are meant such things as the many technological developments and advances in agriculture and industry that have done so much to make our lives easier. In the area of agriculture, for example, improved farming techniques (such as crop rotation and the use of chemical fertilizer), the adoption of new crops (such as the potato, which was first brought to Europe around 1600), and the development of mechanized farming all made it possible to raise more and better food. The greater abundance of food of higher quality reduced the incidence of famine, raised caloric intake, improved the level of nutritional well-being, and raised the general health level of the population so that it was less susceptible to infection.

The development of industry, on the other hand, had both positive and negative effects. On the negative side, the coming of the Industrial Revolution intensified the overcrowded, unsanitary living conditions in urban areas. The factories that sprang up generally had inadequate ventilation, temperatures were often much too high (or else too low), the lighting was bad, the hours were long and exhausting, and the risk of accidents was great. But in the long run these negative effects were offset by other developments that led to a safer and healthier environment, and that were conducive to a decline in the death rate. For one thing, the greater productive efficiency of machine factory industry over the old home handicraft industries greatly increased the amount and variety of products available for public consumption; at the same time, it substantially reduced the cost of such products. The growth of the

textile industry, for example, and the coming of cheap cotton clothing made it possible for the masses of people to afford more than
one or two garments: now people could change their clothes more
often, put on something dry when it rained, keep warmer in the
winter, and so forth. The advent of the factory system also helped
make many agricultural improvements possible through the mass
production of needed farm tools such as the iron plowshare. The
invention of the steam engine permitted many improvements in
transportation and facilitated a wider distribution of the new agricultural and industrial products, thus reducing man's dependence
on his immediate environment. Soap, once a scarce luxury for the
rich, now became available to everybody; iron bedsteads replaced
makeshift wooden frames and floor mats; more adequate housing
was constructed; temperature and humidity control in the house
as well as in the place of work not only made for greater comfort
in living but also may have contributed to a decline in respiratory
infections during winter months; and, more recently, the development of pesticides (such as DDT) have contributed substantially
to a reduction in mortality from particular diseases (such as
malaria).

(2) *Changes in non-material culture.* Mortality reduction has
also been greatly facilitated by changes in the non-material aspects
of culture. As opposed to "material culture" which refers to things,
objects, technological inventions, and so on, "non-material culture"
refers to attitudes, beliefs, values, normative patterns of behavior,
and the like. Although they have different referents (the former
are found in the real world where they can be seen and touched,
while the latter exist largely in men's minds), material and non-
material culture are dynamically interrelated so that a change in one
is generally accompanied by a change in the other. For example,
once people came to accept the belief that sewage disposal systems
would be beneficial to their health and well-being (a non-material
change), a lot of time, effort and money was put into the construction of such systems. On the other hand, the material change
represented by the growth of the textile industry and the provision

of cheaper cotton clothing led to the emergence of an entirely new set of values about how often people ought to change their clothes. Because of this dynamic interrelationship, it is not always feasible to consider particular material or non-material changes apart from one another.

Keeping this relationship in mind, perhaps one of the most significant non-material changes to effect a reduction in the death rate of the modern Western world has been a sort of growing liberalization of philosophy during the nineteenth and twentieth centuries. This was a tendency to move further from an "every man for himself" type of philosophy to a point of view more conducive to a ready acceptance of the responsibility for being our brother's keeper; and it resulted in a number of significant social reforms. The development of this attitude and its influence is clearly visible in the gradual adoption of measures directed toward the eradication of slums and the improvement of housing conditions; in the establishment of minimum wage laws; in the fixing of maximum working hours for men and women; in the establishment of minimum working age laws for children; and in a general alleviation of the working environment through the development and widespread adoption of factory safety devices, as well as the adoption of various lighting, heating, and ventilation codes. Evidence that this liberal social philosophy is still very much in the process of development is clearly revealed by the United States government's declaration of a "war on poverty" in the mid-1960's. One outcome of this war on poverty, it may be hoped, will be a narrowing of the fairly wide differences in life expectancy that still characterize the various social and economic subgroups in the American population.

(3) *Public health and medical science.* By far the most significant factors behind the decline of the death rate in the Western world can be found in the tremendous development and acceptance of preventive public health programs, and in improvements in medical knowledge and practices. Although many of the specific developments in these areas can be included under either material or non-material cultural changes, they have exercised such a pro-

found impact on the death rate that they merit separate treatment. Moreover, the specific developments are so frequently tied to both material and non-material changes that it would be exceedingly difficult to try to separate them as belonging more to one group than to the other.

Public health and medical science as we know them today are of relatively recent origin. It is only since the late eighteenth and early nineteenth century that man has freed himself from many of his traditional beliefs and practices with regard to the protection and care of the human body and its external environment. Any declines in mortality that occurred before the nineteenth century, therefore, must have resulted primarily from developments that were not directly concerned with physical health, for little was known at the time concerning the causes and cures of disease. Since that time, however, a number of important discoveries and inventions have led to a substantial increase in man's ability to control his death rate. No longer are "evil spirits of the night" cited as a chief cause of illness and death, and no longer do medical practitioners apply leeches to their patients to draw off such evil spirits through the letting of blood. Rather, today we live in a world filled with programs and practices specifically aimed at preventing the occurrence of disease (for example, water purification programs and the practice of bathing regularly); and we live in a world where physicians use a wide variety of serums and "wonder drugs" to contain, if not cure, a particular type of infection or one of the specific strains of virus that man has been able to isolate.

If one were to single out a particular development as having exerted the most significant influence on a decline in the death rate, one would be most likely to cite *immunology*. The door to the possibility of developing preventive serums for the various infectious diseases was first opened in 1798 when Edward Jenner reported his discovery of a vaccine for smallpox. But it was not until a full century later that the basic principle of immunization (i.e., that inoculation with a mild strain of a particular virus will produce a minor case of the disease in question but will render the patient relatively immune to contracting a more serious case at some later date) was clarified by Robert Koch (1876) and Louis Pasteur (1877). Following this breakthrough, however, preventive vaccines were soon developed for cholera, anthrax and hydrophobia, diphtheria, tetanus, typhoid, whooping cough, and scarlet fever. These diseases that were once major "killers," particularly among young children, are now virtually nonexistent in the United States. The fight to conquer infection continues even today. More recent years have seen the development of prophylactic serums for influenza, poliomyelitis, and measles, and the years ahead will likely see the development of still others (such as a chicken pox vaccine, perhaps). Nor is current research with prophylactic serums limited to infectious diseases. In the area of fertility control, for example, a significant research effort today is focused on the development of an anti-pregnancy vaccine which would temporarily immunize a woman against her husband's sperm.

The acceptance of Pasteur's "germ theory," which preceded the full development of immunology, also led to the acceptance of the practice of *asepsis,* or the adoption of prophylactic measures which have as their aim the exclusion from the body of bacterial organisms that may carry disease. In the area of cure rather than prevention, it also led to the development of *antisepsis,* or the application of antibiotics and other chemicals for the purpose of destroying or otherwise inhibiting the growth of micro-organisms already present. On the one hand, Joseph Lister revolutionized the entire practice of medicine and surgery and contributed substantially to disease prevention by introducing such simple practices as the wearing of masks by physicians, the washing of hands before operating, and the sterilization of surgical instruments. On the other hand, the curative powers of medical science have been enhanced by the emergence of chemotherapy and the discovery of a wide variety of antibiotic wonder drugs (beginning with Alexander Fleming's 1928 discovery of penicillin); today when illnesses such as influenza and pneumonia do occur they are much less lethal than was the case in earlier times.

The theory and methods of medical practice were not all that changed with the acceptance of the germ theory of disease and the concept of preventive health. On the contrary, these developments were in many instances preceded by a number of significant developments in public sanitation, particularly in urban areas. Early in the nineteenth century cities began to install sewage disposal systems; provisions were made for the collection of garbage and other refuse; drinking water supplies were separated from sewage depositories; water filtration and purification were introduced; and quarantine measures were adopted and enforced in order to prevent the spread of communicable diseases. Today, in the modern countries of the Western world, sanitation measures such as these have practically wiped out infectious, filth-caused diseases such as cholera, typhoid fever, and diphtheria.

The years since the early nineteenth century have also seen the invention of a number of significant medical *tools*. Among them, to name just a few, have been the stethoscope, the microscope, the basal thermometer, the ophthalmoscope, and the X-ray. These inventions, which may be looked upon as material culture changes, contributed to medical progress by greatly enhancing the doctor's ability to *examine* patients rather than merely observe them. This, in turn, facilitated his ability to go beyond superficial symptoms and discover the underlying causes of particular ailments. Developments such as these that made it possible to study the human organism in more detail also served to encourage such study. They helped create an intellectual spirit in medicine that endorsed and encouraged research for its own sake (a nonmaterial culture change); and today research and experimentation have become an inseparable component of medical science.

It is worth stressing at this point that many of the developments just described (for example, immunology, asepsis and antisepsis, and public sanitation control measures) were possible only after man had abandoned the old "evil spirits" explanation of disease causation and had accepted the theory of Pasteur that "life is a germ and a germ is life. . . ." The acceptance of this germ theory represents a major change in man's non-material culture that had many significant ramifications for the material aspects of his culture. Another illustration of the interrelationship between material and non-material culture can be seen in the impact of the decline in the attitude that the human body was a sacred temple that should not be tampered with by man. It was not until this attitude had lessened that the taboos against autopsy were removed, thereby making it possible for man to vastly increase his knowledge of the structure and functioning of the human body. It was also a decline in opposition to cutting the body that permitted the development and spread of therapeutic surgery. Similarly, it was a change in attitudes regarding hygiene and personal cleanliness that encouraged such things as regular bathing with soap, more frequent changing and washing of clothing, and so forth. All of these illustrations indicate the extent to which changes in non-material cultural attitudes and changes in material culture techniques and practices are closely intertwined, especially when it comes to progress in the broad areas of medical science and public health.

In summarizing the many factors responsible for the decline of mortality in the Western world, it is important to note the relative timing and impact of the forces involved. Although the development of medical science and sanitation control have probably exercised the greatest effect on the death rate, an emphasis on these factors should not lead to a neglect of the more basic social and economic changes that underlie them. To give credit where credit is due, it must be stressed that the initial decline in man's death rate came about as a result of rudimentary economic development as reflected in increases in the quantity and variety of agricultural products, and in simple improvements in transportation and communication facilities which made famine control easier. Only much later did medical progress begin to exert its influence on mortality levels.

To simplify this discussion, it is possible to conceive of mortality reduction in the Western world as having occurred in three stages. For the sake of illustration, let us go back to the time when the crude death rate was on the order of 40 to 45 per 1,000 population per year. The first ten-point drop in the death rate occurred during the seventeenth and eighteenth centuries and came about largely as a result of an increase in the amount and availability of the *food supply*. The second ten-point decline in the death rate (from 30 to 35 per 1,000, to 20 to 25 per 1,000) took place during the late eighteenth and early nineteenth centuries and was primarily the result of *public health* measures which led to a decline in the incidence of infection and facilitated the control of epidemic diseases (for example, sewer construction, garbage and refuse disposal provisions, the introduction of purification of public drinking water supplies, and so forth). Finally, in the third stage death rates fell to levels of 10 to 15 per 1,000 (even lower in some areas) as a result of the development of medical science and the spread of improved *individual medical care* (immunization, better personal hygiene practices, the use of antibiotics, and so on).

This third stage of mortality decline, wherein crude death rates fall to levels well below 15 per 1,000, has been reached by the United States and the countries of Europe and Oceania. Japan and the Soviet Union are also characterized by mortality levels of this order. Several of the countries in Central and South America have also achieved very low death rates, whereas the remaining countries are well advanced into the second phase of mortality decline where the introduction of modern public health measures has lowered death rates to levels of 15 to 20 per 1,000. In most Asian countries, however (with the notable exceptions of Japan and the Soviet Union), and particularly in Africa, crude death rates are still fairly high—in many cases in excess of 25 or even 30 per 1,000. It is in these latter countries that the spread of public health environmental improvement programs is likely to have the greatest impact on mortality declines in the immediate future. Declines in these countries in fact are likely to be spectacular, since they can be brought about by the adoption and application of already proven techniques; they do not have to wait for the gradual development of lifesaving methods that led to a reduction of mortality in the Western world. Additional mortality declines are also likely for Latin American countries for some years to come, as individual health care practices improve and further reduce the incidence of infection in this part of the world. But in modern industrial nations like the United States, where the death rate has already achieved a fairly low level, mortality declines in the immediate future are not likely to be very dramatic.

MORTALITY TRENDS IN THE UNITED STATES

One of the measures of a nation's accomplishments in raising the general level of living of the population has traditionally been a lowering of the crude death rate. It has in fact been demonstrated that the level of a nation's death rate (especially the level of mortality in infancy) has been a rough but usable measure of that nation's level of living and the state of its social, economic, and technological development. It must be noted, however, that fairly substantial mortality declines have been experienced in some parts of the world in recent years solely as the result of sanitary improvements (often in the complete absence of any change in the social and economic level of living), and such developments have modified this traditional relationship. Nevertheless, the conquest of disease and the reduction of mortality have been closely associated with the growth and development of American society, and the history of the United States can in part be viewed as a history of declining death rates.

Unfortunately, the lack of adequate vital statistics for the early years of American history makes it impossible to document this mortality reduction with complete precision. Some areas such as the state of Massachusetts have fairly reliable data going back to the early nineteenth century, but the availability of national mortality data is of fairly recent origin. Although some efforts were made by the United States Census Bureau to collect national data on mortality (characteristics of decedents and causes of death) in conjunction with the decennial censuses from 1850 through 1900, the results of these inquiries were not very good and they gave a very imperfect picture of the mortality situation in this country. It was not until 1900 that death statistics began to be compiled by the federal government from registration sources on an annual basis. At that time, a "death registration area" was identified consisting of ten states and the District of Columbia. Over the years other states were added to this registration area as their systems for recording deaths were established and perfected, but it was not until 1933 that all states were included. Thus, dependable nationwide death statistics are not available in the United States for the years before 1933, and almost no official registration statistics are available for years before 1900. In view of this situation, then, it is best to consider mortality trends in the United States in terms of (1) trends before 1900, or before the existence of official national registration data; and (2) trends during the twentieth century, or after the establishment of official registration statistics.

(1) *Mortality trends before 1900*. Several states as well as many cities have maintained birth and death statistics since the early days of the nation's history, but very little is really known about their completeness or accuracy. Thus, what is known about mortality conditions in the United States before 1900 has largely been pieced together from scattered vital statistics reports of questionable validity, which cover only a small segment of the total population. The data available, however, are fairly conclusive in pointing to death rates in the eighteenth and early nineteenth centuries that were fairly high in normal times and that fluctuated rather sharply from one period to another. Records for Boston and New York City, for example, indicate that average annual death rates were between 30 and 35 per 1,000, but often rose to as high as 50 per 1,000 in epidemic years. Other historical sources reveal that the average life expectancy at birth in colonial America varied from a low of twenty-five years (Philadelphia, 1782–1790) to a high

of thirty-five years (Massachusetts and New Hampshire, 1793). These compare with an average life expectancy at birth in the United States today of approximately seventy years.

The first clear indication that the mortality level was declining in the United States was provided by the vital statistics data of Massachusetts. In that state the systematic registration of the vital events of births and deaths by civil authorities was introduced as early as 1639, and by the end of the nineteenth century this system was fairly well established. According to these data, death rates were close to 30 per 1,000 in colonial Massachusetts but had fallen to a level of about 20 per 1,000 by the middle of the nineteenth century, and by 1900 the death rate in that state was still on the order of 18 to 19 per 1,000 (compared to a national rate in 1900 of about 17 per 1,000). The decline in mortality during the nineteenth century is also indicated by a series of death probability tables which have been constructed on the basis of these early Massachusetts statistics. According to these tables, the average life expectancy at birth in 1850 was about thirty-nine years. By 1880 it had risen to approximately forty-three years, and by the end of the nineteenth century the average number of years that a newborn baby in Massachusetts could expect to live had risen to roughly forty-seven or forty-eight years.

These data for Massachusetts should not necessarily be taken as representative of mortality conditions in the United States as a whole. (Massachusetts in the nineteenth century was an industrial state with a relatively high percentage of the population living in urban areas and a high proportion of foreign born. In contrast, the nation as a whole at this time was still predominantly rural and heavily native.) Nevertheless, taken together with what is known about advances in medicine and public health, it supports the conclusion that the overall level of mortality in the United States was definitely on the decline during the nineteenth century.

(2) *Mortality trends in the twentieth century.* The data in Table II-1 indicate the nature of the trend in the United States crude death rate since 1900. A quick glance at these data reveals that the

Table II-1: Crude death rates in the United States, 1900–1965
(deaths per 1,000 population).

Year	Crude death rate	Year	Crude death rate	Year	Crude death rate
1900	17.2	1922	11.7	1944	10.6
1901	16.4	1923	12.1	1945	10.6
1902	15.5	1924	11.6	1946	10.0
1903	15.6	1925	11.7	1947	10.1
1904	16.4	1926	12.1	1948	9.9
1905	15.9	1927	11.3	1949	9.7
1906	15.7	1928	12.0	1950	9.6
1907	15.9	1929	11.9	1951	9.7
1908	14.7	1930	11.3	1952	9.6
1909	14.2	1931	11.1	1953	9.6
1910	14.7	1932	10.9	1954	9.2
1911	13.9	1933	10.7	1955	9.3
1912	13.6	1934	11.1	1956	9.4
1913	13.8	1935	10.9	1957	9.6
1914	13.3	1936	11.6	1958	9.5
1915	13.2	1937	11.3	1959	9.4
1916	13.8	1938	10.6	1960	9.5
1917	14.0	1939	10.6	1961	9.3
1918	18.1	1940	10.8	1962	9.5
1919	12.9	1941	10.5	1963	9.6
1920	13.0	1942	10.3	1964	9.4
1921	11.5	1943	10.9	1965	9.4

SOURCES: *Vital Statistics of the United States: 1961,* II-1, Washington, D.C., 1963; and *Monthly Vital Statistics Reports,* 14:12, *Annual Summary for the United States, 1965,* Washington, D.C., 1966.

most striking trend of the twentieth century has been a rapid and fairly steady decline in mortality in this country. From a relatively high level of 17.2 per 1,000 in 1900, the crude death rate had fallen to 9.6 by mid-century—a decline of nearly 45 per cent. Since 1950, however, the death rate has not changed very drastically. It declined a little further during the early 1950's, reaching an all-time low of 9.2 per 1,000 in 1954; but since then it has risen slightly and hovered consistently between 9.4 and 9.6 per 1,000. This sudden cessation of the historical decline of the crude death rate in the mid-1950's, especially the reasons for the cessation, represents one of the major health problems on which research in the United States is currently being focused.

Closer inspection of the data in Table II-1 reveals that the rate of decline in the crude death rate has not been uniform throughout the twentieth century. On the contrary, it has been extremely erratic. Most of the noteworthy fluctuations in the death rate reflect periodic epidemics of influenza. The best known of these outbreaks was the influenza epidemic of 1918: during that year the crude death rate rose to a level of 18.1 per 1,000 (5 per cent higher than the crude death rate recorded at the beginning of the century and 30 per cent higher than the crude death rate of the preceding year). It has been estimated that this epidemic resulted in nearly half a million deaths in excess of the number that would have occurred with a normal level of mortality. Other years when epidemics of one sort or another seem to have influenced temporary upward swings in an otherwise declining death rate were 1904, 1923, 1926, 1928, 1936–1937, 1943, and 1957 (in that latter year a mild epidemic of "Asian flu" was experienced throughout the nation). In 1963 the crude death rate again rose as high as 9.6 per 1,000, suggesting that there was an unusually high incidence of some form of flu during that year.

In spite of the fact that the general pattern is a fairly erratic one, it is still possible to identify at least four distinct phases in the decline of the United States crude death rate during the twentieth century. The first phase, and also the most dramatic, lasted from 1900 until just after the 1918 influenza epidemic (1900–1921). During this phase the crude death rate declined from 17.2 to 11.5 per 1,000, or by approximately one-third. Although there were slight upturns in several of these years, the only major reversal of the pronounced downward trend during the first two decades of the twentieth century was the temporary rise occasioned by the

1918 influenza epidemic. All in all, this period of rapid and substantial decline in the crude death rate accounted for roughly three-fourths of all the mortality reduction that has occurred in the United States since 1900.

During the second phase, from 1921 to 1937, the crude death rate remained relatively stable. Although there were no major upswings in this period, neither were there any notable declines. Rather, the 1921 crude death rate of 11.5 appears to have become an established plateau, and during these years the crude death rate fluctuated between a low of 10.7 in 1933 and a high of 12.1 in the years 1923 and 1926. In 1936 the crude death rate was 11.6 per 1,000, or one-tenth of a point higher than at the start of the period. In 1937, however, the death rate dropped to a level of 11.3 per 1,000, and another period of declining mortality began. This third phase of the mortality experience of the United States, lasting from 1937 to 1954, saw sulfa and some of the other modern wonder drugs come into fairly widespread use, and the crude death rate in this country declined by another 20 per cent— falling from 11.3 in 1937 to an all-time low of 9.2 per 1,000 in 1954. Since then the downward trend has ceased, and the United States appears to have embarked upon another era of relatively stable death rates. During this most recent phase the crude death rate rose from its all-time low level of 9.2 in 1954 to 9.6 in 1957. In 1961 it had fallen back to 9.3 per 1,000, but since then it has remained between 9.4 and 9.6 per 1,000.

In summary, then, the mortality experience of the United States population during the twentieth century can be described in terms of four distinct periods: (1) a period of fairly rapid and substantial mortality decline between 1900 and 1921; (2) a period of relatively stable death rates between 1921 and 1937; (3) a second period of fairly marked mortality decline from 1937 to 1954; and (4) a second period of relatively stable death rates after the cessation of mortality decline in the mid-1950's. As indicated earlier, this most recent leveling-off of the crude death rate and the reasons behind it represent one of the major public health concerns in the

United States today, and it will be discussed more fully in a later section of this chapter. Before this problem can be discussed adequately, however, it is necessary to have some knowledge of the various differences that characterize the mortality experience of particular subgroups in the population. In the following section, therefore, we consider some of the major mortality differentials characterizing the American population.

MORTALITY DIFFERENTIALS IN THE UNITED STATES

It was noted earlier that the general decline in mortality in the modern era has been largely characteristic of the urban-industrial nations of the Western world. In the non-Western world, although death rates are currently declining (often quite rapidly), mortality levels are still substantially higher than in the West. This does not mean that Western countries have no mortality problems or that there is no longer room for improvement. On the contrary, in spite of the fact that the death rate in the United States has been cut nearly in half since 1900, this reduction in mortality has not affected all segments of the population equally: some groups are still characterized by death rates considerably above the rates for other groups. For those groups that have already achieved a relatively low death rate there appears to be little prospect for any further appreciable reductions in the near future. But there is a definite possibility that fairly substantial reductions can be realized for those groups that are still characterized by comparatively high death rates. The very fact that some groups have managed to achieve a lower level of mortality than others indicates that further reductions of the rates for high mortality groups are feasible. Such reductions are also desirable and necessary if the United States is to provide all of its citizens equality with regard to the most basic of all human rights—the right to live.

Research on the mortality experience characterizing the different segments of the American population has established the existence of several differentials which are now widely recognized. It has even been suggested that some of these differences in mortality levels have so consistently distinguished various segments of the population throughout the years that they have achieved the status of verified hypotheses. As will be seen below, the differences in mortality levels that may be observed in the general population are associated with a variety of social, economic, and demographic factors. Before discussing these differences, however, it may be noted that there are two basic reasons for being concerned with the existence of mortality differentials. First, there is the purely *humanitarian* reason already cited: if some segments of the population have achieved very low death rates, it should be possible for other groups to achieve the same low death rates, and this is an end toward which we are all morally compelled to work. Specifying mortality differentials is important in the first place, then, because they tell us which groups are better or worse off than other groups regarding their life chances; that is, they identify the "high-risk" groups in the population on whom research and remedial action programs should be concentrated.

In the second place, there is the more *practical* reason that the elimination of the differences is one avenue toward the attainment of still further reductions in the overall death rate. Among the low death rate groups it does not seem likely that mortality levels will undergo any appreciable reductions in the very near future. As noted above, however, the very fact that some groups have achieved a lower level of mortality than others may indicate that further reductions in mortality are possible for the high death rate groups; and as the mortality levels of high death rate groups are brought under control, it could lead to an even further reduction in the overall death rate. In fact, it might even be said that the elimination (or at least the narrowing) of some of the currently existing differentials will be a major factor in bringing about further declines in the overall level of mortality characterizing the population as a whole. Some of the more significant mortality differentials existing in the United States today are discussed below.

(1) *Age.* One of the most obvious variables to which mortality

levels are related is age. Death rates tend to be fairly high during the first year of life. From this relatively high level in infancy they fall to almost negligible levels during the early childhood years, and they remain low until about age thirty-five. Thereafter, the death rate begins to rise with advancing age until it becomes very high at the oldest ages. In the United States in 1960, for example, the death rate for the population under one year of age was 26 per 1,000, but it dropped to less than 2 per 1,000 for all groups between ages one and thirty-four years (see Table II-2). After age

Table II-2: Age-specific death rates for the United States, 1900 and 1960.

Age	Crude death rates		Per cent decline, 1900–1960
	1900	1960	
All ages	17.2	9.5	44.8
Under 1 year	162.4	26.0 *	83.4
1-4	19.8	1.1	94.4
5-14	3.9	0.5	87.2
15-24	5.9	1.1	81.4
25-34	8.2	1.5	81.7
35-44	10.2	3.0	70.6
45-54	15.0	7.6	49.3
55-64	27.2	17.4	36.0
65-74	56.4	38.2	32.3
75-84	123.3	87.5	29.0
85 and over	260.9	198.6	23.9

SOURCES: *Vital Statistics of the United States: 1950*, I, Washington, D.C., 1954; and *Vital Statistics of the United States: 1960*, II-1, Washington, D.C., 1963.

* Deaths under 1 year per 1,000 live births.

thirty-five, however, it began to increase rapidly with advancing age: at ages thirty-five to forty-four, 3 out of every 1,000 persons died during 1960; this figure rose to 17 per 1,000 for persons fifty-five to sixty-four, and among persons eighty-five years of age and over there were nearly 200 deaths for every 1,000 people.

Although this general U-shape is characteristic of the age-specific death rates in all nations and for all time periods, there can be great variations as to the height of the curve at each age. The data in Table II-2, for example, indicate that the height of the United States age-specific death rate curve for 1960 would be substantially lower at every age than the one for 1900. But a closer examination of these data reveal that the decline in mortality has not been evenly distributed among all of the various age groups. For ages under thirty-five, the death rate has declined by 80 per cent or more, and for ages one to thirty-four years this decline has meant a near elimination of deaths (the rates for 1960 at these ages were all well below 2 per 1,000). The greatest decline has characterized the group one to four years of age: the 1960 death rate of this group (1.1 per 1,000) was 94 per cent less than it had been at the start of the century. At the other end of the age spectrum, the decline in mortality has been much less pronounced. Among persons fifty-five years of age and over, the 1960 death rate was, on the average, only about 30 per cent lower than it had been in 1900; and at ages eighty-five and over, mortality decline during the present century has amounted to less than 25 per cent.

The fact that mortality declined at different rates for specific age groups is largely a reflection of the developments of medical science since the late nineteenth century. Following the pioneer work of Pasteur and Koch in the field of bacteriology, medical science has made tremendous progress in the cure and prevention of the acute and infectious diseases that formerly took such a heavy toll among the younger members of the population. Much less success has been achieved in preventing deaths from such chronic ailments as heart disease and cancer; and since these diseases are characteristic of older persons, the death rates at the advanced ages have fallen at a much slower rate than the death rates in infancy, childhood, and young adulthood. It is clear that the marked reduction in mortality at the younger ages, particularly in infancy, has contributed most to the overall decline in the death rate and to the corresponding increase in average life expectancy. In view of the major role it has played in past mortality reductions, and particularly in view of the recent cessation of mortality decline in the United States, it is desirable to look more closely at the trends in infant mortality.

(2) *Infant mortality.* The extent of mortality during infancy is commonly measured by the *infant mortality rate,* which is defined as the number of deaths under one year of age per 1,000 live births occurring during a calendar year. As such, it measures the probability that a newborn baby will survive the hazards of infancy and live to celebrate his first birthday. According to the data in Table II-3, the infant mortality rate in the United States has de-

Table II-3: Infant mortality rates by age for the United States, 1915, 1950, and 1960 (deaths per 1,000 live births).

Age	1915	1950	1960
Under 1 year	99.9	29.2	26.0
Under 1 day	15.0	10.2	10.3
Under 1 month	44.4	20.5	18.7
1 to 2 months	9.0	1.8	1.7
3 to 5 months	16.9	2.8	2.4
6 to 8 months	12.5	1.7	1.2
9 to 11 months	9.5	1.0	0.7

SOURCES: *Infant Mortality Statistics: United States, 1950, Vital Statistics Special Reports, National Summaries,* 37:18, Washington, D.C., 1954; and *Vital Statistics of the United States: 1960,* II-3, Washington, D.C., 1963.

clined considerably in the present century, falling from a level of 99.9 per 1,000 in 1915 (the first year for which official infant mortality data are available for the nation) to 26.0 in 1960. This represents a decline of approximately three-fourths during a forty-five year period, or an average decline of slightly more than 1.5 per cent per year. Moreover, there is evidence that even the fairly high rate for the year 1915 was considerably below the levels that had prevailed throughout the early years of the nation's history. The remarkable progress that has been made in reducing the loss of life during infancy may be more fully appreciated if one realizes that in colonial America roughly one out of every six babies failed to survive until its first birthday. By 1915 this had been reduced to one in ten, and by 1960 only about one infant in forty died during the first year of life.

Table II-3 also shows that the rate of mortality in infancy is highest during the first few hours and days of life. In 1960 more than one-third of all infant deaths in the United States occurred during the first day of life, and approximately three-fourths took place during the neonatal period (i.e., during the first month of life). Most deaths at these early ages are due to causes associated directly with the physiological processes of gestation and birth (for example, birth injuries, prematurity, postnatal suffocation); substantially less progress has been made in combating these causes of death than in combating infection. As compared with a 74 per cent decline in mortality for infants in general between 1915 and 1960, the death rate during the first month of life (the neonatal death rate) declined by only 56 per cent, whereas mortality during the first twenty-four hours after birth was only one-third lower in 1960 than it had been in 1915. For ages between one month and one year (the post-neonatal period), the decline in mortality has been much greater. For ages one to two months, the 1960 death rate was 81 per cent less than it was in 1915; this percentage difference increases with age, so that at ages nine to eleven months the 1915–1960 mortality decline amounted to 93 per cent.

Closer examination of these infant mortality rates reveals that most of the declines since 1915 had taken place by mid-century, and that *since 1950 there has been relatively little progress in bringing about further reductions in mortality during infancy.* The declines in recent years are certainly much less spectacular than those that occurred before World War II. If the trend prevailing during the 1940's had continued, the infant mortality rate in the United States today would be about 15 per 1,000 live births. Although such a low infant mortality rate has actually been achieved in both Sweden and the Netherlands, it is considerably below the rate of 26 per 1,000 live births recorded in this nation for 1960, and clearly reflects the existence of a major health problem in the United States today. This deceleration in the rate of the decline recently prompted the United States Public Health Service to undertake a special study of the infant mortality situation in the United States. According to this report, a major factor behind the deceleration has been an increase in the proportion of total births occurring to women belonging to groups where infant mortality is higher than that of the general population (for example, teen-age girls, unwed mothers, women who have had several pregnancies, and nonwhites of all ages and parity levels).

A second factor that has been suggested as contributing to a deceleration in the rate of mortality decline in infancy has been what may be called a stagnation in medical progress since 1950 and a weakening of the many maternal and child health action programs that had been strengthened during the 1940's. According to the report just cited: "In the 1950's a general attitude that significant progress in reducing infant mortality required, above all, new insights to basic biological processes tended to dampen the fervor for action programs. The 1950's might also be characterized as a decade in which earlier medical and program advances continued without significant innovations. This occurred in the absence of major scientific breakthroughs that could have been expected to produce broad effects through immediate application." [3]

Finally, some of the very conditions that were considered beneficial for further declines in infant mortality actually had the reverse effect. The most notable example of this has been the fairly heavy movement of nonwhites into the large cities since the end of the Second World War. This movement, which brought a larger proportion of the lower socioeconomic classes closer to the large urban medical centers with their highly trained physicians, could logically have been expected to result in further declines in the overall infant mortality rate. But such declines did not occur. On the contrary, there have actually been increases in the infant mortality rates for some groups (urban nonwhites, for example). The reasons for this increase are complex and involve a variety of social, economic, and cultural factors. Without a doubt, a major cause is that community medical facilities have not fully adapted to the special needs of a rapidly and substantially increasing number of lower socioeconomic status families; and the groups that have moved into the cities have not taken full advantage of the medical and health care facilities available. On the one hand, the size of the patient population in most of our large urban areas has increased faster than health facilities have been expanded. This has increased pressures on already overcrowded clinics and overworked medical personnel, and has resulted in a watering down (albeit unintentional) of the quantity and quality of care. Nursing personnel are also in short supply, and among other things the limited public health nursing manpower has led to a reduction in the amount of prenatal and postnatal care at home. On the other hand, rural migrants to the cities, many of whom have had little or no formal schooling, may often be completely unaware of the need for prenatal care or of the existence of publicly supported clinics to provide this care. Even if they are aware, many factors may interfere with their adequate utilization of facilities (lack of transportation, ignorance or insufficient motivation, aversion to submitting to examination by male physicians, inability to find someone to take care of other children, dissatisfaction with impersonal treatment received in an overcrowded clinic environment, and so forth).

Although no answer has yet been found for this situation, it can at least be noted that the deceleration in the rate of infant mortality decline has recently been recognized as a major health problem in the United States. As a result, recent years have witnessed a significant increase in research aimed at identifying the special health needs of the high infant mortality groups (for example, unwed teen-agers, nonwhites, multigravida mothers), and at improving the quality of prenatal and postnatal medical care facilities and services available to these less fortunate members of the society. A major research goal is to uncover the various sociocultural attitudes and practices that currently result in poor health care practices and inadequate utilization of existing health facilities.

(3) *Sex.* The death rates in Table II-4, which are age-adjusted

Table II-4: *Age-adjusted death rates by color and sex for the United States, 1900, 1950, and 1960.*

Color and sex	1900	1950	1960
All classes	17.8	8.4	7.6
Male	18.6	10.0	9.5
Female	17.0	6.9	5.9
White	17.6	8.0	7.3
Male	18.4	9.6	9.2
Female	16.8	6.5	5.6
Nonwhite	27.8	12.3	10.4
Male	28.7	13.6	12.1
Female	27.1	10.9	8.9

SOURCE: *Vital Statistics of the United States: 1960,* II-1, Washington, D.C., 1963.

rates and therefore are not influenced by marked differences that may characterize the age composition of the population groups involved, clearly show that mortality levels have long been closely related to sex and color. Considering sex first, it is readily apparent from these data that the female of the species has long enjoyed a mortality advantage. Not only has she consistently managed to outlive her male counterpart, but she has also been increasing her advantage. Between 1900 and 1960 the death rate of American women was reduced by 65 per cent (from 17.0 to 5.9 per 1,000), whereas the 9.5 deaths per 1,000 population recorded for men in this country in 1960 was only 49 per cent lower than the rate of 18.6 experienced in 1900. This increasingly favorable mortality experience of females is further demonstrated by the fact that the male death rate was 61 per cent greater than that of females in

1960, as compared with a difference of only about 10 per cent in 1900.

In the past, higher mortality among males has frequently been explained in terms of the more strenuous role that men play in the life of society, or in terms of such things as occupational hazards affecting males, military deaths in wartime, and greater tensions among men because of the greater pressures to achieve that our society places upon them. But there is ample evidence to suggest that differences in the life experiences of the two sexes cannot completely account for the higher mortality of men. The fact that the male death rate is higher in infancy as well as in old age, for example, and the fact that male stillbirths are more common than female stillbirths, would suggest that the lower mortality level of females stems at least in part from some unknown but inherent biological superiority. The possible significance of such a biological difference is further suggested by the fact that the female advantage has been increasing during a period when women have gradually been assuming a role and status in industry and business much more similar to those of men. (Between 1940 and 1960, for example, the proportion of women age fourteen and over who were members of the labor force in the United States rose from 25 per cent to 31 per cent). In short, the increasing participation of women in the labor force has not been accompanied by an equalization of the mortality experiences of the two sexes. Moreover, although there may be insufficient evidence to justify citing the native frailty of males as the sole cause of their higher mortality, at least one study, under carefully controlled conditions, has provided strong evidence in support of the claim that the biological factors are much more important than sociocultural pressures and strains in relation to the male-female mortality differential.[4] Thus, contrary to popular mythology, the female may not be the weaker sex after all. This would certainly seem to be the case as far as the death rate is concerned.

It is important to point out that while the biological superiority of the female may be a major factor behind the sex mortality differential, the causes of the widening of this differential must be sought elsewhere. A recent examination of trends in causes of death for males and females has suggested that the widening of the overall sex differential is due mainly to a particularly pronounced widening at ages fifteen to twenty-four and forty-five to sixty-four years.[5] The increase in the sex mortality differential at ages fifteen to twenty-four years is seen to be the result of a decline in the female death rate for tuberculosis and also of a decline in maternal mortality (or mortality due to complications of pregnancy or childbirth). At the same time, there has been a substantial increase in male mortality resulting from motor vehicle accidents. For the age group forty-five to sixty-four, the increase in the sex mortality differential can be attributed mainly to an increase in male deaths from lung cancer and coronary heart disease (perhaps reflecting a greater prevalence of smoking and obesity among men than women). It is also due to a decrease in female mortality due to cancer of the uterus (reflecting an improvement in prenatal care and delivery practices when women are going through their childbearing period). Thus, while biological factors may be behind the sex mortality differential in general, the increase in the differential during the present century may be explained by material and nonmaterial cultural changes (or by reference to such things as the rise of the automobile and a new attitude regarding the need for prenatal care).

Although the prominence of biological factors makes it difficult to visualize any immediate narrowing of the sex mortality differential, this is nonetheless a possibility. As the study of the causes of the differential continues, the findings of medical science could conceivably lead to greater declines in the male death rate, narrowing the gap that now exists between the sexes and perhaps contributing to a further reduction in overall mortality. In recent years, for example, some evidence has come to light suggesting that the sex differential may be explained in part by reference to differences in *morbidity* and also to differences in *temperament*. On the one hand, women are more likely than men to admit to being sick and to seek treatment for minor aches and illnesses. That is, a woman with a cold is more likely to stay in bed than a man who is more likely to feel compelled to get up and go to work. On the other hand, not only are men less likely to be bothered by minor aches and pains, they are also more likely to keep their emotions bottled up inside themselves. Women cry a great deal more than men, and it may be that such emotional releases are beneficial for their general level of health and thus contribute positively to their greater longevity. In any case, there is still much to be learned about this differential; and until more is learned one should not completely rule out the possibility of a future equalization of the life chances of men and women.

(4) *Color.* The death rates in Table II-4 also show that non-whites have long been characterized by substantially higher levels of mortality than the white population. It has been demonstrated on many occasions that this color mortality differential is not so much due to any inherent biological inferiority. Rather, it is related to other social and economic differences between whites and non-whites. In the United States in 1960, for example, the median family income of the white population was $5,088, or more than twice the median income of $2,520 recorded for nonwhite families. To cite another difference, the median number of years of school completed by whites in 1960 was 10.9, compared with only 8.2 years for nonwhites. A major concomitant of these educational and income differences is likely to be a substantial difference between whites and nonwhites in general standard of living and quantity and quality of medical care. To illustrate: as compared with the white population, nonwhites often cannot afford adequate housing (and where they can afford it, they are often denied access to it). Nonwhites eat more food of poorer quality and lower nutritional value, partly because of ignorance of what is required for a proper diet and partly because of an inability to afford anything better. Vitamin supplements are often absent from nonwhite diets for the same reasons. These same factors (lack of knowledge and lack of

money) frequently result in nonwhites not knowing when they should seek medical attention, and being less apt to seek it when they know they should. Furthermore, when they do receive medical assistance they are often likely to get it from overworked public health personnel in overcrowded clinics, a situation that is not conducive to high-quality medical care.

Although the nonwhite death rate continues to be notably higher than that of the white population, it is encouraging to note that this differential is narrowing, especially in the most recent period. During the first half of the twentieth century, for example, the age-adjusted death rate of nonwhites declined from 27.8 to 12.3 per 1,000 population, or by 56 per cent. This compared to a decline of 55 per cent for whites and resulted in a very slight narrowing of the mortality differential characterizing these two color groups (i.e., in 1900 the nonwhite death rate exceeded that of whites by 58 per cent, but by 1950 this difference had been reduced to 54 per cent). Between 1950 and 1960, however, the rate of mortality decline was substantially greater for nonwhites (15 per cent) than for whites (9 per cent), with the result that the excess of the nonwhite death rate over that of the white has been reduced to only 43 per cent during the most recent decade. In other words, the narrowing of the white-nonwhite differential since 1950 has been roughly three times as great as that which took place during the entire first half of the twentieth century.

Earlier in this century, improvements in medicine and in public health sanitation (with the general rise in living standards that facilitated the overall decline of the death rate in the United States) probably did not affect nonwhite mortality as much as that of the whites. But the fairly rapid decline of the nonwhite death rate since 1950 may be taken as evidence that there has been some improvement in the status of nonwhites in general. Among other things, they are becoming more and more able to take advantage of the many medical and health benefits available in modern society. Should this trend continue—and we must do everything in our power to see that it does—Americans can look forward to the day when the difference between the death rates of whites and nonwhites is reduced even further (perhaps even eliminated), or when the nonwhite segment of the population is able to share more equitably all of the advantages of our modern society. In the meantime, the fact remains that the nonwhite segment of the American population is characterized by a substantially lower socioeconomic status than the white population. Moreover, reflecting these socioeconomic differences, the nonwhites have a generally lower level of health, they receive lower-quality medical care, and they die at a substantially faster rate than the general population.

(5) *Marital status.* It has long been known that persons who are married have a lower death rate than persons in other marital status categories (single, widowed, or divorced). In the United States in 1959, for example, the death rate for married men at ages forty-five to fifty-four was 8.3 per 1,000. In contrast, the death rate for males in this age group who had never married was 13.9, while for men who were widowed or divorced the death rate was 25.1 per 1,000 population. For females in this age group, comparable marital status death rates per 1,000 population were 4.6 (married), 5.6 (single), and 7.6 (widowed or divorced).

This marital status mortality differential, which characterizes both males and females in all age groups, is generally explained by reference to two sets of factors: selective mating, and home environment differences among married and unmarried persons. On the one hand, it is generally assumed that marriage selects the healthier people in the society. Men who are sickly or physically infirm are less likely to be married—not only because they may be hesitant about assuming the responsibilities of providing for a family, but also because they are less likely to find a woman willing to accept them as a mate. Similarly, reasonably good health would seem to be an important factor regarding female marriageability, if only because most men would generally prefer to marry a healthy woman rather than a sickly one. On the other hand, it is customary to explain the marital status differential partly in terms of differences in the home environment of married as opposed to unmarried persons. Married people generally adhere to a more orderly schedule in their daily living. A married man, for example, is likely to eat more regularly, eat a more nutritionally adequate diet, keep more regular hours, and get more sleep than his bachelor counterpart. Marriage also represents a better physical and mental adaptation to life than does celibacy (either self-imposed or involuntary); and there is likely to be a certain amount of comfort and satisfaction derived from the companionship of marriage and family living —that contrasts quite sharply with the loneliness so often characteristic of the lives of the unmarried.

Persons who are widowed or divorced may have an added disadvantage over ordinary single persons. Not only do such people not have the social, biological, and emotional advantages of a happy family life, but they also must frequently adjust to the sudden, often traumatic, loss of these advantages. This may further impair their chances for survival and may account for the fact that their death rates at all ages are higher than the rates of the comparable group of persons who never married. Widowed persons may have had their health adversely affected by the death of the spouse (such as being weakened through caring for the spouse during a protracted period of illness prior to death) as well as by failing to overcome the hardships of widowhood. On the other hand, the divorced group obviously contains a disproportionate number of persons who have been unable to make a satisfactory adjustment to life—a fact which may be both a cause and an effect of physical weakness. Whatever the reasons, there would appear to be a sound basis for believing that a significant proportion of men and women who either do not marry or whose marriage becomes dissolved are relatively poor health risks and thus have higher death rates than married persons.

(6) *Nativity*. At the beginning of the present century the death rate for foreign-born males was 18.9 per 1,000, compared with a rate of 17.4 per 1,000 for men who had been born in the United States. For females, the corresponding rates were 18.4 among

foreign born and 15.7 among native women. These rates, which indicated an excess of foreign-born mortality over that of the native population—from 9 per cent for males to 17 per cent for females—were interpreted by some people as evidence that the immigrants flocking to this country at that time from southern and eastern Europe possessed inferior biological characteristics. But sufficient evidence has been amassed today to repudiate completely these earlier theories of racial or ethnic inferiority. For example, some evidence suggests that the different cultural backgrounds of the various immigrant groups, by determining their reactions to illness, may have played and may still play a detrimental role as far as their levels of mortality are concerned. To illustrate, the higher rate of infant mortality among Spanish-speaking peoples in the United States today is probably due in part to an attitude that regards pregnancy and childbearing as part of the natural and normal life experience of a woman, and that there is, therefore, no need to seek prenatal medical advice or assistance. Similarly, a generally fatalistic value orientation among such people (*que sera sera,* whatever will be, will be) may result in their failure to seek and adopt preventive health care practices.

Although the cultural factor may be an important one, most of the relevant data accumulated seems to indicate that social and economic differences between the immigrants and the native stock were primarily responsible for much of the former group's higher rates of mortality. For example, the foreign born tended to congregate in cities, and it is likely that urban slum conditions contributed to their generally higher death rate. Also, the hardships of trying to get settled and start a new life in a new and strange environment (for example, language barriers, lack of knowledge pertaining to available health care facilities, economic deprivation, and similar factors) probably prevented the foreign born from taking full advantage of many of the facilities and services available even then.

Since 1900, in contrast to the native population which has been characterized by a pronounced decline in mortality, the crude death rates of the foreign-born group have risen considerably. The explanation of this markedly atypical pattern must be sought not in terms of some set of ethnic factors—nor in terms of a worsening of the socioeconomic situation. Instead, it must be sought in terms of the changing age composition of the foreign-born population. Following the adoption of federal restrictive legislation shortly after World War I, the number of immigrants entering the United States each year underwent a substantial decline. Only about 1.5 million persons entered this country between 1930 and 1950, as opposed to well over 10 million immigrants during the previous twenty-year period. Meanwhile, those who came earlier had aged to such an extent that the proportion of the foreign-born white population over forty-five years of age increased from slightly more than one-third in 1900 to approximately 70 per cent in 1960. (Only about one-fourth of the native white population was over forty-five years of age in 1960.) It would thus seem that any nativity mortality differential that exists today is largely a function of the unfavorable age composition of the foreign born. An examination of the age-specific death rates (i.e., rates that express the number of deaths at a given age per 1,000 people alive at the same age) of the two nativity groups supports this explanation. In 1950, for example, the death rate of foreign-born males at ages twenty-five to forty-four was either identical to or less than the corresponding native male death rate. Moreover, although the foreign-born death rate is higher for males under twenty-five and over forty-four, and higher for females at all ages, the differences are not very large. As has already been indicated, they can probably be accounted for mainly in terms of cultural and especially socioeconomic differences between the two groups.

(7) *Place of residence.* Historically, cities have always had bad reputations as places where one's life chances were less than in the country. This was because the extremely unsanitary living conditions so widespread in the past (for example, using the same source of water for sewage as well as for drinking purposes) were most pronounced in the larger cities. Although the difference is not as

great for some of the other differentials, and although the same
central factors may not be operating to the same degree, there is
evidence that the traditional urban-rural mortality differential continues to persist in the United States today. In 1960, for example,
the death rate in those areas of the country classified as urban was
slightly more than 20 per cent higher than the rate recorded for
rural areas (10.3 per 1,000 in the former, as opposed to 8.4 per
1,000 in the latter). Moreover, within urban areas there was a
marked tendency for mortality levels to vary directly with size of
community. When cities are grouped according to size of population, the lowest death rate in 1960 was found for those containing
from 25,000 to 50,000 inhabitants (9.2 per 1,000). For cities
having a population of 50,000 or more, the death rate for all size
classes was in excess of the national average (9.5 per 1,000): it
was 9.8 per 1,000 for places having populations of 50,000 to
100,000, and became progressively higher as population size increased, reaching 11.5 for cities of a million or more persons.

Part of this relationship may be due to differences in the age
composition of the population in the various residence categories.
In 1960, for example, the median age of the urban population
was 30.4 years, as opposed to 27.3 years in rural areas; since the
urban population was "older," one would normally expect it to
have a higher death rate. On the other hand, since the relationship
has been observed so consistently over time, for all races and both
sexes, it might be that the urban-rural mortality differential stems
partly from the less favorable environmental conditions that can
still be found in many American cities, where the congestion and
smog contrast sharply to the open spaces and fresh air of the
country. It might also be a reflection of the greater tempo and
strain commonly associated with urban living in the United States
today. Finally, the persistence of this differential may very likely
be associated with a decline in the overall socioeconomic status of
the population in many of our larger cities. A major population
trend since the end of World War II has been a movement of
middle and upper socioeconomic groups out of the cities into the

surrounding suburban and rural fringe areas, *and* an opposing movement of lower socioeconomic groups (especially nonwhites) away from rural areas into the larger cities. Between 1950 and 1960, for example, the nonwhite population living in urbanized areas increased by 65 per cent, compared with an increase in the nonwhite population as a whole of only 27 per cent.

In short, we are today faced with a situation where all indications point to the persistence of an urban-rural mortality differential, but where there is little information pertaining to the precise causes of this differential. Although it is possible to list, as we have just done, a number of factors that are probably related to urban-rural mortality differences, it is not yet possible to specify the relative influence of each factor or set of factors. This, then, is one of the many areas where additional research is needed before the mortality situation in the United States can be completely understood and evaluated.

Several differences can be noted among various geographic regions and individual states in this country with regard to mortality levels. For the most part, however, these geographic differentials can be explained in terms of differences in ethnic composition or differences in the degree of urbanization. In 1960, for example, death rates were lowest in the northwestern part of the United States where urbanization is relatively low and where the number of nonwhites is negligible. At the other extreme, death rates were highest in the highly urbanized Middle Atlantic states and in the deep South. Among individual states, the 1960 age-adjusted death rate was lowest in the three western farm states of Iowa, Kansas, and Nebraska (6.6 in each state), and highest in the District of Columbia (9.1) and in South Carolina (9.2).

(8) *Socioeconomic status.* A particularly significant mortality differential, one that has already been referred to in the discussions of color, nativity, and residence differentials, concerns the variations in mortality associated with differences in socioeconomic status. This differential is particularly significant for two reasons. First, many of the previously observed differences in death rates

(as between whites and nonwhites) can be explained largely in terms of corresponding differences in socioeconomic status. Second, this differential is an indication of the extent to which all members of the society are sharing equally in the growing affluence of the society. But in spite of its importance, and in spite of the fact that the study of mortality in different socioeconomic groups has long occupied the attention of many scholars in a variety of fields, there is today a major gap in our knowledge pertaining to the precise influence of socioeconomic factors on mortality rates. In contrast to an abundance of fairly reliable published material showing the relationship of such characteristics as sex, age, and color to mortality rates, studies relating to socioeconomic status are relatively rare. Although people have long been aware of the generalization that mortality is inversely related to socioeconomic status, very few empirical studies have sought to examine this relationship more thoroughly. This is clearly a topic on which the need for research is especially acute.

This lack of information about the relationship between socioeconomic status and mortality is due in part to the difficulty of obtaining the necessary data. Aside from occupation, no information is provided by the death certificate currently in use that would enable a researcher to determine a decedent's social class. But a man's occupation is an extremely crucial factor in determining his socioeconomic status, and it has long been recognized that people in the higher social classes, as indicated by their occupation, have an appreciably lower death rate than those at the other end of the social scale, and that a man's occupation is one of the major factors determining the state of his health and fixing the length of his life. For this reason, there have been several attempts in this country to study the relationship between occupation and mortality. The most recent of these is a United States Public Health Service study that analyzes variations in mortality levels among occupations in the United States as of 1950.[6] The general results of this study are revealed by the *standard mortality ratios* for men at ages twenty to sixty-four in the following major occupation groups:

All classes	100	
Professional	88 ⎫	
Managerial	89 ⎪	White collar
Clerical	84 ⎬	
Sales	96 ⎭	
Craftsmen	99 ⎫	
Operatives	96 ⎪	Blue collar
Service	118 ⎬	
Laborers	163 ⎭	

These standard mortality ratios measure the mortality level of a particular population subgroup relative to the mortality level of all groups which is set at 100. In this way, one can determine at a glance both the direction and magnitude of the deviation of subgroup mortality levels from the general average (for example, the mortality level of professional workers is 88, or 12 per cent below the mortality level of the general population, whereas the mortality level of laborers is 163, or 63 per cent higher than the general average).

Although a consistent gradient is absent, these standard mortality ratios reveal a general inverse relationship between mortality levels and occupational status in the United States. All white-collar occupations as well as the higher-status blue-collar occupations have mortality levels below that of the general public, with the deviation being most pronounced for the white-collar occupations. On the other hand, the two lowest blue-collar occupational groups are characterized by mortality levels substantially higher than that of the general population. Clearly, persons in the lower status occupations have a much higher mortality risk than persons with a higher-status occupation.

If one bears in mind that differences in occupation are associated with differences in education and income (i.e., higher status occupations generally require more education and command a larger salary than lower status occupations), then it is easier to understand the forces underlying the occupational mortality differential. That is, men in the higher-status occupations have lower mortality levels partly because their education and income enable them to know more about better health and to pay for better medical care.

The knowledge of how socioeconomic factors are related to levels of health makes it possible to understand many of the previously observed differences in mortality between various ethnic groups or between various residential areas. For example, the white-nonwhite differences in median family income in 1960 ($5,088 for whites as opposed to $2,520 for nonwhite families) and in median years of school completed (10.9 as opposed to 8.2 years for whites and nonwhites, respectively) makes it easier to understand why the nonwhite age-adjusted death rate in 1960 was about 40 per cent higher than that of the white population. By the same reasoning, neighborhoods in a city (or even whole cities) where particular occupation, education, and income groups were concentrated would be almost certain to have different levels of mortality than other neighborhoods (or cities) where different occupation, education, and income groups were concentrated. In one recent study, residential areas within Hartford, Connecticut, and Providence, Rhode Island, were compared on the basis of the occupation, education, and income composition of their resident populations. The various neighborhoods were grouped into five broad socioeconomic areas in each city and then compared in terms of their age-adjusted death rates. On the one hand, this comparison revealed a pronounced inverse relationship between mortality levels and the overall socioeconomic status of the population in both cities (see Table II-5). In both Hartford and Providence, age-adjusted death rates increased consistently from the highest to the lowest socioeconomic area, with death rates in the latter area being approximately 40 per cent higher than in the highest status areas. On the other hand, the age-adjusted death

Table II-5: *Age-adjusted death rates for five socioeconomic areas in Hartford, Connecticut, and Providence, Rhode Island (1949–1951).*

Socioeconomic areas		Age-adjusted death rates	
		Hartford	Providence
All areas		9.2	10.1
(High status)	I	7.7	8.7
	II	8.8	9.6
	III	9.2	9.9
	IV	10.0	11.0
(Low status)	V	10.6	12.1

SOURCE: Edward G. Stockwell, "A Critical Examination of the Relationship Between Socioeconomic Status and Mortality," *American Journal of Public Health* (June 1963).

rates for all socioeconomic levels were notably higher in Providence than in Hartford. This intercity variation in mortality levels is also explainable in terms of socioeconomic differences. To illustrate, in 1950 less than three out of ten members of the Providence labor force (28.6 per cent) were working at occupations in *non*-manufacturing industries, whereas more than two-thirds of the Hartford labor force (68.7 per cent) held jobs in non-manufacturing industries. Similarly, the median number of years of school completed by adults was less in Providence (9.4) than in Hartford (9.7); and this same relationship was noted with regard to the median income level of the population ($2,434 in Providence, $2,953 in Hartford). That is, Providence ranked notably lower than Hartford in terms of the overall socioeconomic status of its population in 1950, and these socioeconomic status differences probably explain a large part of the intercity mortality differentials.

Although it has long been known that the lower socioeconomic status groups in the population have substantially higher death rates than the higher status groups, and although the most recent studies confirm the persistence of this socioeconomic differential, there are still significant questions pertaining to this differential for which there are no satisfactory answers. If one were to review the relevant research, for example, one would find conflicting evidence as to whether or not such a differential does in fact exist. Moreover, even where the existence of a socioeconomic differential is agreed upon, there is disagreement concerning such things as the magnitude of the differential, whether or not it is becoming smaller, whether it characterizes all groups within a socioeconomic ranking (i.e., women as well as men, infants as well as adults), and whether it is in evidence for all causes of death or for only a few selected causes. This situation clearly stresses the need for additional research. In view of this need it is not surprising to note that the major studies of mortality in the United States today have incorporated socioeconomic factors as being among the most significant independent variables in the research design.[7]

Hopefully, the findings of current research will enable us to obtain a more comprehensive picture of mortality differences among the various areas and subgroups of the population of the United States, and of the relationship of these mortality differences to other demographic, social, and economic characteristics. In the meantime, we must face the fact that there are many groups within the American population that do not share the low levels of mortality enjoyed by other groups. With the exception of such factors as the obvious age differential (and perhaps also the sex differential, which seems to be in large measure a function of some inherent biological differences between the sexes), the mortality differentials in the United States are closely related to a variety of social and economic factors. Since the influence of such factors is not fixed, it follows that they are subject to modification. This means that it should be possible to eliminate these differentials and thereby effect a further reduction in the overall level of mortality.

THE END OF MORTALITY DECLINE

In spite of the fact that the crude death rate in the United States has been cut nearly in half during the present century, there is little justification for sitting back to admire the progress we have made. Differentials within the general population represent one reason why we can ill afford to adopt a complacent attitude. Another reason is the recent end of the decline in mortality. The failure to experience continued declines in mortality since 1954 is very disturbing to many experts, particularly since the postwar years have been characterized by a number of major medical breakthroughs (such as the polio vaccine) as well as by substantial improvements in both the quantity and quality of public as well as private medical care. Since the end of the Second World War ". . . there has been a growth in the volume and scope of health services in prevention, diagnosis, medical and surgical therapy, and rehabilitation, and also an improvement in their quality. The rapid growth of health insurance plans has made high-quality medical care readily accessible to ever-increasing numbers of people. The rising level of living has resulted in improvement of work and home environment, quality and variety of food, educational attainment, and facilities for recreation. Developments in medicine arising from the exigencies of a global war have become readily available for application to civilian health problems. At no time in the history of the country have conditions appeared so favorable for health progress." [8]

In spite of this seemingly auspicious situation, the crude death rate has remained relatively stable since the mid-1950's. And this apparent leveling off of mortality levels is not unique to the United States. Many of the advanced nations of western Europe have experienced a similar leveling off of death rates during recent years, and some countries (such as Norway, Denmark, the Netherlands) have even experienced a reversal of the downward trend in the death rate. The questions that need to be faced now are: (a) Does the recent leveling off of the death rate represent a temporary phase in the course of the mortality experience of the United States, or does it mark the end of mortality decline and the attainment of a minimum death rate? (b) If it is only a temporary phenomenon, what factors are responsible for the recent leveling off in the United States?

Considering these questions in order, the first thing to note is that it is not likely that the crude death rate in the United States has reached an irreducible minimum level. The overall crude death rate summarizes the mortality experience of a number of different subgroups in the population, many of whom have substantially lower death rates than other groups. The very fact that some groups have lower death rates than others means that there is room for further mortality reductions simply by eliminating current differentials. Further evidence to support the conclusion that the United States has not reached an irreducible minimum death rate lies in the fact that lower death rates have on occasion been achieved by other countries of the Western world.

Turning to the second question, if the end of mortality decline in recent years does not mark the attainment of an irreducible minimum death rate, then the problem becomes one of understanding and explaining the causes underlying this temporary halt in the downward trend. The latest investigation of this problem has suggested that the leveling off of the crude death rate since 1954 is the result of a combination of two sets of factors, each of which relates to the trend in mortality from particular *causes* of death. Thus, to fully comprehend the significance of the recent leveling off, it is necessary to examine the mortality situation in terms of the influence of the various causes of death.

(1) *Cause of death trends.* In discussing the mortality situation in the United States so far, we have considered only trends in total mortality, with particular emphasis on the various differentials that currently exist in American society (age, sex, color, marital status, nativity, place of residence, and socioeconomic status). But the total mortality picture is not a single whole. Instead it is made up

of many separate parts, each of which represents deaths from a particular cause. Generally speaking, there are two broad classes of diseases that ultimately lead to death: (1) *acute* diseases, which are the result of some sort of virus or bacterial infection (influenza and pneumonia, tuberculosis, diphtheria, typhoid fever, and so forth); and (2) *chronic* diseases, or those that reflect some sort of organic disintegration (heart disease, stroke, and cancer, for example). A third group of causes sometimes singled out for special analysis includes deaths involving physical violence (for example, accidents, suicides, and homicides). The data in Table II-6 reveal

Table II-6: Death rates from selected causes in the United States, by decade, 1900–1960 (deaths per 100,000 population).

Cause of death	1900	1910	1920	1930	1940	1950	1960
All causes	1,719.1	1,468.0	1,298.9	1,132.1	1,076.4	963.8	954.7
Influenza and pneumonia	202.2	155.9	207.3	102.5	70.3	31.3	37.3
Tuberculosis	194.4	153.8	113.1	71.1	45.9	22.5	6.1
Gastritis and related causes	142.7	115.4	53.7	26.0	10.3	5.1	4.4
Diphtheria	40.3	21.1	15.3	4.9	1.1	0.3	0.0
Typhoid fever	31.3	22.5	7.6	4.7	1.0	0.1	0.0
Heart disease	142.7	165.1	163.4	216.7	293.9	356.8	369.0
Cancer	64.0	76.2	83.4	97.4	120.3	139.8	149.2
Vascular lesions	106.9	95.8	93.0	89.0	90.9	104.0	108.0
Diabetes mellitus	11.0	15.3	16.1	19.1	26.6	16.2	16.7
Accidents	72.3	84.2	70.0	79.8	73.2	60.6	52.3
Motor vehicle accidents	......	1.8	10.3	26.7	26.2	23.1	21.3

SOURCE: Same as Table II-4.

that the overall decline of mortality in the United States during the twentieth century has come about largely because of man's growing ability to control infection. To illustrate, the cause-specific death rate (i.e., the number of deaths due to a particular cause per 100,000 population) for influenza and pneumonia, the leading cause of death in 1900, has been reduced by 82 per cent during this century. Even more spectacular declines have occurred in tuberculosis and gastritis death rates (both have declined by 97 per cent since 1900); and deaths from such parasitic diseases as diphtheria and typhoid fever have been virtually eliminated in this country.

Man is not immortal, however, and the partial elimination or reduction of certain causes of death has only meant that others have increased in importance. For example, although the death rates for infectious causes such as influenza and pneumonia have been substantially reduced since 1900, the rates for many of the chronic type diseases have undergone marked increases. The death rates for heart disease and cancer, for example, have more than doubled since the beginning of the century. This means that the killers of the old have replaced the killers of the young as the leading causes of death. This increasing prominence of diseases characteristic of middle and older age has brought about a refocusing of medical research; as progress is made in uncovering the causes and improving the care and treatment programs of these chronic causes of death, it may be that we can look for further declines in the overall level of mortality. An encouraging illustration of what can happen is the trend in the death rate for diabetes mellitus. The diabetes death rate increased steadily up to 1940, at which time it was well over twice as high as it had been at the beginning of the century. It has declined since then, however, and in 1960 the death rate from this cause was 37 per cent lower than it had been in 1940 (although it was still substantially higher than it had been in 1900).

The trend in accident mortality is interesting to note. The accident death rate has declined from 72.3 per 100,000 population in 1900 to 52.3 per 100,000 in 1960, or by slightly more than one-fourth. But this decline would have been much greater—well over 50 per cent—if it were not for motor vehicle fatalities. Automobile accidents, nonexistent at the beginning of this century, were responsible for some 38,000 deaths in the United States in 1960. They account for approximately 40 per cent of all accident fatalities in this country today and are in large part responsible for accidents now ranking as the fourth leading cause of death in the United States. It is thus apparent that the overall mortality situation in this country could be partially improved through efforts entirely unrelated to biology or medicine.

(2) *Cause of death trends and mortality stabilization.* A closer examination of the trend for particular causes of death suggests that the end of the decline in the death rate since the mid-1950's can be attributed to two sets of factors. First, the accelerated decline in the death rate for infectious diseases, such as influenza, pneumonia, and tuberculosis, has lost its momentum in recent years. The death rate from influenza and pneumonia together, for example, fell from 194.4 per 100,000 population in 1900 to 31.3 in 1950. It reached an all-time low of 25.4 per 100,000 in 1954, but since then it has risen and remained consistently at a level in the mid-30's. The low influenza and pneumonia death rate of 37.3 per 100,000 recorded in the United States in 1960, for example, is nearly 50 per cent higher than the all-time low rate achieved in 1954.

Other infectious respiratory diseases have also ceased to decline since the mid-1950's. The bronchitis death rate rose from 1.8 per 100,000 in 1954 to 2.4 in 1960, or by approximately one-third. Other infectious causes have remained at fairly constant levels (for example, the death rate from gastritis and related causes was 4.9 in 1954 and was still as high as 4.4 in 1960). Finally, the death rate for still other infectious diseases has experienced a marked reduction in the rate of decline. During the first half of the 1950 decade, for example, the tuberculosis death rate declined from 22.5 to 9.1 per 100,000, or by a rate of about 12 per cent per year. But since 1955 the rate of decline has fallen to only 7 per cent per year. These infectious diseases still account for a fairly large proportion of deaths among infants and preschool children (approximately 9 per cent of all deaths under one year in 1960 were due to influenza and pneumonia, whereas they accounted for 15 per cent of the deaths between one and four years of age). As the proportion of the total population in the younger age groups has increased (the proportion of the population under five years of age in the United States rose from 10.7 to 11.3 per cent between 1950 and 1960), it has contributed disproportionately more to the overall crude death rate. Thus the failure of the major infectious diseases to continue declining as the proportion of youth in the population increases may be cited as one of the factors behind the leveling off of the overall death rate. To this possible explanation must be added the fact that the death rate for these infectious diseases has leveled off at all ages. At the time of this writing, this phenomenon represented a newly emerging health problem in the United States for which there was no satisfactory explanation.

The second factor, of course, relates to the continued increase in death rates from chronic causes of death such as heart disease and cancer, particularly respiratory cancer. Between 1950 and 1965, for example, the death rate for all forms of cancer increased from 139.8 to 152.0 per 100,000, or by 9 per cent; during this same period the death rate for respiratory cancer (for example, lung cancer) increased from 14.1 to 25.3 per 100,000 population, or by 80 per cent. Although this trend has been partly attributed by some sources to such things as an increase in smoking and air pollution, not enough is yet known to be able to specify the exact influence of these factors. Nevertheless, the fact remains that the rapid rise in the lung cancer death rate in recent years (as well as the increased mortality from other chronic respiratory diseases such as bronchitis and emphysema) has been recognized by the United States Public Health Service as indicating one of the most serious mortality problems in the nation today.

Respiratory diseases are not the only chronic ones to undergo substantial increases between 1950 and 1965. During this same period the death rate from all forms of heart disease increased 4 per cent (from 356.8 to 371.3 per 100,000), whereas the mortality from arteriosclerosis increased by as much as 37 per cent (from 213.0 to 293.0 per 100,000 population). These diseases which are the leading causes of death today (heart disease and cancer account for well over half of all deaths in the United States every year) are difficult to prevent. As the diseases for which there are no effective preventive serums have replaced infectious diseases as the major causes of death, the downward trend in the overall death rate has ceased. In other words, although the leveling off of the death rate for diseases such as influenza and pneumonia has contributed some to the end of mortality decline in the United States, the increase in the death rate from chronic diseases, such as heart disease and cancer, is much the more important factor. This means that a revival of a downward trend will come only when we have achieved a measure of control over chronic diseases analogous to that which has been achieved since 1900 with infectious diseases.

(3) *Outlook for the future.* There are several reasons for anticipating still further reductions in the mortality level of the United States population. One reason lies in the simple fact that other population groups have achieved lower death rates, and what is possible for others to achieve is possible for us. To illustrate, recent estimates have shown that if the lowest age-specific death rates ever recorded for males and females in any country were applied to the United States in 1960, we would have had a crude death rate of 7.3 per 1,000—a rate 23 per cent below the crude death rate actually recorded in that year. For the most part, the lowering of the overall crude death rate to a level as low as 7 per 1,000 will come about largely through the narrowing (perhaps even the elimination) of many of the earlier noted mortality differentials, particularly those associated with differences in socioeconomic status. One of the best possibilities for further declines relates to deaths before, during, and after the birth process, for the socioeconomic differential is most pronounced with regard to infant and childhood mortality. (In 1960 the age-adjusted death rate of the nonwhite population was 42 per cent higher than the white death rate, whereas the nonwhite infant mortality rate was 98 per

cent higher.) Mortality reductions at the older ages may also be possible, but these will be less significant and will depend on the outcome of current research into the causes of the major chronic diseases.

In speculating about the reduction of chronic disease mortality, it must be stressed that the greatest contributions medical science and public health have so far made in gaining control over mortality have been in the area of disease prevention rather than treatment. Naturally, curative powers have increased (witness the power of penicillin); but they have not increased anywhere near as much as preventive powers. It was not a miraculous cure that eliminated smallpox as a major cause of death; rather, it was the development of a serum that prevents the disease from occurring. Similarly, it is the preventive aspect of infant DPT shots that have more or less done away with diphtheria, whooping cough, and tetanus as major killers of young children. In other words, man's greatest progress in reducing deaths due to particular disease has come through eliminating the disease. Future declines in chronic disease mortality will depend upon finding ways to prevent the occurrence of those diseases that are the leading causes of death today. One recent step in this direction is the identification of the causal relationship between smoking and lung cancer. It must be stressed, however, that chronic diseases are in the long run due to a disintegration of the organic tissue as the body grows older, so we are not likely to witness any major breakthrough similar to those that have led to the conquest of many infectious diseases. Nevertheless, as medical science continues to learn more about the many factors that are causally related to the various chronic ailments, it is possible to anticipate minor breakthroughs. These will result in some reductions in the death rate at the older ages, and will thereby perhaps influence a further decline in the overall crude death rate.

MORBIDITY

Any discussion of mortality is incomplete without some reference to morbidity (illness). Not only is morbidity important because it is a precursor of death; it is also of interest because of its relationship to economic productivity and the general welfare of the family (i.e., illness often entails absence from work and a loss of earnings). In this sense, morbidity may act as an underlying cause in the circular chain of events leading to higher death rates among many lower socioeconomic status groups: ill health → inability to work steadily → low income → inability to maintain a level of living conducive to good health → ill health, greater risk of mortality, and higher death rate. That is, ill health may be both a cause and effect of the low socioeconomic status associated with higher mortality levels.

Although morbidity is an important topic, discussion of it must necessarily be limited by the *relative* nature of illness. One person's "ill health" may not be another's, and this makes it extremely difficult to obtain reliable morbidity data from all segments of the population. The information that we have been able to collect (through the United States National Health Surveys and other sources) suggests that although we cannot generalize from mortality to morbidity, there is a close similarity to their patterns. Thus, if we know that one population subgroup has a higher death rate than another subgroup, we will generally not be wrong if we assume that it also has a higher illness rate. For example, where poor housing and other adverse environmental conditions are associated with higher death rates from infectious respiratory diseases such as tuberculosis, it can generally be assumed that a higher incidence of the disease in question is associated with the same environmental conditions. To cite a more specific illustration, recent National Health Survey findings in the United States have shown that the average number of days spent in bed due to illness, as well as the number of work days lost, decreases as family income rises.[9] That is, the lowest mortality groups tend to have the lowest incidence of disabling morbidity, and vice versa.

One notable exception to the preceding general rule relates to sex, where the morbidity differential is commonly the reverse of what it is for mortality: men may die at a faster rate, but women get sick more. As suggested earlier, this morbidity differential may be one reason women in fact live longer than men. That is, women have lower death rates because they take better care of themselves —because they are more likely to stay in bed if they are not feeling well.

With this one notable exception, however, morbidity differences tend to parallel the mortality differentials that currently exist in American society. The implication here is that a more equitable sharing of our current knowledge and techniques for preventing and treating illness among the less privileged members of the society would not only lead to a reduction in their death rate; the resulting improvement in their overall level of physical well-being would also reduce the incidence of illness, and this in turn might affect such things as enhanced ability to find and hold a job. This, of course, would benefit not only the individual and his family but also the society at large: the latter would profit both by the individual's increased productivity and by the reduction of unemployment and other welfare expenditures frequently associated with ill health.

REFERENCES AND SUGGESTIONS FOR FURTHER READING

Donald J. Bogue, *The Population of the United States,* Glencoe, Ill., 1959, Chapter 9.

Louis I. Dublin, Alfred J. Lotka, and Mortimer Spiegelman, *Length of Life,* New York, 1949.

Conrad and Irene B. Taeuber, *The Changing Population of the United States,* New York, 1958, Chapter 14.

Ralph Thomlinson, *Population Dynamics,* New York, 1965, Chapters 5–7.

Warren S. Thompson and David T. Lewis, *Population Problems,* New York, 1965, Chapters 12 and 13.

United Nations, *Determinants and Consequences of Population Trends,* ST/SOA/Series A/17, New York, 1953, Chapter 4.

U.S. National Center for Health Statistics, National Vital Statistics Division, *Vital Statistics of the United States,* II. Annual compilation of mortality statistics for the United States.

U.S. National Center for Health Statistics, Vital and Health Statistics, Series 3, No. 1, *The Change in Mortality Trends in the United States,* Washington, D.C., 1964; and Series 3, No. 4, *Infant and Perinatal Mortality in the United States,* Washington, D.C., 1965.

3

Fertility

The second basic demographic process is fertility. Like mortality, fertility is basically a biological process, but unlike death it is not inevitable. On the contrary, whether or not a married couple has a baby can frequently be a matter of their own choice. Thus it is necessary to consider fertility in relation to human attitudes and desires regarding the bearing of children.

At the outset, we may specify some of the more commonly used terms and concepts. To begin with, one should be aware of the distinction between the two terms *fertility* and *fecundity*. When one speaks of a woman's fertility one refers to the number of children she has actually borne. Fecundity, on the other hand, refers to the number of children a woman is biologically capable of having— provided an artificial check to childbearing is not imposed on her. Most layman would think in terms of "fertile" and "sterile" as being opposites; but for demographers the opposite of fertile is childless, whereas the opposite of sterile is fecund. A woman may be fecund, or capable of bearing children, but she does not become fertile until she has actually had a baby.

The level of fertility in any population is most commonly measured by the *crude birth rate*. This rate is analogous to the crude death rate and is defined as the number of live births occurring per 1,000 people in a given population during a calendar year. To illustrate, there were 4,257,850 live births in the United States during the twelve months from January 1 to December 31, 1960. The average number of people living in the country during that year (i.e., the midpoint population, or the population as of July 1, 1960) has been estimated at 180,684,000. The crude birth rate can thus be computed as $4,257,850 \div 180,684,000 \times 1,000 = 23.57$. This means that in 1960 there were roughly 23.6 births for every 1,000 people in the United States.

The highest fertility levels in the world today are found in the economically underdeveloped countries of Asia, Africa, and Latin America, where it is not uncommon to find birth rates on the order of 45 or even 50 per 1,000. At the other extreme, many of the low-fertility countries of Europe and Oceania have crude birth rates as low as 16 or 17 per 1,000. The 1960 crude birth rate in the United States of 23.6 would thus represent a moderate level of fertility.

HISTORICAL FERTILITY CONDITIONS

As revealed in the preceding chapter, the population history of the Western world shows that economic growth and improvements in the standard of living have been followed closely by a gradual— but sustained—decline in the death rate. Fertility, however, was much slower to respond to these changes. It was not until several generations had passed that the birth rate also began to decline; and the interim period was one of rapid and substantial population growth. The tendency of mortality to decline earlier and more rapidly than fertility results, in large measure, from differences in human attitudes toward death and procreation. People have generally been quite willing to adopt practices that would postpone the evils of death. But the birth of a child has almost universally been looked upon as a wondrous and blessed event; and people have traditionally been reluctant to adopt measures to limit their fertility. This reluctance has its roots deep in antiquity, where conditions of life were so harsh and death rates so very high that a correspondingly high birth rate was a necessary condition for the survival of the species, and it was to the advantage of every society to encourage maximum childbearing. Many aspects of the social and cultural structure functioned, therefore, to promote a high level of fertility, and birth rates throughout the ancient world generally approached the biological maximum—in many cases exceeding 50 per 1,000.

The strongest inducements to high fertility in the premodern world (and also the primary inducements to high fertility among economically underdeveloped countries now) lay in the fact that societies were characterized by a strong familistic rather than an individualistic orientation. Emphasis was on promoting and maintaining the strength and solidarity of the extended kinship group. This subordination of the individual to the kinship unit had several consequences conducive to high fertility. For one thing, in such a setting the economic cost of rearing children did not impinge solely on the young parents but was spread among all members of the family. Similarly, the time and effort involved in caring for young children did not have to be borne entirely by the parents. Perhaps most important, however, was the simple arithmetical fact that the more children that were born in a family, the more workers it would have to contribute to the common treasury, and the more soldiers it would be able to field to defend against external threats to the family's welfare. Thus, early marriage coupled with early and regular childbearing was strongly encouraged: the prestige and security of the women in the family were determined directly by the number of children they bore (especially by the number of sons); and barrenness was about the worst possible sin of which a wife could be guilty.

An additional influence on fertility in pre-industrial societies was the tendency to differentiate sharply between the roles of men and women. Women were confined largely to the household and were identified primarily with the tasks of housekeeping and of bearing and raising children. Finally, the religious values in the pre-industrial world generally supported the other structural features of the society that encouraged high fertility behavior. Among such positive inducements to childbearing were (a) the stress on filial piety, or the need to have children to perpetuate the family name and to care for the ancestor shrines; (b) the Old Testament injunction to "be fruitful and multiply"; and (c) various religious taboos that discouraged the practice of contraception.

Not all features of primitive societies were geared to encourage high fertility. Frequently, in fact, there were many aspects of the social structure that functioned to *prevent* the attainment of maximum fertility. Such things as prohibitions against the remarriage of widows, restrictions on having intercourse during specified periods (such as during the first year after the birth of a child), and taboos on a woman having children after she had become a grandmother are some of the beliefs and practices that served to keep actual fertility below the fecundity potential. But in spite of such checks on the attainment of maximum fertility, birth rates were very high throughout the pre-industrial world. Only fairly recently has this situation changed and birth rates declined to a relatively low level—and only in the more advanced Western countries. In Sweden, for example, which has one of the lowest birth rates in the world today (16 per 1,000 as of 1964),[2] vital statistics data reveal that the crude birth rate was about 30 to 35 per 1,000 a scant hundred years ago. Most European countries, in fact, had birth rates on the order of 30 or more as recently as the middle of the nineteenth century, and it was not until the decade immediately preceding the Second World War that birth rates of less than 20 per 1,000 ceased to be a rarity. Today, however, nearly every major country in Europe has levels of fertility as low as or even lower than this rate. In Rumania, for example, the birth rate in the mid-1960's has been estimated at 15.2 per 1,000; it was as low as 13.1 in Hungary, while in the city of

West Berlin in 1964 there were only 12.2 live births for every 1,000 inhabitants.

FERTILITY DECLINE IN THE MODERN WORLD

A high birth rate has historically been a functional prerequisite for the very survival of the human species: as long as death rates are high, a correspondingly high birth rate is necessary to prevent the population from dwindling into extinction. Where death rates are low, however, this necessity is absent. With the coming of death control, therefore, one of the most compelling forces promoting high birth rates was diminished; and as mortality decline became firmly established it was soon followed by corresponding declines in the level of fertility. But simply citing the emergence and spread of death control as "the cause" of the historical decline of the birth rate in the modern Western world is a gross oversimplification. It does not adequately consider the many changes in human social life (especially in the family) that have influenced the fertility reduction of the past 100 to 150 years. As with the causes of mortality decline, the more important changes that have contributed substantially to the lowering of the birth rate in the industrially advanced countries of the Western world can be grouped into three broad categories: (1) changes in the *material* aspects of culture; (2) changes in the *non-material* aspects of culture; and (3) changes related to the development and diffusion of improved techniques of *birth control*.

(1) *Changes in material culture.* Many of the material changes associated with the emergence and growth of modern urban-industrial society at first had a positive effect on the fertility level. One result of the many changes that accompanied this transition, for example, was an improvement in agricultural productivity. An important corollary of the increase in the quantity and quality of food available for personal consumption was an improvement in the nutritional status of the population. This not only led to a decline in childlessness due to sterility but also contributed to a

reduction in reproductive wastage through a lowering of both infant mortality and the incidence of miscarriage. A particularly significant development was the appearance of the common potato in Europe. This crop, first introduced in Spain in the late sixteenth century, can not only be grown in marginal soil but also has a per acre yield that is four to six times as great as that of the major grain crops. Thus, a man who switched from planting grain to planting potatoes could easily double the number of dependents he was capable of supporting without changing either the extent of his labors or the amount of land area under cultivation.

The emergence of the factory system of production also encouraged an increase in the birth rate. One consequence of this development, for example, was the creation of industrial employment opportunities at a time when improvements in agricultural technology were displacing large numbers of people from farm occupations. The availability of this employment made it possible for a man to become economically self-sufficient at an early age, and this was a positive inducement to early marriage. At the same time that industrialization was creating more jobs, the coming of power-driven machinery in manufacturing was causing a breakdown in the old skill hierarchy of the craft industries. This meant an end to the apprentice system with its long training requirements (and its proscriptions on marriage during the training period), thereby adding several years to a man's working (and married) life. The earlier start on marriage made possible by these two developments meant that couples were exposed to the risk of childbearing for longer periods; and at a time when methods of birth control were little known (and often less appreciated), this longer period of exposure was conducive to higher fertility.

In spite of these initial effects, however, the long-run impact of the technological changes that marked the transformation from an agrarian to an industrial society was a reduction in the level of fertility. The emergence of the factory system cited above, for example, signified an end of the earlier cottage industries as well as the apprentice system, and the former meant a sharp separation between place of residence and place of work. This represented an inducement to a lower birth rate in that a woman who wanted to augment the family's income could do so only with difficulty if she had many children to care for in the home. Fertility decline was also influenced by the growth in productivity that accompanied the rise of industrialization. This increase in productivity meant that less human labor was required to yield a given amount of either agricultural or industrial goods. A farmer who wanted to increase the output of his fields, for example, could now do so through the application of technology rather than through the application of more labor, and this removed one of the major incentives for having large families.

The entire phenomenon of *urbanization* (by which is meant an increase in both the number of cities and the proportion of the population living in them) also served as a major stimulus to fertility reduction. Historically, fertility has always been lower in cities than in the countryside. Partly this is because a large number of children is less likely to be an economic asset in the city than on the family farm. It is also because the extremely overcrowded housing and generally unsanitary living conditions characteristic of the early industrial centers did not encourage people to bring more children into the world. Thus the mass movement of population away from rural areas in search of more lucrative employment in the factories of the growing cities meant that an increasing proportion of the population was exposed to the lower fertility values of urban areas.

The gradual emergence of death control, discussed in the previous chapter, was another material cultural change that influenced a reduction in the birth rate. On the one hand, a lower mortality rate among infants and children meant that a larger proportion of births survived to adulthood; thus it was no longer necessary for a couple to have a large number of children to be assured of having one or two survive to help care for them in their old age. On the other hand, the extension of adult life meant that "children" who had to wait for their inheritance before they were in a position to marry and assume family responsibilities had to wait longer. The classic illustration of this phenomenon is offered by the experience of Ireland, where a late age at marriage has long been characteristic of males. In that country a man generally did not marry until he had gained his inheritance, and this did not usually occur until the death of his father. As medical progress increased the ability to postpone death, it became necessary for the young man to delay marriage until later and later in life, thereby reducing the number of married years he would actively be siring children.

Finally, a decline in the birth rate would have been very unlikely if a reduced death rate had not removed the necessity of a high level of fertility for the survival of the species. Thus, although a variety of factors were influential, one has to regard the decline of the death rate as one of the major developments underlying the subsequent decline in the birth rate.

(2) *Changes in non-material culture.* Although it is admittedly difficult to separate one from the other, there is some basis for suggesting that the greatest influence on fertility reduction can be found in the changes in attitudes and values associated with the material culture changes discussed above (i.e., subjective wants and desires are much more important in determining births than deaths). This is the reverse of the situation with regard to mortality: the most significant causes of the reduction in the death rate are to be found in those material changes in medicine and public health that greatly enhanced man's control over the leading infectious causes of death.

As far as fertility is concerned, perhaps the most significant non-material cultural change was the emergence of a set of attitudes and values that favored smaller families than had traditionally been regarded as ideal. This *small family ethos* (as this attitudinal development is called) reflected a very fundamental transformation in the organization and function of the family in Western society. In part it was associated with a decline in the importance of the family as the primary economic unit. As industrialization progressed, and as the factory system replaced the earlier cottage industries, the significance of large numbers for the economic well-being of the family declined, and this gave rise to the nuclear family rather than the extended kinship group as the dominant productive unit. The decline in the economic significance of large families was accompanied by a decline in their social significance as well. This is reflected in such changes as a lessening of the importance attached to having many sons to ensure perpetuation of the family name, and an increase in the tendency to evaluate an individual on the basis of his own accomplishments rather than on the basis of his group membership. In short, values shifted from an emphasis on the well-being of the group to an emphasis on the welfare and development of the individual.

Related to the growth of individualism was the general growth in intellectual freedom, both caused and further enhanced by the agricultural and industrial revolutions of the eighteenth and nineteenth centuries. For example, the growing secularization of religion characteristic of the post-Renaissance period saw, among other things, a decline in the importance traditionally attached to such biblical commands as "be fruitful and multiply." Today it is relatively rare to come across a woman who has borne six to eight children, whereas only a few generations ago it was relatively rare to come across a middle-aged married woman who had *not* borne this many offspring. The epitome of this intellectual development is found in what Max Weber has called the *Protestant Ethic*—a system of values and beliefs rooted in Calvinism which places a premium on individual achievement and on man's ability to exercise a fairly large measure of control over his own destiny. The whole Protestant religious revival, in fact, played a key role in upsetting the traditional balance in which dogma and spiritual considerations held primacy over reason and worldly interests; and it brought about a new equilibrium that was generally more favorable toward worldly interests and more inclined to place a positive value on man's ability to think and act rationally for himself. The changing status of women in society provides an interesting illustration of how the growing emancipation of the human mind from traditional beliefs and dogmas had a depressing influence on fertility and family size. An increase in women's rights was one of the many consequences of the growth of intellectual freedom. As women more and more came to regard themselves as being on an equal basis with men, it naturally followed that they would demand a say in determining how many children they would bear, and this had a profound influence on Western fertility reduction. As has been noted elsewhere: "To ignore the changes in the general intellectual atmosphere which made women demand rights as persons is to overlook one of the underlying causal factors in the decline of the birth rate." [3]

Finally, the overall rising *standard of living* generated a set of attitude changes that had a significant influence on fertility reduction. As the level of living rose and a better way of life became more easily attainable, more people sought to attain it. In fact, the previously mentioned values associated with the Protestant revival and its emphasis on achievement encouraged such a desire. All else being equal, nonparents are economically better off than parents. Thus, persons who wished to take optimum advantage of the emerging opportunities for a higher standard of living were quick to see that their economic resources would go further if they had fewer children with whom to share them.

(3) *Development and diffusion of modern birth control methods.* The various material and non-material cultural changes cited above as factors influencing the historical decline in Western fertility could not have exerted the influence they did had it not been for (a) the existence of effective methods of birth control, and (b) an attitude that accepted as proper the use of such methods to limit deliberately family size. Something like the small-family ethos, for example, could not really have emerged unless the means to achieve a small family were available and unless people approved of using these means to achieve their smaller families. Thus, the changes associated with the development and diffusion

of modern birth control techniques are the most important factors influencing the decline of the birth rate in the Western world.

Changes related to birth control, like those discussed in the preceding chapter relating to public health and medical science, involve both material and non-material aspects of culture. That is, they involve both *techniques* of preventing conception and human *attitudes* toward the use of the various methods. To begin by considering the technological aspects, one of the first things to note is that the many methods of population control that have been (and are being) used can be divided into two broad classes: (a) those used after the fact of conception or birth (such as *abortion* and *infanticide*); and (b) those used before, during, or immediately after intercourse to prevent conception from taking place. Attention will here be focused on the latter. Although the former have long been known and used (abortion continues to be a major means of limiting fertility in many parts of the world today—notably in Japan), they are not properly methods of birth control in the sense usually understood today. When one speaks of birth control today one generally has in mind the prevention of conception.

Ever since he has been aware of the association between sexual intercourse, conception, and birth, man has looked for ways to avoid the end product of this relationship through the prevention of conception. Although some of the earlier methods were quite effective (for example, *coitus interruptus,* or withdrawal, has been successfully used for centuries and is still one of the most widely used methods of birth control today), many of them were pretty farfetched. Among the ancient Greeks, for example, a woman not wanting to become pregnant would wear a tube containing the liver of a cat tied to her left foot; whereas Bavarian peasant women believed that turning the wheel of a grain mill backward four times at midnight was a good way to prevent conception.[4]

Other relatively simple methods of birth control that have long been in use throughout different parts of the world include various spermicidal *douches* (for example, warm water and soap) and the Roman Catholic–approved *rhythm method* according to which couples abstain from sexual intercourse during the middle of the wife's menstrual cycle, when the probability of conceiving is greatest.

The development of more reliable means of contraception came with the emergence and spread of industrialization. Among the first of the modern appliances to be perfected was the *condom.* Although there is evidence that condoms were in use as early as the sixteenth century, they did not become popular on a mass level until the middle of the nineteenth century when the invention of the vulcanization of rubber permitted its low-cost mass production. The mid-nineteenth century also saw the invention of the *pessary* and the *diaphragm,* as well as considerable improvements in the effectiveness of chemical spermicides. Used correctly in conjunction with a spermicidal cream or jelly, these two devices are virtually 100 per cent effective in preventing conception, and they (especially the diaphragm) are widely used as methods of birth control in the United States today.

More recently, continued technological progress and increased knowledge of the mechanisms of the human reproductive system have led to the development of the *contraceptive pill.* These pills, which block conception by preventing the female ovaries from releasing eggs, represent a safe, reliable, and relatively inexpensive method of birth control. Although some women occasionally experience unpleasant side effects when they first begin using them (headaches, nausea, spotting), these side effects generally disappear after a couple of months' usage. Moreover, the pills are more convenient than any of the appliance methods. Research is still going on in this area, including experimentation with an oral contraceptive that would induce temporary sterility in males. Also being developed is an anti-pregnancy vaccine for women that would temporarily immunize a wife against her husband's sperm.

Still another recent development in birth control technology is progress in the area of *contragestion,* or prevention of the growth of life after fertilization has occurred. The *intra-uterine devices*

(IUD's) that are becoming increasingly popular today fall into the contragestive category in that they act to prevent the fertilized egg from becoming implanted in the uterus.

In discussing these newer methods of birth control, one must be careful not to overemphasize their impact on fertility. History has clearly shown us, for example, that "where there is a will there is a way," and if people do not want to have children they will not have them. Similarly, there are too many reasonably effective "old-fashioned" methods of fertility control (*coitus interruptus,* for example) to warrant the expectation that the sudden unavailability of condoms, diaphragms, pills, and IUD's would lead to any substantial change in the birth rate. But the fact remains that these newer methods, by being virtually 100 per cent effective, have vastly enhanced man's ability to regulate the size of his family. With respect to pills and IUD's, it should be noted that their use as a means of controlling fertility has the added advantage of being separated in time from the act of intercourse. This not only reduces the likelihood of an accidental pregnancy resulting from a moment of passionate weakness but also enhances the enjoyment of marital relations by promoting a generally greater "freedom from worry."

One other highly effective method of fertility control needs to be mentioned, and that is *sterilization.* This is an operation that involves severance of the tubes (vasa deferentia in men or fallopian tubes in women) through which the sperm or ova pass. In spite of its relative permanence, sterilization is becoming very popular in some parts of the world today—notably among the economically underdeveloped countries where problems of overpopulation are particularly acute. It has not gained widespread popularity in modern Western industrial nations, however, partly due to the easy accessibility of a variety of inexpensive and effective alternative methods of preventing conception. This is the important point to stress: today, in sharp contrast to pre-industrial times (either in the Western world two hundred years ago or in many parts of the non-Western world today), there is a wide variety of relatively inexpensive and highly effective methods available to couples who wish to determine not only how many children they will have but also when they will have them.

Turning to a consideration of non-material developments, the major factor behind the easy accessibility of various birth control methods today is the more or less open approval of the principle of family limitation. This has not always been the case. On the contrary, the dominant attitude of Western culture in the past was that deliberate attempts to prevent conception were immoral. This attitude, primarily religious in origin, dated from the fifth century and the writings of Saint Augustine, who stressed that the sole purpose of sexual intercourse in marriage was the procreation of children. Not until 1917 did the Code of Canon Law (Canon 1013, paragraph 1) add a secondary purpose—that of "mutual aid and the quieting of concupiscence"; but since then the position of the Catholic Church has become increasingly liberal. A clear illustration of this changing attitude was an address by Pope Pius XII before the Italian Catholic Union of Midwives in 1951. After emphasizing that the primary end of marriage is the procreation of children, he went on to note that ". . . under certain circumstances a husband and wife may be excused from exercising the primary function of their marriage and thus limit the number of their children." He further noted that it is possible to be exempt from the obligation of procreation for a long time, ". . . even for the whole duration of married life, if there are serious reasons such as those provided in the so-called indications of the medical, eugenical, economic, and social order." This clearly takes the decision either to have or not have children out of the realm of morality alone and gives it some very practical dimensions. In the words of one leading Catholic theologian: "This means that such factors as the health of parents, particularly the mother, their ability to provide their children with the necessities of life, the degree of population density of a country, and the shortage of housing facilities may legitimately be taken into consideration in determining the number of offspring." [5]

These developments, nevertheless, have had no effect on Catholic adherence to natural law. Although married couples are in principle permitted to limit the size of their families, the Church rejects all methods of birth control except the periodic abstinence of the rhythm method.[6] Among Protestants, however, there is more or less universal acceptance of the use of artificial means to regulate fertility and family size. This attitude represents a radical departure from the late nineteenth century when Protestants, under the leadership of Anthony Comstock and his New York Society for the Suppression of Vice, led the more or less successful crusade to have the dissemination of birth control methods and information outlawed as obscene. Most of the laws passed at this time (the "Little Comstock Laws" as they came to be called) have either been repealed, revised, or overruled; and most Protestant (and also Jewish) leaders today not only openly support family planning but also encourage it as being a positive religious duty. The clearest statement of this attitude came from the 1958 Lambeth Council of the Protestant Episcopal Church. A major conclusion of the report issued by the participants of this council was that a primary obligation of Christian marriage was not so much procreation as making sure that children were born "within the supporting framework of parental love and family concern, with a right to an opportunity for a full and spiritually wholesome life." The council went even further and strongly censured those couples "who carelessly and improvidently bring children into the world trusting in an unknown future or a generous society to care for them."

One final indication of the change in attitudes toward birth control is found in American government policy. Until fairly recently the official position was that birth control was strictly an individual matter and not something with which the government should be concerned. Today, however, reflecting the growing awareness of the extremely serious crisis facing many of the underdeveloped nations (see Chapter 5 below), not to mention the increasing concern over poverty and social welfare here in our own country, the federal government has adopted a much more permissive policy.

A good illustration of this is the fact that in June 1966 both the Senate and House of Representatives acted favorably on bills authorizing the use of federal funds not only to finance family planning research programs but to provide technical assistance in the control of population growth. Even more significant is the statement made by President Johnson in his 1967 State of the Union Message to the effect that the governments of underdeveloped countries such as India and Pakistan *must* exert an all-out effort to encourage the widespread practice of fertility control.

Clearly we have come a long way from the attitude expressed by Martin Luther when he wrote that "propagation is not in our will and power." Today we have reached the point where the rational control of fertility has not only been accepted as morally right but has been given the stamp of official public approval. The emergence of this attitude coupled with the development of more effective methods of contraception is the basic factor underlying the long-term decline of the birth rate in the Western world.

FERTILITY TRENDS IN THE UNITED STATES

National statistics on births, like those on deaths, are not available for the United States before the twentieth century. This means that statements pertaining to historical fertility conditions in this country must be based on fragmentary evidence at best. Even so, estimates, both historically and more recently, all agree that fertility in colonial America was high by any standards. Both because of the relative youthfulness of the population and because of an abundance of opportunities for self-sufficiency, people tended to marry at an earlier age than their European contemporaries and to have larger families. It is generally believed that the annual birth rate during the colonial era in America approximated 55 or more per 1,000 inhabitants, and the women of the time are estimated to have given birth to an average of eight children by the time they passed out of the childbearing ages.

Fertility remained generally high throughout the first two decades of the nineteenth century. At that time, however, in response to developments discussed in the previous section, a fairly rapid decline began. As of 1820 it is estimated that the United States still had a crude birth rate on the order of 55 per 1,000 population.[7] Available data indicate that the annual number of births per 1,000 was down to 52 in 1840, 44 in 1860, and 40 in 1880. By the end of the century it is estimated that the crude birth rate in this country was only 32 per 1,000 population. The statistics available

Table III-1: Crude birth rates in the United States, 1909–1965 (births per 1,000 population).

Year	Crude birth rate	Year	Crude birth rate	Year	Crude birth rate
1909	30.0	1928	22.2	1947	26.6
1910	30.1	1929	21.2	1948	24.9
1911	29.9	1930	21.3	1949	24.5
1912	29.8	1931	20.2	1950	24.1
1913	29.5	1932	19.5	1951	24.9
1914	29.9	1933	18.4	1952	25.1
1915	29.5	1934	19.0	1953	25.0
1916	29.1	1935	18.7	1954	25.3
1917	28.5	1936	18.4	1955	25.0
1918	28.2	1937	18.7	1956	25.2
1919	26.1	1938	19.2	1957	25.3
1920	27.7	1939	18.8	1958	24.6
1921	28.1	1940	19.4	1959	24.3
1922	26.2	1941	20.3	1960	23.7
1923	26.0	1942	22.2	1961	23.3
1924	26.1	1943	22.7	1962	22.4
1925	25.1	1944	21.2	1963	21.7
1926	24.2	1945	20.4	1964	21.0
1927	23.5	1946	24.1	1965	19.4

SOURCE: *Vital Statistics of the United States: 1961*, I-1, Washington, D.C., 1963; and *Monthly Vital Statistics Reports*, 14:13, *Annual Summary for the United States, 1965*, Washington, D.C., 1966.

for subsequent years (see Table III-1) clearly show that the long-term downward trend in the birth rate continued on into the twentieth century. But they show with equal clarity that the decline has not been consistent. In order to better understand the trend in American fertility during the present century, it is convenient to distinguish three periods: (1) the period before the Second World War; (2) the postwar decade from 1947 to 1957; and (3) the years since 1957.

(1) *Fertility trends before World War II.* Annual estimates of births and birth rates in the United States are available beginning with 1909. In that year there were an estimated 30 live births per 1,000 persons living in the country. This is slightly lower than the birth rate at the beginning of the century and is consistent with the long-term downward trend that continued, with only occasional minor upswings, until an all-time low level (18.4 per 1,000) was reached during the 1930 depression decade. This long-term decline represents a real demographic revolution and, as indicated above, has been a major concomitant of the development of our modern urban-industrial society and the emergence of a more rational attitude toward life. The explanation of the particularly low level of the mid-1930's must be sought in adverse economic conditions that motivated many people to postpone marriage and childbearing. But as the nation slowly recovered from severe economic depression, the birth rate bounced back a little, and by the time the United States entered the Second World War it was again at the level it had occupied at the start of the 1930's.

(2) *The baby boom.* From its all-time low level of between 18 and 19 per 1,000 reached during the 1930's, the crude birth rate in the United States rose gradually until it reached 23 in 1943. This moderate increase was followed by two years of declining fertility, and it appeared that the initial fertility recovery following the end of the depression and America's entrance into the war had given way to a revival of the historical downward trend. The declines during the latter years of the war, however, were in part

due to the absence of large numbers of men from the country. The demobilization of the armed forces at the end of the war, in a period of economic prosperity, was followed by a sudden and pronounced increase in the birth rate. From a level of 20.4 in 1945 the crude birth rate rose to a peak of nearly 27 per 1,000 in 1947—a level that had not been attained for a quarter of a century.

Up to this point the experience of the United States is consistent with that of other nations in the modern Western world: fertility declined steadily throughout the nineteenth and early twentieth centuries, reached a low point during the 1930's, then rose to moderately high levels during the immediate postwar period. There, however, the similarity ends. In most European countries the higher postwar birth rates lasted for only one or two years—just long enough to give people a chance to get caught up on the families they had postponed during the earlier depression and war years—and then fertility returned to its low prewar level. In Sweden, for example, the crude birth rate rose from less than 15 per 1,000 during the 1930's to a postwar high of approximately 20 per 1,000 in 1946. But by 1954 it was once again less than 15, and it has remained close to this low level ever since. In the United States there was a slight dip from 1948 to 1950, but from then until 1957 the crude birth rate remained consistent at 25 per 1,000 population.

This decade (1947–1957) of unexpected high fertility has come to be known as the "baby boom" era. Although the postwar fertility revival occurred in both Europe and America, it was the result of slightly different causal factors, and these differences largely explain why the boom ended in Europe so much earlier than in the United States. In Europe a return to normalcy after several years of depression and war resulted in many people *making up* marriages and childbearing they had earlier postponed. In the United States this making up of earlier marriages was accompanied by a *moving ahead* of marriages and childbearing that would ordinarily have taken place at a later time. This moving ahead reflects the especially favorable economic climate that prevailed in the

United States during the postwar decade. Developments such as improvements in unemployment compensation and retirement benefits, and expanded health and accident insurance programs did much to promote an atmosphere of economic security. These feelings were further strengthened by such other developments as the increasing bureaucratization of society, one corollary of which was that the mobility process became more visible, more orderly, and more predictable. Another factor was the tremendous expansion of credit opportunities. Installment buying, with its "buy now but pay later in small convenient sums," made it easier for large numbers of young people to get married, buy a car, buy a house, furnish it, and fill it with a couple of children—all for a relatively small cash investment.

Many of these developments that encouraged relatively high birth rates in the United States were also evident in other European countries where fertility returned to low levels shortly after the end of the war. The "welfare state," for example, is particularly well developed in the Scandinavian countries. But the general climate of well-being was never as pronounced in Europe as it was in the United States. For one reason, although living levels are high in the Western world in general, they are much higher in the United States than in any European country. Furthermore, Europe has been devastated by two world wars during the twentieth century, neither of which resulted in any real material damage to the United States. The people of Europe have also had to live much closer to the danger that the Cold War might blossom into a full-scale shooting war. As a result, a much less optimistic climate has prevailed in Europe during the 1950's and 1960's, and this atmosphere has been less conducive to having children than that which prevailed in the United States. A good illustration of the difference is offered by the experience of Hungary, a country that has suffered particularly harshly during the postwar struggle for power in eastern Europe. In that country it is estimated that the number of abortions each year exceeds the number of annual births by roughly 25 per cent.[8]

In discussing the persistence of relatively high birth rates throughout the postwar decade, it is essential to stress that it did not signify any return to the larger families of an earlier era. On the contrary, the proportion of women having four or more children today is substantially less than the proportion having this many babies a generation ago. What has happened, rather, is that there has been a decline in the proportion of women remaining childless, both because of the improved economic situation and because the fruits of medical progress have helped to reduce involuntary sterility. There has also been an increase in the proportion of women having a second and third child—very likely for the same reasons that explain the decline in childlessness.

(3) *Fertility since the baby boom.* As the United States entered the 1960's, it gradually became apparent that, in spite of continued prosperity, the postwar baby boom was coming to an end. The birth rate began to decline after 1957, and by 1965 it had fallen back to the prewar level of less than 20 per 1,000 population. The magnitude of the recent fertility decline is further revealed by the fact that ever since 1961 the absolute *number* of births has also been declining: in 1965, for the first time since 1953, there were fewer than 4 million live births in the United States.

In trying to explain this decline it is easy to put the blame on the broader dissemination of birth control information and the development of improved contraceptive methods—particularly "the pill." But the pill was not put on the market until 1960 and could not have had any appreciable influence on the birth rate until 1962—at which time the birth rate decline had already been in evidence for five years. Rather, the reasons for the recent decline can probably be found in the same reasons that led to a prolongation of the baby boom. As indicated above, part of the higher fertility of the 1947–1957 decade was due to a "borrowing from the future." Because of the particularly favorable economic climate, this period saw a marked increase in the proportion of women marrying as well as a marked decline in the age of marriage and childbearing. To illustrate, in 1940 only seven out of every ten women in the United

States had ever been married, and the age at first marriage was roughly twenty-two years. As of 1960, eight out of every ten American women had been married at least once, and the median age at first marriage was slightly less than twenty years. The main point, however, is that these women usually had all the children they wanted fairly early in their marriage. To illustrate, among women aged twenty-five to twenty-nine, the proportion who had borne three or more children (three is approximately the average number of children that most American couples want) was 29 per cent in 1957 but 37 per cent in 1963.[9] These young women who had contributed to the high birth rates during the postwar decade stopped having children toward the end of the 1950's, and this is one of the major factors influencing the decline in the birth rate after 1957.

Another factor is the changing age composition of the population. Because of the sharp reduction in births during the depression, there were fewer women at the heaviest childbearing ages. In 1940 there were nearly 6 million women at ages twenty to twenty-four in the United States, but in 1960 there were only 5.5 million women in this age group. Since women at these ages account for approximately one-third of all births in this country, the simple fact that there were fewer women would be sufficient to influence a reduction in the overall crude birth rate, even if there were no change in the rate at which women were having babies.

Added to this is the fact that the women who entered the reproductive ages during the late 1950's and early 1960's have had lower birth rates than the women who preceded them a decade earlier. Two reasons may account for this development. First, these young couples may have decided to space their children further apart instead of having them as rapidly as those couples who began their families earlier in the postwar period. Second, it may be that these younger couples have actually decided to have fewer children than their immediate predecessors. If the former is the major reason, then the 1970 decade is likely to be characterized by a higher level of fertility than that which prevailed during the 1960 decade. If the latter is the major factor, then the 1970's will probably see a continuation of the relatively low birth rates of the mid-1960's. The problem is that we do not know which of these two explanations is more nearly correct; therefore, we cannot say with any certainty what the birth rate will be during the years ahead.

In speculating about the future course of the American birth rate, there is one other element in the current situation that deserves mention. As of 1965 the babies that were born in 1947 attained eighteen years of age; the larger birth cohorts of 1948 and subsequent years will follow right behind them, thereby greatly increasing the number of women at the young childbearing ages. Whereas the number of women twenty to twenty-four years of age declined from 6 million in 1940 to 5.5 million in 1960, the aging of the postwar baby boom cohorts will result in there being roughly 8.5 million women in this age group by 1970 (over 50 per cent more than in 1960)! This trend will not necessarily influence the *rate* at which women at particular ages are having babies, but it will affect the total number of children born in subsequent years. Moreover, it is conceivable that the increase in the number of women in this age group (twenty to twenty-four years), which accounts for approximately one-third of all live births, will be sufficient to influence an increase in the overall crude birth rate. The extent of this potential increase will depend on whether the present rates at each age remain the same, decline even further, or perhaps increase.

To summarize: at the middle of the 1960's the crude birth rate of the United States was back at the prewar level of less than 20 live births per 1,000 population per year. This was partly because the women who were over twenty-five were having low birth rates to compensate for the higher birth rates they had had earlier. It was also due to fertility declines at the younger childbearing ages (under twenty-five), because couples either were postponing childbearing until later ages or were planning to have fewer children than their immediate predecessors. Even though fertility levels were relatively low, there was a potential for an increase in both the number of births and the crude birth rate during the 1970's. When such an increase would begin and what magnitude it would assume were questions that could be answered only speculatively. The most important fact is that fertility can be controlled; and in an era when birth control knowledge is so widespread and when more and more people are coming to adopt some method of family planning, no one can say with any certainty what the future birth rate will be.

FERTILITY DIFFERENTIALS IN THE UNITED STATES

Not all societies nor even all segments of the same society are characterized by the same level of fertility. On the contrary, wide differences exist in any population, and these differentials are of major importance for the demographic study of fertility. There are at least three basic reasons why demographers are interested in knowing the nature of existing fertility differentials. First, a knowledge of existing group differences in fertility levels is useful in the identification of the "causes" of reproductive behavior. For example, if there are two groups with markedly different birth rates, a comparison of these groups may reveal other differences (as in religious regulations concerning the use of birth control) that are helpful in explaining their different birth rates. Second, fertility differentials provide clues concerning possible trends and changes with regard to certain aspects of population composition. If there are two subgroups, for example, each representing 50 per cent of the total population, and one is reproducing at a faster rate than the other, then (all else being equal as far as mortality and migration are concerned) this even distribution will soon be upset in favor of the group with the highest level of fertility. Third, the existence of different birth rates among the various subgroups of a population may have important implications for the future trend in the fertility of the entire group. For example, if urban people have lower birth rates and smaller families than rural people, and if the population is becoming more urban, the implication is that the overall level of fertility will fall as rural residents move to cities and adopt the lower urban fertility patterns. This, in fact, is precisely what concerned persons hope will happen in those rapidly growing, economically underdeveloped countries of the non-Western world that have only just begun to make the transition from a rural-agrarian to an urban-industrial society.

In the United States several variables affect differences in fertility. Moreover, not only do certain groups have higher levels of fertility than others, but some are experiencing greater (or lesser) declines in fertility than others. Unfortunately, however, many of the most important differences and differential trends cannot be documented statistically for the entire country. This is because the groups that can be studied comparatively are necessarily limited by the data collected on birth certificates. The standard birth certificate currently in use in the United States does not contain any information about such things as the religion of the mother or the financial status of her family; and, as will be seen in a subsequent section, these two variables—religion and socioeconomic status—are the most important determinants of differential fertility behavior in the United States today. At present, however, the only major population groups whose fertility can be studied on the basis of information collected on birth certificates are those identified by race and residence. Some of the other major fertility differentials can of course be documented by using other data (such as sample survey data, or statistics on age composition and family size from the decennial census of the population); and some consideration will be given to the differentials revealed by these data. But this does not detract from the problem that much information extremely relevant to the sociological study of fertility is not being provided by the standard birth certificate being used throughout the United States today.

(1) *Age.* Although age does not properly designate different population subgroups, it does relate to fertility in a very definite way. Moreover, the same general pattern of age variations is more or less consistent among the several subgroups in the population—regardless of the overall level of fertility of any particular subgroup. For these reasons, the present discussion of fertility differentials in the United States will begin by considering the influence of age.

The relationship between age and fertility is such that the resulting curve is just the reverse of the U-shaped curve depicting the relationship between age and mortality (see Table II-2 in the preceding chapter). Birth rates start out relatively low at the younger childbearing ages, rapidly reach a peak during the twenties, but then decline quickly and consistently as the age of the mother increases (see Table III-2). In the United States in 1960, for example, the birth rate for women fifteen to nineteen years of age was 89 per 1,000 women, but at ages twenty to twenty-four it was roughly three times as high—258 per 1,000 women. Thereafter, each succeeding age group had fewer births proportionately than the one preceding it, so that by age forty to forty-four there were only about 16 live births per 1,000 women in the United States.

The data in Table III-2 show that this general pattern is characteristic of the age-specific birth rates for every period shown. Al-

Table III-2: Age-specific birth rates for the United States, 1940–1960.

Age, years	Births per 1,000 women				
	1940	1945	1950	1955	1960
15-44	79.9	85.9	106.2	118.0	118.0
15-19	54.1	51.1	81.6	89.7	89.1
20-24	135.6	138.9	196.6	240.4	258.1
25-29	122.8	132.2	166.1	190.8	197.4
30-34	83.4	100.2	103.7	115.8	112.7
35-39	46.3	56.9	52.9	59.5	56.2
40-44	15.6	16.6	15.1	15.7	15.5

SOURCE: *Vital Statistics of the United States: 1960,* I-1, Washington, D.C., 1962.

though the magnitude of the rates at particular ages can and does vary as patterns of childbearing change (for example, the previously noted trend toward earlier childbearing is revealed by the increase in the birth rates at ages twenty to twenty-nine between 1955 and 1960 and the corresponding declines at ages thirty and over), this general pattern is likely to remain. One reason why this is so is that age differences in fertility are in part due to variations in fecundity. Although women are technically ready to conceive and bear children beginning with their first menstruation (at about ages eleven, twelve, or even younger), not very many do. Even in societies where it is not uncommon for girls to marry at such tender ages, their birth rate tends to be much lower than that of women in their late teens and early twenties. This is not because the younger girls are particularly skilled practitioners of birth control; rather it is simply because it generally takes a few years after the onset of puberty for a girl to start producing fully developed, healthy eggs on a regular basis. That is, the years between the onset of puberty and the late teens are years of *adolescent subfecundity* during which the probability that a girl will be able to conceive and bear children is relatively low (but *not* entirely absent).

At the other extreme, just as it generally takes a while for a maturing girl to start producing fully developed eggs on a regular basis, there comes a time in the life of every woman when regular egg production begins to falter and ultimately ceases altogether. From about age thirty to the onset of menopause, women go through a period of *senescent subfecundity* during which the viability of the eggs produced tends to be substantially less than those produced during her prime reproductive years (ages twenty to twenty-nine). During this period the probability that a woman will be able to conceive and bear children declines progressively with each passing year.

Not only women go through these phases of adolescent and senescent subfecundity. Men also require a little time after the onset of puberty before they reach full sexual maturity; and the viability of the spermatozoa (like that of female eggs) declines with age. But these phases of subfecundity are much less pronounced in the male. On the one hand, once sexual development begins it takes place much more rapidly in males than in females: the peak of sexual potency is generally reached in the early or mid-teens among men, as opposed to the late teens and early twenties among women. On the other hand, there is nothing in the male experience corresponding to the menopause. Instead of the conclusive physical (and sometimes emotional) change that occurs in women, men are characterized by a slow steady decline in sexual potency right from their teens. Moreover, although the decline begins earlier in males, it is more common for men to retain their generative powers to very advanced ages. Many men have been able to sire children after their sixtieth birthday, but comparatively few women have become mothers this late in life.

The pattern of age variations in fertility described above is also due partly to age variations in the extent to which women deliberately try to prevent conception. As women get older and gradually have all the children they want, there is a tendency to intensify efforts to avoid giving birth to additional children. To illustrate, the results of one recent large-scale study showed that among fecund couples the proportion who were using some form of contraception rose from 71 per cent at ages eighteen to twenty-four to 84 per cent at ages twenty-five to twenty-nine, and to 90 per cent at ages thirty to thirty-four and thirty-five to thirty-nine years.[10] Similarly, although it may be less pronounced, it is not uncommon for young couples getting married today deliberately to postpone child-bearing until two or three years after marriage in order to give themselves an opportunity to "get settled" (for example, until they have completed their education or accumulated the down payment for a house).

It was noted earlier that medical science has recently made a great deal of progress in increasing our knowledge of the human reproductive system. Not all of this knowledge has been used to perfect man's ability to prevent conception. On the contrary, the now famous contraceptive "pill" was developed as the by-product of research aimed at helping subfecund women conceive and bear children. Thanks to this research many couples who would have had to remain childless a generation ago are now able to have children of their own. Moreover, as research in this area continues, we may see further declines in the incidence of childlessness due to involuntary sterility. The use of hormone products to enhance fecundity at age thirty could conceivably have the same effect at ages fifteen and forty-five. One implication of this in terms of the present discussion is that the persistence of current age-fertility differences will come to be less due to variations in fecundity and more and more the result of deliberate efforts among women at the youngest and oldest childbearing ages to avoid conception.

The main point here is not so much man's ability to prevent conception as the extent to which he chooses either to avail or not to avail himself of this ability, or, more significantly, the extent to which he is able to exercise such a choice. As will become apparent in subsequent paragraphs, whether or not couples are in a position realistically to make a choice concerning how many children they will have and when they will have them lies at the bottom of the major fertility differences in the United States today.

(2) *Color.* The fertility of the nonwhite population in the United States is substantially higher than that of whites.[11] As of 1960, for example, nonwhites had a crude birth rate of 32.1 per 1,000, compared with a rate of only 22.7 per 1,000 for whites—a difference of 41 per cent. This color differential has been observed consistently ever since appropriate statistics have been available in this country. Moreover, the trend during recent years has been for these two groups to move even further apart. To illustrate, in 1963 the nonwhite crude birth rate of 29.7 per 1,000 population exceeded the corresponding white rate (20.7 per 1,000) by nearly 44 per cent, compared with the 1960 difference of only 41 per cent. That is, the post–baby boom fertility decline observed for the na-

tion as a whole has been less pronounced for nonwhites than whites, thus widening the traditional color fertility differential.

The persistence of the color differential over the years is not, it should be stressed, because of any racial variations in fecundity or the ability to bear children. On the contrary, all of the available evidence suggests that nonwhites have historically had greater fecundity impairments than whites. Evidence to support this is the relatively high proportion of nonwhite married women who remain childless throughout their reproductive years (28 per cent according to the 1960 census of population, compared with only 20 per cent for whites).[12] The greater incidence of involuntary childlessness among nonwhites is due to such factors as nutritionally less adequate diets and the greater prevalence of venereal disease —factors which are in turn due to the socially and economically disadvantaged lives that many nonwhites live.

Neither does the white-nonwhite fertility differential reflect a desire among nonwhites to have more children. Here again contrary evidence is available from a recent study which showed that nonwhite married women would *like to have* an average of 2.9 children as compared to an average of 3.3 for married white women. The existence and persistence of the color fertility differential reflects, instead, different family planning practices among whites and nonwhites. At least four essential differences may be noted, all of which are clearly revealed by data collected in a sample survey during the summer of 1960 (see Table III-3).

First, nonwhites are less likely to take any steps to try and limit their fertility. Less than six out of every ten nonwhite couples interviewed in 1960 had ever used some method of contraception, as opposed to eight out of ten white couples. Moreover, the proportion of couples planning never to use contraception was roughly twice as great among nonwhite couples (24 per cent) as among white couples (13 per cent).

Second, nonwhite couples who do try to limit fertility tend to use less effective methods of contraception than white couples. A particularly important difference here is the much greater reliance of nonwhite couples on douche: half of the nonwhite couples who have practiced contraception have used this method of particularly low effectiveness, compared with only one-fourth of the white couples.

Third, contraceptive usage among nonwhites is more likely to be adopted "too late" (i.e., after an unwanted conception has

Table III-3: Selected family planning characteristics of whites and nonwhites in the United States (1960 survey results).

Family planning characteristics	White	Nonwhite
Total number of couples	2,414	270
CONTRACEPTIVE USAGE *		
Number of couples having used some method	1,948	160
Per cent	81	59
Per cent having used:		
Condom	50	58
Diaphragm	38	30
Rhythm	35	18
Douche	24	50
Withdrawal	17	21
Jelly alone	11	19
Suppositories	6	16
Per cent of couples who do not expect ever to use contraception	13	24
EXCESS FERTILITY		
Per cent of all couples whose last conception was unwanted		
Total	17	31
Before contraception	4	13
After contraception	13	18
Accident during regular use	6	4
Unplanned (irregular use)	7	14

SOURCE: P. K. Whelpton, A. A. Campbell, and J. E. Patterson, *Fertility and Family Planning in the United States*, Princeton, 1966.
* The survey from which these data were obtained was conducted before the widespread adoption of "the pill" and IUD's; hence, statistics concerning the differential usage of these relatively new but very popular methods of birth control were not available.

already occurred). The survey data presented here, for example, show that 31 per cent of all nonwhite couples had experienced one or more unwanted pregnancies and that nearly half of these (13 per cent of all nonwhite couples) had experienced the unwanted pregnancy before the adoption of any method of contraception. For whites, the corresponding proportion having an unwanted conception was only 17 per cent, and less than a fourth of these (4 per cent of all white couples) had taken place before the use of contraception.

Fourth, nonwhites are likely to be less regular in their use of contraception than whites. To illustrate this difference: among couples using some method of contraception, 14 per cent of the nonwhites as compared to only 7 per cent of the white couples reported at least one unwanted pregnancy due to the irregular use of contraception.

The explanation of these group differences in birth control practices must be sought in both the cultural backgrounds of the nonwhites (the majority live in the South and most come from rural backgrounds) as well as in their present low socioeconomic status (see Chapter 6 for specific details on the socioeconomic differences between whites and nonwhites in the United States). Many nonwhite couples, for example, are reluctant to use contraception even though they have nothing against it from a moral or ethical point of view. This reluctance stems from a long cultural tradition of frequent childbearing coupled with the fatalistic attitude that another baby or two (or three, or four, or even more) is not going to make that much difference in their daily lives. Closely related to this is the extremely low socioeconomic status of the nonwhite population relative to that of whites: not only are nonwhites more apt to be ignorant of methods of contraception (particularly the newer, more effective methods), but they have less opportunity to learn about them and are less able to afford them even if they do learn about them. This situation with regard to nonwhites has been aptly summarized as follows: "It is clear that these women and others like them do not want unusually large families, but their culture has accustomed them to frequent child-bearing and they have no ready means of learning about methods of family limitation. Also, it is doubtful whether they are strongly motivated to try and limit family size. They seem to regard the burden of numerous children with the same fatalism (and, per-haps, despair) with which they 'accept' their extreme poverty." [13]

Another factor, for Negroes, is their past history of slavery and its de-emphasis of the family as a major social unit. Thus, Negro culture has emerged as more matriarchal than that of whites, and the responsibility for contraception is frequently left up to the women. This accounts for the disproportionate reliance on the less effective "female methods" that are readily available (douche, jelly, and suppositories).

To summarize: the nonwhite population of the United States has long been (and still is) characterized by a substantially higher level of fertility than the white population. This is not because nonwhites are more fecund than whites; nor is it because non-whites want to have more children. Rather, this traditional fertility differential is the result of different family planning practices: non-whites are less likely to be motivated to limit their fertility, more likely to rely heavily on the least effective methods of contracep-tion, and less likely to practice birth control regularly and effec-tively. These differences reflect in part the unique past experiences of the nonwhite population of the United States (for example, their relative inability to get ahead because of color discrimina-tion—regardless of individual abilities and efforts). They also re-flect their present low socioeconomic status which has severely limited their access to birth control information and techniques. (The importance of socioeconomic status for fertility and family planning is discussed more fully in later sections of the present chapter.) The basic implication of these observations is that before the white-nonwhite fertility differential can be appreciably reduced it is necessary to raise substantially the latter's present level of social and economic well-being—not only so nonwhites can have more equitable access to the more effective methods of fertility control, but also so there will be a realistic basis for motivating nonwhite couples to limit their fertility.

(3) *Religion.* Differences in fertility levels among various religious groups are, and long have been, extremely pronounced throughout the world. In spite of their importance for a completely adequate understanding of fertility behavior, however, it is difficult to document such differentials for the United States. This is because the United States decennial censuses have not been able to include a question on religion. This has been partly because some groups and organizations have established strong lobbies against it on the grounds that asking a person his religious affiliation is an infringement of the constitutional guarantee of freedom of religion. Also, some people fear that census records showing a person's religion could be used as a basis for discrimination or even persecution. Such fears are completely unfounded, for other records indicating one's religious preferences are readily available to anyone willing to take the time to look for them (for example, elementary and secondary school records, college records, marriage certificates, burial permits, military service records—not to mention church membership registers—all contain data that could be used to determine a person's religious affiliation). In any case, information on religious differences in fertility in the United States must come from data collected in a sample survey (either government-sponsored or private). Such surveys have been undertaken periodically, however, and their results clearly show that religion is an extremely important, if not *the* most important, variable influencing fertility behavior in the United States today.

The nature of the religious fertility differential is shown in Table III-4. According to these data, collected in a sample survey by the Bureau, of the Census in the spring of 1957, fertility was highest among Roman Catholics and lowest among Jews. Protestants as a whole were intermediate between the other two

Table III-4: Number of children ever born per 1,000 women age 45 and over, by major religious groups, United States, 1957.

Religion	Children ever born per 1,000 women age 45 and over
All classes	2,798
Protestant	2,753
Baptist	3,275
Lutheran	2,382
Methodist	2,638
Presbyterian	2,188
Other Protestant	2,702
Roman Catholic	3,056
Jewish	2,218

SOURCE: U.S. Bureau of the Census, *Statistical Abstract of the United States: 1962*, Washington, D.C., 1962.

major religious groupings. Among Catholics forty-five years of age and over (i.e., persons who had completed their childbearing), each woman had borne an average of 3.1 children. This compared to an average of roughly 2.8 for all Protestants and only 2.2 for Jewish women. Among Protestants the lowest fertility characterized the more liberal groups (such as Presbyterians), whereas the fertility of the more fundamentalist sects (notably the Baptists) was the highest of all: the average number of children ever born to Baptist women age forty-five and over was nearly 10 per cent greater than the corresponding Roman Catholic average and roughly 50 per cent greater than the average number of children ever born to either Presbyterian or Jewish women.

The results of other recent surveys indicate two basic reasons why the members of different religious bodies are characterized by differences in fertility behavior. First of all, there are apparently notable differences in preference concerning desired family size. In general, members of the more conservative groups (Roman

Catholics and fundamentalist Protestants, for example) want larger families than members of the more liberal religious bodies. According to one study, the average number of children desired ranges from 2.7 among Jewish couples to 3.6 among Catholics.[14] Protestants, on the average, want an intermediate number of children (3.0 for couples where both husband and wife were Protestant, but slightly higher—3.1 to 3.2—where either one of the spouses was Catholic). Data from another survey carried on at about the same time also clearly show that fundamentalist Protestant sects want more children (approximately 15 per cent more) than members of liberal Protestant groups.

The fertility extremes to which religious fundamentalism may lead are illustrated dramatically by the Hutterites, an ultra-conservative sect related to the Mennonites. The Hutterites are largely farmers who live in small communal settlements in Montana, North Dakota, and the neighboring part of Canada; and they are characterized by a cultural value system that results in their level of fertility coming very close to the level of maximum fecundity. (For example, economic security and well-being does not depend on individual achievement but is assured by the community; methods of birth control used generally throughout the larger society are regarded as sinful; and large families are looked upon as a source of community strength.) Reflecting this subculture, the Hutterites have a fertility level that is hard to match even among the most socioeconomically backward nations. As of 1950, for example, the average number of children ever born to Hutterite women forty-five and over was between nine and ten!

Differences in attitude toward desired family size are clearly related to the teachings of the various religious bodies. The Catholic Church, for example, clearly emphasizes that the primary purpose of marriage is reproduction; all other purposes are secondary. Moreover, although the Church has no unequivocal ban on fertility control as such, it does teach that only the most serious motives may be used to justify deliberate efforts to avoid conception.

The *welfare of the prospective child* is regarded as the most important consideration in deciding whether to have another baby. Although other reasons are recognized as legitimate (for example, if an additional birth would either be harmful to the health of the wife or be seriously detrimental to the well-being of previous children), such reasons are clearly of secondary importance. Thus, while Roman Catholics are not directly encouraged to have many children, the teachings of the Church make it difficult for fecund couples to prefer—and have—small families and maintain a clear conscience.

Among the more fundamentalist Protestants (many of whom live in rural areas or come from rural backgrounds), the preference for larger families is probably a carry-over from the old agrarian subculture in which large families were looked upon as an economic asset, and in which a married couple could measure the extent to which they were "providing" for their old age in terms of the number of children they had. There is little official dogma among Protestant denominations concerning family size, and where pronouncements have been made they have generally stressed the importance of each couple deciding for themselves—within the framework of their personal, social, psychological, and economic situation—how many children they should have.

The second factor explaining fertility differences among the major religious bodies is that they also differ on their willingness to practice contraception and their ability to plan their families successfully. This is clearly revealed by data collected in the 1960 survey on the Growth of American Families (see Table III-5). These data show that attitudes favoring the use of contraception are nearly twice as prevalent among Protestants as among Roman Catholics, and well over twice as prevalent among Jewish couples. Similarly, although the difference is less pronounced, the proportion who have ever used some method of preventing conception is greatest among Jewish couples (95 per cent) and least among Roman Catholics (70 per cent). Among both Protestants and

Table III-5: Selected family planning characteristics of major religious groups in the United States (1960 survey results).

Family planning characteristics	Protestant	Catholic	Jewish
Total number of couples	1,596	668	106
Per cent favoring fertility control	80	44	95
CONTRACEPTIVE USAGE			
Number of couples having used some method	1,347	466	101
Per cent	84	70	95
Per cent having used:			
Condom	56	28	74
Diaphragm	46	12	51
Rhythm *	27	67	9
Douche	28	17	8
Withdrawal	18	17	4
Jelly alone	14	4	8
Suppositories	8	3	......
* Per cent using only rhythm:	5	45	1
Per cent of couples who do not expect ever to use contraception	10	20	5

SOURCE: Same as Table III-3.

Catholics, approval and use of contraception varies with religious attitudes. To illustrate, although only 44 per cent of Roman Catholic women in the 1960 survey approved of birth control, this proportion was as high as 70 per cent for women who were irregular and infrequent churchgoers. Among Protestants, a similar though less pronounced pattern prevailed: the use of contraception was approved by 85 per cent of liberal Protestants, compared with only 76 per cent among those who were classified as fundamentalists.

Differences in contraceptive usage, like differences in desired family size, reflect basic differences in the teachings and dogma of the various religious groups. These range from the more or less *laissez-faire* attitude of the liberal Protestant and Jewish groups to the ultra-conservative belief common among many fundamentalist sects that children are the gift of God and that no attempt should be made to interfere with God's wishes concerning the number of children particular women have been preordained to bear. Most major religions today lean more toward the liberal position that permits couples to have some say in how many children they will have. But a major difference concerns the particular method or methods that may be used to achieve desired ends; and here religious differences become most pertinent. The most significant fact is the unequivocal stand of the Roman Catholic Church against all forms of birth control other than abstinence—either total abstinence or the periodic abstinence of the *rhythm method.* The impact of this religious teaching is clearly illustrated by Table III-5. Among all couples who have utilized some method of contraception, over half of the Protestants and nearly three-fourths of the Jewish couples have utilized the highly effective condom as opposed to only 28 per cent of the Catholics. Similarly, the diaphragm has been used by roughly half of the Protestant and Jewish couples but by only 12 per cent of the Catholics. At the other extreme, the less reliable rhythm method has been used by two-thirds of Catholic couples as compared to only one-fourth of the Protestants and less than 10 per cent of the Jews. Even more illustrative of this difference is the fact that fully 45 per cent of the Roman Catholic birth control users relied solely on the rhythm method, whereas only 5 per cent of the Protestants and only 1 per cent of the Jewish couples used only this method. Finally, the proportion of Roman Catholic couples who never expect to use contraception is twice as great as the corresponding proportion among Protestants and four times as great as that of Jewish couples. Clearly, one of the major determinants of fertility behavior in the United States today is found in the basic teachings of the major religious groups.

(4) *Socioeconomic status.* Statistics available in official Census Bureau sources clearly reveal marked differences in the fertility

Table III-6: *Children ever born per 1,000 women age 50 and over, by education of women and family income, United States, 1960.*

Education of women and family income	Children ever born per 1,000 women age 50 and over
EDUCATION OF WOMEN, YEARS	
Less than elementary 5	3,860
Elementary 5–high school 3	2,711
High school 4–college 3	1,743
College 4 or more	1,179
FAMILY INCOME	
Under $4,000	2,997
$4,000–$6,999	2,444
$7,000–$9,999	2,314
$10,000 and over	2,252

SOURCE: U.S. Bureau of the Census, *U.S. Census of Population: 1960*, Final Report PC(2)-3A, *Women by Number of Children Ever Born*, Washington, D.C., 1964.

levels of various socioeconomic groups in the United States (see Table III-6). The general relationship is a negative one: the higher socioeconomic status groups have the lowest fertility. Among American women fifty years old and over in 1960 (i.e., women who had completed their childbearing), the average number of children ever born ranged from slightly more than one among college graduates (1,179 children ever born per 1,000 women) to nearly four for women who had completed less than five years of elementary school (3,860 children per 1,000 women). Similarly, women from families with an annual income below $4,000 had roughly a third more children as women in families where incomes were in excess of $10,000 per year.[15]

These socioeconomic differences, like religious differences, can be explained largely by attitudes and practices concerning fertility control. The broadening of one's horizons through education, for example, results in a greater likelihood that birth control will be approved and practiced. Recent data show that roughly four out of five women who graduated from college approve of fertility control and have used some method to regulate their fertility. In contrast, only about two-thirds of the women with no more than a grade school education had ever practiced birth control. Nearly three out of ten grade school women but only 7 per cent of the college graduates do not expect to use any method of contraception during their marriage. Similar differences exist with regard to income: nine out of every ten women whose husbands earn more than $10,000 per year have used some method of birth control (compared to only seven out of ten women whose husbands' incomes are below $3,000); and only one-tenth of the women in the high-income group never expect to practice birth control (compared to nearly one-fifth of the low-income wives).

Although these socioeconomic fertility differentials have persisted over several generations, there is some evidence to suggest that the differences are becoming less pronounced. To illustrate, the average number of children born to American women age fifty and over in 1960 with less than five years of elementary school education (3.9) was over three times as great as the average for college graduates (1.2). At ages forty to forty-four, however, the average number of children born to women at the lowest education level (3.4) was less than twice as great as that for women who had completed four or more years of college (1.8). A similar decline in the magnitude of the fertility differential is also apparent for income.[16] The reasons for this trend toward a narrowing of the traditional socioeconomic fertility differentials can probably be found in the growing liberalization of attitudes during the postwar years and the associated wider diffusion of modern birth control methods. Moreover, as the atmosphere continues to become more liberal, and also as newer, more effective methods such as "the pill" and IUD's become more readily available throughout the general population, it is possible to anticipate an even further narrowing of the traditional differentials. Perhaps, as some recent evidence seems to indicate, there will even be a reversal in the differentials toward a more logical positive association. In the meantime, however, it is evident that the less educated elements of the population and the lower income groups—those who are least prepared both intellectually and economically to provide adequately for their children—are characterized by fertility levels and average family sizes notably greater than those of the general population.

One other point deserves to be mentioned in this section, namely, the socioeconomic fertility differential is particularly significant because of its tendency to *cut across* other differentials. For example, although nonwhites as a whole have a higher level of fertility than whites, there are marked socioeconomic variations within the nonwhite group. In the United States in 1960 the average number of children born to women age fifty and over who were college graduates was roughly the same for nonwhites as it was for the population as a whole (approximately 1.2 children per woman). The reason that nonwhites as a whole had larger families than the general population is simply that there are far more nonwhites, proportionally, in the lower socioeconomic groups where fertility levels are much higher.

In concluding this section it may be noted that the existence of a socioeconomic fertility differential, like the socioeconomic mortality differential discussed in the preceding chapter, has serious implications for a society which puts so much emphasis on granting equal rights to all its citizens. The lower socioeconomic groups not only have high death rates because of their disadvantaged situation; but the disadvantaged status of such groups is perpetuated (at least in part) by excessively high fertility resulting in larger families than can be cared for adequately. One cannot assume, as in the case of some religious groups, that people in the lower socioeconomic segments of society have larger families because they want larger families. On the contrary, according to the frequently cited 1960 survey on the Growth of American Families, the proportion of women who had more children than they wanted was three times as great among women with only a grade school education as it was among college graduates.[17] The available evidence also suggests that a major reason for this situation is that such persons are often completely ignorant of the concept and methods of family planning, or they are unable to afford the cost of consulting a private physician. In spite of increasing efforts to solve the problem, family planning services and facilities are not readily accessible to many economically and culturally deprived groups in the population. In part this is a reflection of the relatively recent general acceptance of birth control; as such there may be a basis for anticipating a more equitable situation in the future. In the meantime, however, the relative scarcity of services for the lower socioeconomic groups amounts to serious discrimination. And until family planning services and facilities are available on a much larger scale than at present, a sizable segment of the American population will continue to be discriminated against, and will not share with the majority the "freedom to choose" not only how many children to have but also when to have them.

THE BIRTH CONTROL ISSUE TODAY

In the past, any discussion of birth control generally had to consider it in terms of its legality and morality, not merely the extent to which it was practiced by various segments of the population. Even in the United States, birth control was until recently outlawed in one form or another in a number of areas. But with the Supreme Court's ruling on the unconstitutionality of the Connecticut anti–birth control law in 1965, followed by the repeal of the Massachusetts statute in 1966, the legality of family planning is no longer questioned. Moreover, since all the major religious bodies today emphasize *responsible* parenthood rather than just parenthood, they give at least tacit approval to the principal of fertility control; hence the morality of family planning is no longer a major issue for debate. This does *not* mean, however, that there are no longer any problems associated with the birth control issue. For one thing, the appropriateness of particular methods is still a point of fairly widespread disagreement. For another thing, as was stressed in the preceding section, the public acceptance of birth control is still fairly new in the United States. Many people—notably in economically and culturally deprived groups—still do not have adequate access (either because of a lack of education or insufficient economic resources) to the more effective means of controlling fertility. It is this fact, not a difference in desired family size or in biological fecundity, that is the major "cause" of most of the fertility differences in the United States. The poor are kept poor because they have so many children, and they have so many children not because they want to or because society has encouraged them to do so, but because society has gone out of its way to prevent them from having recourse to an acceptable alternative to regular childbearing. This problem could well receive more attention if the "war against poverty" begun in the mid-1960's is to be more effective.

There is another, larger problem, however, that concerns the long-range future growth of the American population. This problem relates to the motivation for practicing birth control. The most common justification for the practice is the well-being of the individual or family. Parents are urged to have only as many children as they can adequately care for—not just economically but also socially, psychologically, and, say some, spiritually. Even the most liberal view is one that stresses the *right* of parents to decide for themselves on purely selfish grounds whether or not they want to have children. The idea that a *whole society* has a responsibility for limiting the size of its population, or that couples have a *duty* to practice fertility control for the sake of the well-being of the nation as a whole, is only rarely heard in America. In many underdeveloped countries, where the adverse consequences of too many people are very real and obvious, much more emphasis is given to the individual's responsibility to the larger society. Such consequences have not been felt in the United States; but unless the population stabilizes they will eventually be upon us. Americans must realize that although all couples have a *right* to have children they also have a *duty* to keep their family size down to limits compatible with the best interests of the larger society. For many people, acceptance of this responsibility will mean having fewer children than they may want and than they can easily afford— simply because smaller average families are necessary to enhance the well-being of the nation as a whole. With our traditional emphasis on individual rights, however, Americans are not likely to come to a quick change regarding the strictly personal nature of a couple's decision either to have or not to have another baby. Thus, although Americans do not really have a quantitative "population problem" in terms of sheer numbers and density, we are faced with certain qualitative losses in our way of life (see Chapter 5). More-over, there is a very real danger that we may someday have to face a quantitative problem as well. If the necessary attitude that child-bearing entails a *social* as well as an individual responsibility does not evolve in time to prevent it, the United States could one day find itself having to contend with many of the problems of over-population already facing most of the world's people.

REFERENCES AND SUGGESTIONS FOR FURTHER READING

Donald J. Bogue, *The Population of the United States,* Glencoe, Ill., 1959, Chapter 12.

Ronald Freedman, Pascal K. Whelpton, and Arthur A. Campbell, *Family Planning, Sterility, and Population Growth,* New York, 1959.

Conrad and Irene B. Taeuber, *The Changing Population of the United States,* New York, 1958, Chapter 13.

Ralph Thomlinson, *Population Dynamics,* New York, 1965, Chapters 8–10.

Warren S. Thompson and David T. Lewis, *Population Problems,* New York, 1965, Chapters 9–11.

U.S. Bureau of the Census, *United States Census of Population: 1960,* Final Report PC(2)-3A, *Women by Number of Children Ever Born,* Washington, D.C., 1964.

U.S. National Center for Health Statistics, National Vital Statistics Division, *Vital Statistics of the United States,* I. Annual compilation of fertility statistics for the United States.

U.S. National Center for Health Statistics, Vital and Health Statistics, Series 21, No. 8, *Natality Statistics Analysis: United States, 1963,* Washington, D.C., 1966.

Charles F. Westoff, Robert G. Potter, Philip C. Sagi, and Elliot G. Mishler, *Family Growth in Metropolitan America,* Princeton, 1961.

Charles F. Westoff, Robert G. Potter, and Philip C. Sagi, *The Third Child: A Study in the Prediction of Fertility,* Princeton, 1963.

Pascal K. Whelpton, Arthur A. Campbell, and John E. Patterson, *Fertility and Fertility Planning in the United States,* Princeton, 1966.

Dennis H. Wrong, *Population and Society,* New York, 1961, Chapters 4 and 5.

4

Migration and mobility

The third and final demographic process is migration, or the movement of people from one geographic area of residence to another. There are two basic reasons for leaving the discussion of migration until last. On the one hand, it is a more complex process than either mortality or fertility. Migration is neither inevitable (as is mortality), nor necessary for the continued survival of the species (as is fertility); hence, individual motivation plays a much greater role in determining migration. On the other hand, the study of migration is made more difficult by the scarcity of relevant data. Statistics on fertility and mortality are more or less readily obtainable from local or federal vital records, but no such records are available in the United States for migration. In some countries persons wishing to move must fill out a migration certificate that is somewhat analogous to birth and death certificates, and in such countries migration trends and differentials can be studied in much the same manner as fertility and mortality. But in the United States, where there is no such migration registration system, data on migration trends and the characteristics of migrants must be obtained from other sources (for example, census data on place of birth cross-tabulated by place of residence) which for many purposes are not as adequate as birth and death records.

THE SOCIAL SIGNIFICANCE OF HUMAN MIGRATION

In spite of the data problem, migration is an extremely important topic for investigation. From a sociological point of view, migration often creates problems of *assimilation* (i.e., the process whereby the beliefs, customs, and behavior patterns of one group are merged with those of another, generally larger, group). These problems are reflected in such things as the existence of ethnic ghettos, marginal men (people caught between the conflicting values of two cultures), and higher incidences of deviant behavior among migrant groups. Although not all the world's ills result from a loss or breakdown of primary associations, the necessity of abandoning familiar surroundings for a new and perhaps strange environment when one migrates often leads to personal and social disorganization; so it is not surprising to find that migrants are often characterized by higher rates of delinquency, adult crime, mental illness, prostitution, divorce, and other social ills.

On the more positive side, migration has historically served as a major mechanism bringing people from diverse cultures (with different customs, knowledge, skills, technology) into contact with one another. Although this occasionally has had adverse consequences (as illustrated by the destruction that accompanied the Mongol invasions of Europe), this intermingling and interstimulation of diversity has generally exerted a positive influence on the growth and development of human civilization. Thus, human migration may be regarded as a major mechanism of social and cultural diffusion. Migration has also played a key role in helping mankind maintain a more or less even balance between the distribution of numbers and resources. In the pre-industrial world the number of people that could be supported in a given area was determined largely by the food-producing capacity of that area. If the population increased to the limits that could be supported, it became necessary for some people to migrate to a new area: the alternative was for the surplus to be killed off in some fashion (such as war, disease, or starvation). In more modern times, the role of migration in maintaining a balance between numbers and resources is illustrated by the rural-to-urban movement of the population. As improved agricultural techniques reduce employment opportunities in rural areas, surplus farm workers move to the cities where the growth of non-agricultural industries creates jobs to absorb them. Similarly, the decline of foreign immigration to this country after the First World War created a large number of employment opportunities in many of the industrial centers of the urban Northeast, and this influenced the emergence and growth of a major movement of Negroes out of the southern states (see Chapter 7). Because of this function of redistributing numbers in relation to available resources and opportunities, migration is often referred to as "The Great Equalizer."

From a purely demographic viewpoint, migration is significant because it is one of the three major processes through which changes in population size, composition, and distribution are effected. The population of the United States, for example, would hardly be as large as it is today if it had not been for the millions of European immigrants of the past two centuries. Moreover, since migrants usually are younger than the general population, areas that are losing people through out-migration (rural farm areas, for example) will find themselves becoming "older" than areas into which migrants are moving. In the early days of the twentieth century, when large numbers of persons were entering the United States from Europe (an average of roughly 1 million immigrants per year during the decade preceding the First World War), the median age of the population was about twenty-four years. This compares to a median age of thirty years in 1960, sev-

eral decades after the adoption of federal restrictive legislation.[1]
Finally, as already indicated, the vast shift in the distribution of
population from rural to urban areas as industrial development
progresses is brought about entirely by migration.

BASIC MIGRATION CONCEPTS

Before we can adequately understand the determinants and consequences of migration behavior, it is necessary to become acquainted with some of the basic migration concepts. In particular,
it is necessary to be familiar with the various forms that the
movement from one geographic area to another may assume. This
is not only because the causes of migration will differ, but also
because different types of migration will generally be associated
with different types of problems.

To begin with, migration may take place on a *group* basis
(such as the exodus of Moses and the Hebrew tribes out of
Egypt, or the more recent movement of the Mormons in this
country to Utah), or it may take place on an *individual* or family basis (United States foreign immigration, or the world-wide
cityward movement away from declining rural areas). Most migration in the modern era has been individual migration and has
involved the movement of persons and their immediate families
rather than the movement of larger groups of people. This is in
contrast to the pre-industrial era when the survival of the individual was so much more dependent on the group and when migration more often entailed the movement of larger groups—such as
entire clans or tribes.

These two types of migration also generally differ in terms of
their underlying causes. People move from one area to another
either because some set of forces or circumstances drives them
out of the old habitat (*push* factors), or because a different set of
forces of circumstances attracts them to a new area (*pull* factors).
In the case of group migration, the underlying cause was generally

a push of one sort or another—such as religious or political persecution (for example, the initial colonization of the United States by the Pilgrims, or the westward movement of the Mormons). Often, especially in the pre-industrial world, the motivating force behind a group migration was an ecological push arising either from a depletion of resources in the local environment (such as soil exhaustion or disappearance of game), or from some sort of natural disaster (drought, flood, locust plague). In the case of individual migration, however, the underlying causes are more commonly pull factors—a promise of a better life in the new home or a chance to get rich quickly. Such were the reasons behind the California Gold Rush of the 1850's, for example, or the mid-twentieth-century movement of American Negroes out of the rural South to the larger urban-industrial centers of the Northeast. Somewhat different pull factors underlie the more recent movement of young women to heavily male-dominated Alaska.

More often than not, both push and pull factors are found in some degree, with the magnitude and location of the two complementary forces determining the volume and direction of migratory streams. For example, in explaining the causes of the "great Atlantic crossing" that involved the transfer of some 20 million persons from Europe to the United States during the nineteenth century, one can cite a number of significant push factors in the various sending countries. Among them would be political and religious persecution, economic instability, and rural overpopulation as major advances in agricultural technology reduced the size of the farm labor force more rapidly than the excess could be absorbed into still infant industries. Balanced against these were the strong pull forces exerted by the United States—political and religious freedom, rapid economic expansion, the availability of large tracts of undeveloped lands, and a surplus of relatively high-paying jobs in developing industries. To take a more recent example, the postwar refugee exodus from East Germany (and from mainland China to Hong Kong) involves both a push from polit-

ical oppression and a pull toward the promise of political freedom and better economic opportunities. Thus, a really adequate
analysis of the determinants of *all* migratory movements must
consider the relative importance of both push and pull forces.

Another way of looking at migration is to consider whether it
is *voluntary* or *involuntary*. Much of the group migration that
occurred in the ancient world was "forced" in the sense that the
exhaustion of the environment's food-producing capacity necessitated a move to a new habitat. Examples of forced migration in
the modern era would be the nineteenth-century slave trade, the
westward movement of the Mormons in search of freedom from
religious persecution, and, more recently, the deportations carried
out all over Europe by the Nazi government during World War
II. Compared to these are those cases of migration in which there
is no element of force—cases where individuals or groups move
not because they have to but because they want to and because
they believe they can better their life chances by moving. In contrast to the push associated with forced migration, voluntary migration is more often the result of some positive pull toward a new
and hopefully better home. Although there are exceptions—
dramatically illustrated by the presence even today of large numbers of refugees from war (in Viet Nam, for example), or political oppression (refugees fleeing East Berlin and Red China)—
most migration in the world today tends to be both individual and
voluntary, and is largely motivated by positive pull factors.

Still another basis of classifying migration is in terms of whether
it occurs between different countries (*international migration*) or
within the confines of a single country (*internal migration*). Most
migration in the world today is internal migration—the internal
movement of *individuals* on a *voluntary* basis who are *pulled* to
areas of greater opportunity. International and internal migration
are further distinguished by the terms applied to migrants. On
the international level, a person who enters a given country is
called an immigrant, whereas a person who leaves a country

is called an emigrant. On the internal level, however, a person who moves into one area from another area in the same country is called an *in-migrant,* whereas a person who leaves one area for another within the same national territory is called an *out-migrant.* The use of this distinct terminology simplifies discussions of migration patterns for areas (like the United States) where there has been a good deal of both international and internal migration. This international-internal dichotomy is generally regarded as the major classification of migration. For one thing, it provides a ready scheme for discussing those movements that alter the distribution of world population (international migration) as opposed to more localized movements that have only a slight impact on the world population situation—but which can have profound significance for the local areas involved. For another thing, it is a dichotomy into which all other types of migration can be fitted.

(1) *A formal definition.* Migratory moves could be classified in many other ways. One could distinguish among migrants on the basis of *distance* covered by the move (for example, long- versus short-distance moves); or one could make a distinction in terms of the type of areas between which migration takes place (rural-to-urban, urban-to-rural, and so forth). One contemporary American demographer has recently formulated a classification of migration based on a combination of the forces impelling particular moves and on whether they preserve an old or create a new way of life (i.e., a classification based on both the determinants and consequences of particular moves).[2] One could go still further and identify more specific types of migrants such as refugees, migrant farm workers, intrastate versus interstate migrants, or even *transmigrants* (i.e., persons whose move from one area of origin to a specific area of destination takes place in stages—such as Europeans who migrate to the United States by way of Canada).

In spite of the fact that there are many different types of migration and many different ways of classifying it, all such moves have one thing in common. By definition, all migration entails the movement of individuals or groups from one area of residence to another with a view toward a *permanent change of residence*. This qualification concerning the permanency of a move eliminates groups such as tourists, college students, and military transfers who may move into or out of particular areas but who generally do not have any *permanent impact* on the size, composition, or distribution of the population. Moreover, persons in these types of groups do not consider themselves migrants and generally have plans to return "home" in the future. When the term "migration" is used in this book it refers to a change of residence that is intended to be permanent and that results, therefore, in a definite change for the population in both the sending and receiving areas. In the remainder of this chapter the discussion will focus on the determinants and consequences of both migration *into* the United States from other countries and migration *within* the political confines of the nation.

UNITED STATES IMMIGRATION TRENDS

Speaking in the broadest sense, if it were not for human migration there would not be a United States today. All Americans are either immigrants themselves or the descendants of earlier immigrants (or colonists, as the case may be). It may be said, therefore, that immigration has been a most persistent and most pervasive influence in the development of the United States. It may even be said that the whole of American history has been molded by the successive waves of immigrants who responded to the lure of the "new world." The labors of the immigrants and their descendants have transformed an almost empty continent into the world's richest and most powerful nation. Other countries have experienced heavy immigration (Australia and Argentina, for example), but no country has had such a large and diverse number as the United States; and in no country (with the possible exception of Israel in the post–World War II years) has immigration had the pervasive influence on population growth and socioeconomic development that it has had in America.

The United States has passed through three distinct phases or eras of immigration and is currently in the midst of a fourth. These eras, which are discussed more fully in the following paragraphs, are: (1) initial colonization and early settlement; (2) the nineteenth-century era of mass immigration; (3) the era of federal restrictions on immigration; and (4) the recently emerged era of *controlled* immigration.

(1) *Colonization and early settlement.* The first era of United States immigration can be identified roughly as the period lasting from the arrival of the first settlers in the early seventeenth century until the end of the Napoleonic Wars early in the nineteenth century. Although there are no official statistics showing their exact numbers, the evidence indicates that immigration during this early period of American history did not involve a very large number of people. For one thing, when the first federal census was taken in 1790 (well over a century and a half after the first settler landed) only about 4 million people were enumerated. Given the relatively high birth rates of the early colonists (50 to 55 per 1,000), it is highly unlikely that the population would have been that *small* if there had been any large-scale immigration. There are many reasons for this relatively small immigration during the seventeenth and eighteenth centuries. Among the most important are: (a) the lack of a really strong pull prior to the Industrial Revolution and the opening of the American West; (b) poor transportation facilities for the difficult Atlantic crossing; (c) ignorance, especially among landlocked European peasants, of the nature of conditions in the colonies; and (d) restrictions on emigration in a number of European countries of origin (many European governments, for example, looked upon emigration as a loss of potential soldiers and taxpayers).

Although this first era of immigration did not involve a very large number of people, it did have a special significance for the type of society into which the United States ultimately developed. Specifically, this early immigration laid the foundations for what we call the "American Way of Life." The United States has long been regarded as the classic land of equality and opportunity for all; and this "American Ideal," with its religious and political freedom and its emphasis on a classless society, is largely an outgrowth of the initial pattern of immigration and settlement. With regard to "freedom of thought and belief," it may be noted that the United States was initially settled by basically bigoted groups —groups who came in search of religious freedom but who themselves were frequently intolerant of dissenting views. But as the number and diversity of religious groups seeking asylum increased, it became impossible for one group to dominate another; hence a tolerance of diverse views emerged more or less by necessity. With regard to the "equality for all" ideal, the important point is that colonial America had an almost limitless supply of land; virtually everyone could become a property owner if he so desired. Although the early United States had a social structure resembling Europe's, the widespread ownership of land made class lines less rigid. And since land was the basis of political power as well as wealth in the pre-industrial world, the relative ease with which it could be obtained inhibited the rise of a landed aristocracy and virtually assured the development of our democratic form of government. In short, the fact that the United States was a sparsely settled country with plenty of available land, plus the diverse nature of early colonial settlement, virtually necessitated the emergence and development of America as a land of social, political, economic, and religious freedom.

(2) *The era of mass immigration.* Shortly after the War of 1812, immigration to the shores of America began to assume mass proportions. There are several reasons why the volume of immigration began to swell at this time. On the one hand, various push factors were operating in the European countries of origin (rural overpopulation, economic instability, political unrest, and so on).

On the other hand, very strong pull forces were exerted by a rapidly expanding American economy—particularly during the last half of the nineteenth century. "The great land areas beyond the Mississippi were available for agricultural use. Rapid industrialization created major demands for unskilled labor to work in factories, build canals and roads, and later railroads, and carry on many tasks not yet mechanized. At this same time conditions in Europe were becoming more improved, and more and more people learned of the opportunities in the United States. Improved transportation within Europe facilitated movement to the coast, while steamships permitted quicker, safer, and cheaper passage across the ocean than had the sailing ships of earlier days." [3]

This era of mass immigration lasted roughly one hundred years from about 1820 (when attempts to collect immigration statistics were first initiated) to 1920 (when the emergence of restrictive legislation led to a sharp decline in foreign immigration). During this century it is estimated that close to 35 million aliens entered the United States (see Table IV-1). During the first decade of this era (1820–1829) the number of immigrants averaged slightly more than fifteen thousand per year. This figure rose rapidly and substantially as the country expanded westward, so that it surpassed 300,000 per year during the decade preceding the Civil War. Immigration declined slightly during the war years but thereafter continued to increase at a rapid rate. By the beginning of the twentieth century the average number of immigrants per year was in excess of 800,000; and it remained at roughly this level until America's entry into the First World War, whereupon the era of mass immigration came to a sudden halt.

In discussing this era of mass immigration, it is customary to divide it into two periods: pre–Civil War and post–Civil War. This distinction is not significant simply because it tells us *when* immigrants came. Rather, it tells us *where* they came from: those who came prior to the Civil War came almost entirely from northern Europe (Great Britain, Ireland, Germany, Scandinavia),

Table IV-1: Number of immigrants to the United States since 1820.

Period	Number of immigrants	
	Total	Annual average
1820-29	151,636	15,164
1830-39	572,716	57,272
1840-49	1,479,478	147,948
1850-59	3,075,900	307,590
1860-69	2,278,612	227,861
1870-79	2,742,137	274,214
1880-89	5,248,568	524,857
1890-99	3,851,150	385,115
1900-09	8,202,388	820,239
1910-19	6,347,380	634,738
1920-29	4,295,510	429,551
1930-39	699,375	69,938
1940-49	856,608	85,661
1950-59	2,499,268	249,927

SOURCE: U.S. Bureau of the Census, *Historical Statistics of the United States: Colonial Times to 1957,* Washington, D.C., 1960; and *Historical Statistics of the United States: Continuation to 1962 and Revisions,* Washington, D.C., 1965.

whereas the postwar decades saw a larger and larger proportion of immigrants coming from the countries of central and southeast Europe (Poland, Italy, Russia, Lithuania, and other Baltic nations). These two groups are generally designated "old" immigrants and "new" immigrants. Finally, this distinction derives added significance in that the Civil War marked a turning point in the official immigration policy in the United States, for it was after this internal conflict that native agitation to restrict foreign immigration really began.

The volume of immigration to the United States from particular countries of origin was determined by the whole process of socioeconomic and demographic change that spread across Europe during the nineteenth and twentieth centuries. Given that the pull

forces in the New World remained more or less constant throughout the period of mass migration, the major factors influencing
emigration from Europe were (a) rapid population growth as a
declining death rate created a widening gap between levels of
fertility and mortality; (b) innovations in agricultural technology
which displaced large segments of the rural farm labor force; (c)
land reform programs (such as the British Enclosure Acts and the
French Primogeniture Laws) that aggravated the displacement
of the rural population; and (d) widespread urban unemployment
as emerging industries failed to expand rapidly enough to absorb
the excess population. These developments occurred first in the
British Isles and in the countries of northwest Europe that had already established social, cultural, and economic ties with the young
republic on the other side of the Atlantic. It is thus not surprising
that these parts of the world were the first to contribute to the
mass immigration of the nineteenth century: at the time of the
Civil War, roughly nine out of every ten United States immigrants
were coming from either Great Britain, Ireland, or Germany (see
Table IV-2).

In the ensuing decades, however, the situation changed radically.
On the one hand, the above cited socioeconomic and demographic
changes began to spread across Europe to the south and east where
they created a tremendous push to emigrate. On the other hand,
the push from the countries of northwest Europe began to decline.
In part this was because their developing industries began to reach
maturity and were thus more able to absorb surplus populations.
It was also because the birth rate began to fall, thus slowing down
the rapid rate of population growth that had characterized these
countries during the early years of the nineteenth century. With
these developments came a gradual shift in the source of United
States immigrants. During the 1880's only 63 per cent of European immigrants to America came from the three countries cited
above (Great Britain, Ireland, Germany). This trend continued
throughout the remainder of the nineteenth and into the twentieth

Table IV-2: Per cent of European immigrants coming from selected countries, by decade, United States, 1820–1959.

Decade	Total number of immigrants from Europe	Per cent coming from:				
		Great Britain	Ireland	Germany	Italy	Poland, USSR, and the Baltic States
1820-29	99,291	26.5	52.0	5.8	0.4	0.1
1830-39	422,779	17.6	40.4	29.5	0.5	0.2
1840-49	1,369,304	16.0	47.9	28.1	0.1	*
1850-59	2,619,774	17.0	39.3	37.3	0.3	*
1860-69	1,877,853	28.4	22.8	38.5	0.5	0.2
1870-79	2,252,197	25.7	18.7	33.4	2.1	2.1
1880-89	4,640,057	17.5	14.5	31.1	5.8	4.8
1890-99	3,579,958	9.2	11.3	16.2	16.9	15.6
1900-09	7,634,425	6.2	4.5	4.3	25.3	19.7
1910-19	5,056,560	7.4	3.3	3.4	24.3	21.9
1920-29	2,576,710	13.1	8.0	15.0	20.5	12.1
1930-39	445,273	12.2	8.0	26.7	19.1	7.8
1940-49	473,043	26.4	4.7	25.3	10.7	2.6
1950-59	1,407,230	13.1	4.0	41.0	13.1	0.9

SOURCE: Same as Table IV-1.

* Less than 0.1 per cent.

century, and during the 1910 decade these three countries accounted for only 15 per cent of all European immigrants, whereas the proportion coming from the southeast (Italy, Poland, Russia, and the Baltic states) was up to 46 per cent.

(3) *Twentieth-century restrictions on immigration.* After the First World War there was another pronounced change in the character of American immigration. The nature of this change is revealed by: (a) a sharp drop in the total *number* of immigrants; and (b) a shift back to the earlier pattern wherein the majority of the immigrants came from northwest Europe. (During the 1930 decade Great Britain, Ireland, and Germany alone accounted for

47 per cent of the European immigrants.) Unlike earlier immigration trends, however, this change was not caused by either socioeconomic or demographic developments in either Europe or the United States. On the contrary, the era of mass immigration came to an end at a time when the push from southeast Europe was at its height, and the decline in the volume of immigrants was determined largely by legislative developments in the United States. From the days of earliest settlement until well into the twentieth century, the United States did not have any real official immigration policy. Beginning shortly after the First World War, however, the federal government placed severe restrictions on immigration. This in itself would not be cause for concern. The tragic aspect of these restrictions was the basis on which persons were barred. Specifically, the 1920's marks the beginning of an era which saw ethnic and racial discrimination become official government policy in a nation that supposedly represented the classic example of a land where freedom and equality prevailed for all persons.

The main reason for the emergence of a restrictive immigration policy lies in the shift in the source of American immigrants; and the adoption of restrictive legislation may be regarded as both an economic and a sociocultural response to the "new" immigration from southeast Europe. When the "new" immigrants began to arrive in ever-increasing numbers toward the end of the nineteenth century, the United States had more or less completed its transition from a rural-agrarian to an urban-industrial society. The vast majority of immigrants arriving at this time from southeast Europe were largely rural peasants. When the "old" agricultural peasants had arrived during earlier decades the United States was still largely an agricultural country; hence the immigrants fitted in quite readily. But the "new" peasants did not fit very well into the industrial mold of American society. There are a number of reasons why: (a) most of them were illiterate and possessed no industrial skills; (b) all were poor; (c) the American frontier was closing, which meant that large tracts of cheap agricultural land were no longer available; (d) the "new" immigrants were easily identified by their strange languages, customs, modes of dress, and so forth (many of the "old" immigrants came from the British Isles and were barely distinguishable from the natives); and (e) labor was becoming organized in this country, and organized labor was very much opposed to the immigration of poor foreigners who would be willing to work for lower wages and who would thus have a depressing effect on wages in general. For such reasons, people all over the country began to show concern over the hordes of "strange and ignorant peasants" flocking to our shores; and movements to restrict immigration began to gain strength. The growing agitation eventually led to the adoption of ethnically discriminatory legislation which remained until the mid-1960's as part of the law of the land.

The first major piece of restrictive legislation came toward the end of the First World War. In response to the growing agitation, Congress set up its first large-scale immigration commission out of which came the Immigration Act of 1917. Among the many provisions of this act were: (a) the establishment of an Asiatic Barred Zone to exclude orientals; (b) the establishment of Ellis Island as a clearing house for all European immigrants; and (c) the establishment of the literacy test requirement which banned illiterate persons from entering the country. In view of the fact that most potential immigrants from southeast Europe were illiterate (full-scale industrial development and its accompanying emphasis on education had not yet evolved in that part of the world), one can regard the literacy test requirement of the 1917 legislation as a deliberate attempt to limit immigration from this part of the world. But the literacy test was still aimed at individuals rather than groups as such: the attempt to improve the "quality" of immigrants by restricting on a group (ethnic) basis was—except for orientals —still a few years away.

Agitation for even more stringent restrictions continued to mount after World War I had ended. To the earlier socioeconomic motives (fear that immigrants would depress wages, or general aversion for the "strange" ways and customs of the alien peasants) were added political motives. The postwar period was characterized by a growth of anti-foreignism (let Europe take care of its own problems, and so forth), and this was aggravated by a growing fear of the "Red Menace" in Russia. Many bills designed to bring about sharp reductions in immigration were introduced to the Congress at this time; and out of all the legislative efforts came the now infamous Immigration Act of 1924, which not only substantially lowered the number of immigrants to be allowed into the country each year but also established the basic pattern of the *national origins* system whereby ethnic characteristics became the basis for restricting immigration. On the one hand, the 1924 act established an annual quota of 150,000 immigrants. On the other hand, it set quotas for each country based on the number of people enumerated in the census of 1890 who were born in each country. Since most of the foreign born in 1890 were from northwest Europe (approximately one-third were born in the British Isles alone), this provision clearly amounted to discrimination against those countries of southeast Europe that had, as of 1890, sent only a very few nationals to the United States.

The Immigration Act of 1924 contained provisions for even more stringent restrictions to go into effect as of July 1, 1929. The legislation that became official American policy in 1929 also authorized the admission of about 150,000 immigrants per year. Furthermore, it reaffirmed ethnic discrimination by setting quotas for each country determined not on the basis of the number of American residents born in particular countries but on the basis of the proportion of the *total* white population of 1920 who could trace their national origins to that country. This specification of national origins, or ancestry, as the criterion for setting quotas clearly implied a belief that some ethnic groups are superior to others. Moreover, the use of total whites rather than just the foreign born as the base population for setting quotas clearly discriminated against the "new" immigrants who had not been in this country long: they had not had time to produce the second and third generations that the "old" immigrants had produced and that helped to increase the quotas allotted to the "old" immigrant countries of northwest Europe.

The restrictive legislation of the 1920's had a pronounced effect on the total volume of immigration to the United States. In contrast to the 1.3 million aliens admitted in 1907 (the peak year during the era of mass immigration), the number of immigrants arriving each year since 1929 has exceeded 300,000 only twice (in 1956 and 1957); and in most years it has been well below 250,000 per year. Ironically enough, however, the national origins quota system did not achieve its desired end with regard to the origin of American immigrants. The ultimate purpose of this legislation was to restore an ethnic composition of immigrants similar to that of the white population of the United States in 1920, but this purpose has never been realized. To illustrate, roughly 80 per cent of the total immigration quota was allotted to the countries of northwest Europe, but these countries have accounted for only about 40 per cent of *all* immigrants admitted since 1929. In part this is because high-quota countries like Great Britain and Ireland have seldom filled their quotas. In part it is because of a large amount of *nonquota immigration*. On the one hand, countries exempted from quota regulation (such as Mexico and other Western Hemisphere nations) have contributed a great deal more to total immigration than was initially anticipated (roughly one-fourth since 1929 as compared to the 6 per cent designated by the national origins legislation). On the other hand, a fairly large number have been allowed in under special legislative provisions (such as the Displaced Persons Act of 1948 and the 1953 Refugee Relief Act); and the majority of these persons have been from southeast Europe. To illustrate, of the more than 600,000 European refugees admitted to the United States between 1945 and 1965, nearly three-fourths came from the southeast European countries of Poland (154,000), the Baltic states—Latvia, Estonia, Lithuania (74,000), Italy (62,000), Hungary (60,000), Yugoslavia (45,000), the USSR (38,000), and Rumania (21,000).[4]

(4) *Current immigration policy.* The national origins system was never very popular among American liberals, and it has been opposed from many sides ever since its inception. The struggle for repeal was not an easy one, however, and as recently as 1952 Congress passed the McCarran-Walter Act which perpetuated the system of ethnic discrimination. This act slightly increased the total annual quota to 154,657 (determined as one-sixth of 1 per cent of the 1920 white population); but the allocation of quotas was still determined by the national origins formula laid down in 1929. Agitation for the repeal of this discriminatory legislation continued to mount in the United States, and throughout the 1950's and early 1960's this agitation gained strength as more and more people came to realize that our immigration legislation was not helping our image as a world leader. Not only the East Europeans but also the peoples of the underdeveloped countries of Asia and Africa could not help but be affronted by a policy that excluded them from immigration on the basis of more or less arbitrary racist principles; and a number of countries (for example, the Philippine Republic) have used official diplomatic channels to point out "certain irritating inequalities" in our immigration laws. In the face of such arguments it became more and more apparent that the restrictionist view that any sovereign nation has the right to regulate immigration as it sees fit was not the strong arguing point it had been during the isolationist days of the 1920's. Rather, it became more and more obvious that the United States could not afford to ignore the opinion of other countries, and that for the sake of our national interests we had to try to establish and maintain a maximum of friendly cooperation among all non-totalitarian powers. This growing moral and political pressure on the United States eventually had the desired effect in the summer of 1965. At that time Congress adopted a new immigration policy that struck

down the national origins quota legislation and finally put an end to what had long amounted to officially sanctioned ethnic discrimination.

According to the new legislation, the national origins system is scrapped as of July 1968. At that time all nations outside the Western Hemisphere will be allotted 170,000 immigrant visas on a first-come, first-served basis, with twenty thousand being the maximum allowed to any one nation. While the present legislation is not likely to alleviate the problem of overpopulation in many of the underdeveloped nations, it at least means that the United States can now hold its head up among free nations everywhere, and that responsible Americans seeking to help the poverty-stricken masses of many nations need no longer apologize for American immigration policy.

SOME CONSEQUENCES OF UNITED STATES IMMIGRATION

When one hears reference to the "consequences" of migration, the most common reaction is to think of its role in maintaining a balance between the spatial distribution of numbers and resources (or opportunities). But this is a very narrow perspective, and as far as American immigration is concerned it is very inadequate. Foreign immigration has had many and varied consequences for the growth and development of the nation. The present section will consider briefly some of the more significant consequences.

(1) *Immigration and population size.* One of the most obvious consequences of immigration is its effect on population size. It is only natural to deduce that emigration leads to a reduction in population size, whereas immigration brings about an increase. In the short run this deduction would certainly be valid, but in the long run it is questionable. No one can refute the impact of migration on the ethnic composition of the United States today; but there has long been disagreement concerning its impact on size. On the one hand, history has shown that population losses due to migration

have soon been replaced by natural increases (an excess of births over deaths) resulting from either a rise in the birth rate or a drop in the death rate. This fact should be kept in mind when considering migration as a possible solution to the problems of overpopulation plaguing many of the economically underdeveloped nations in the world today. Although emigration may be of value as a temporary solution to give these young economies a chance to get started (as it was for many European countries during the nineteenth century), the only long-run solution to current problems of overpopulation is to reduce the rate of population growth through the rational control of fertility. (These problems are discussed more fully in the following chapter.)

Turning to the opposite issue, scholars in this country have long debated the effect of foreign immigration on the size of the United States population. Opposing those who argue that immigration was a major factor in American population growth have been men like Francis Walker, a nineteenth-century conservative who wrote numerous essays and magazine articles criticizing our then relatively free immigration policy. Walker maintained that immigration had little or no effect on the long-run growth of the population because one of its consequences was to encourage a reduction in the level of native fertility. The general argument was that for every immigrant there would be one less baby born to the native group; thus, rather than contributing to population growth, immigration merely lowered the "quality" of the population by replacing a "native son" with a "foreigner."

Since the birth rate in the United States was declining at a time when the volume of immigration was swelling to a peak during the late nineteenth and early twentieth centuries, it is difficult to refute such xenophobic arguments. There is in fact some validity to them if one realizes that immigration, by hastening the processes of industrialization and urbanization, did contribute indirectly to fertility decline. Even so, these arguments can be criticized because of their failure to consider adequately one crucial fact: most of the immigrants were young adults who came to this country at a time when an expanding economy was desperately in need of a larger labor force. In the absence of immigration, the needed labor would not have been available—because the native births that the critics argue would have taken place in the absence of immigration would not have contributed to the adult work force until a generation later. The most significant point, then, does not concern the question as to whether the population of the United States today would be as large if there had not been such heavy immigration during the nineteenth and early twentieth centuries. Rather, the important point is that this mass immigration did have a positive impact on the economic growth of the nation. This subject will be considered in greater detail in the following section.

One final point concerning the impact of immigration on the demographic structure of the population relates to composition. America today is a "nation of nations" in that it comprises people whose ancestors came from all over the world. Out of this mingling of widely different sociocultural backgrounds has come a unique kind of Americanism that is homogeneous by virtue of its heterogeneous background. With the exception of a few full-blooded Indians, we are all descendants of immigrants. Rare indeed is the American today who, when asked what his origin is, can cite a single country; many of us, in fact, can list several different countries where our several grandparents (or even earlier ancestors) were born. Added to this overall effect are the more specific contributions of individual immigrants. This topic will also be discussed more fully in a later section of this chapter.

(2) *Immigration and economic growth.* One aspect of American immigration that merits special consideration is its role in the economic growth and development of the nation. It was noted earlier that the economic prosperity of the United States was a major factor motivating people to leave their homelands during the nineteenth century and migrate to the "land of opportunity." But this heavy immigration was also a major factor behind the rapid

economic growth of the nation during that era. Immigration provided a continuous supply of fresh labor when and where it was most needed. In other words, the relationship between immigration and economic growth in the United States has traditionally been a two-way relationship: economic growth has encouraged immigration, and this immigration has promoted further economic growth.

This positive relationship does not always exist, and there have been many historical instances where too large a volume of immigration has had the opposite effect of retarding economic growth. In both West Germany and Israel during the postwar decade, for example, the influx of refugee immigration was so great that it placed a severe strain on the economy, and it was several years before this immigration provided an impetus to economic expansion. Whether or not immigration is favorable for the economy of any country depends on its *carrying capacity* (i.e., the capacity of a given country to absorb additional laborers—either through immigration or natural increase—without putting a serious strain on the economy). In the case of West Germany and Israel, their postwar economies were just getting off the ground, and the flood of incoming refugees tended to slow down rather than promote their development. In nineteenth century America, however, the economy was very well developed for that time, and its rate of expansion was in large part determined by the rate at which labor became available. There are a few countries today (Canada, for example) that might likewise benefit from immigration that would increase the size of the labor force and permit a more optimal development of available natural resources. For the most part, however, potential immigration areas are virtually nonexistent today because there are so few nations willing to accept immigrants. Moreover, even in those few instances where immigrants are actively sought, their number and characteristics are rigidly controlled. Even in the United States, where the ethnic basis of our national immigration policy has finally been removed, the number of immigrants we will accept each year is limited, and preference is given to persons such as doctors, engineers, chemists, and others who possess various technical skills. Thus, although the United States certainly benefited from the mass immigration of a previous era, it is doubtful if the world will ever again witness such a phenomenon of comparable scale.

(3) *Sociocultural contributions of immigration.* Most discussions stress (with some justification) the economic consequences of immigration for the historical growth and development of the nation. But we should not neglect the fact that the immigrants also made many contributions to American social and cultural development. For one thing, the heavy immigration of unskilled peasants at a time when the United States was undergoing a rapid transition to an urban-industrial society was a major factor contributing to the maintenance of a highly mobile and open class society during the nineteenth and early twentieth centuries. Thus, one contribution of immigration was its role in the emergence of America as the classic example of a "classless" democratic society with virtually unlimited opportunities. Similarly, as mentioned briefly above, whatever homogeneity exists in the United States today is not solely the outgrowth of our colonial American heritage. Rather, it is the result of the interstimulation between the native population and the millions of immigrants who came from vastly different social backgrounds. These diverse traditions were mingled with one another and ultimately synthesized into a new cultural tradition that was uniquely American. Another significant contribution of immigration, then, lies in the role it has played in promoting civilizational growth by necessitating a synthesis of differences.

The sociocultural contributions of immigration become more apparent when considered on an individual level.[5] What would American *music* be like today, for example, without the benefit of immigrants such as Bela Bartok, Jascha Heifetz, José Iturbi, Serge Koussevitzky, Fritz Kreisler, Sergei Rachmaninoff, Artur Rubinstein, Leopold Stokowski, Igor Stravinski, Arturo Toscanini, Bruno

Walter—not to mention Irving Berlin—to cite just a few? Similarly, who can deny the influence on the American *theatre* and movie industry of immigrants like William Fox, Otto Preminger, Max Reinhardt, and the Warner brothers? And who is to say where America would stand as a world power today if it had not been for the work of immigrants such as atomic scientists Enrico Fermi and Edward Teller, and rocketeer Wernher von Braun? In every conceivable field of endeavor, in fact, immigrants have left their mark. To cite a few others who have come to the United States and made significant contributions to their various fields: Sholem Asch, Lion Feuchtwanger, and Erich Maria Remarque in *literature;* Salvador Dali and Karl Bittner in *art* (painting and sculpture); Jacob Riis and Joseph Pulitzer in *journalism;* Felix Frankfurter in *law;* Victor Borge, Greta Garbo, and Jean Hersholt in *entertainment* and the dramatic arts; Bruno Rossi in *physics;* Knute Rockne in *athletics;* Igor Sikorsky in *aeronautics;* Bronislaw Malinowski in *anthropology;* Florian Znaniecki and Pitirim Sorokin in *sociology.* The list could go on for hundreds of pages (thousands of pages if we were to include the contributions of the sons and daughters of immigrants); but the few who have been cited should be sufficient to illustrate the point: immigration has played a major role in the sociocultural development of America and the American way of life, as well as in the economic growth of the nation.

(4) *The problem of assimilation.* Although no one can deny the importance of immigration in the growth of the United States, it is also true that it created its share of problems for the society. In the first place, whenever two or more diverse cultural groups come into close contact, they must develop some sort of composite culture with regard to various attitudes, values, behavior patterns, and so on. This usually means that the smaller group must modify many of its beliefs and traditions to coincide with those of the larger dominant group. This transformation process (the various degrees of which are indicated by such terms as *accommodation, adjustment, assimilation,* and *integration*) is a difficult, often pain-

ful process that entails both personal and social readjustment to new situations. In general, the magnitude of the problems involved reflects the extent of the differences between the minority and majority groups. Where differences in such obvious traits as language and skin color are minimal, the adjustment process will be relatively easier. Where such differences are pronounced, adjustment will be slower and more difficult to achieve—if it is achieved at all. The most poignant illustration of this is the American Negro who even after hundreds of years has not been able to become fully assimilated into American society.

Reference has already been made to the higher crime rate of many ethnic minorities (either native nonwhites or various foreign-born white groups), their higher death rates, their higher rates of prostitution and illegitimacy, and so forth. Although statistics would tend to bear out these facts, they do not reveal the most important fact: *the greater incidence of deviant behavior is not an inherent ethnic trait but is a reflection of the problems encountered in the assimilation process.* Broadly speaking, there are two basic sources of problems relating to the assimilation of ethnic minority groups: (1) resistance by the dominant group; and (2) resistance by the minority group. The former leads to such things as segregation in ghettos where differences are reinforced. It also leads to other discriminatory practices (for example, nineteenth-century help-wanted ads with the note "No Irish Need Apply," or Jim Crow practices that still exist in many parts of the United States). All of these, of course, promote resentment of the majority and may encourage lack of respect for the majority laws. This in turn influences a greater incidence of lawlessness or other forms of deviant behavior.

The other source of problems is resistance to assimilation on the part of the minority group which often does not want to modify any of its traditions. This is most prevalent among the older foreign born, and it is frequently a source of intergenerational conflict within immigrant groups. The nature of this conflict is represented by the *marginal man,* a term used to describe persons caught between two conflicting cultural groups. The native-born children of immigrants have often found themselves caught between the old world of their parents and the new world in which they are trying to make their way. Often the marginal person facilitates assimilation by acting as a bridge between the two cultures. Not infrequently, however, such persons may seek to escape the conflict by rejecting both cultures. This rejection generally takes the form of some socially deviant behavior (crime, prostitution, drug addiction); and it is basically this marginal group that accounts for the generally greater incidence of personal and social disorganization among immigrant ethnic groups.

When there is widespread marginality as a result of efforts of the older immigrants to maintain their old cultural traditions, it may often be because they have had unpleasant experiences in their dealings with the larger society. Many immigrants came to this country not knowing the language, not having much money, and not possessing many technical skills; and they frequently encountered a native population that regarded their poverty and lack of knowledge of American ways as a sign of laziness and stupidity. The immigrant's only defense against such hostility was to retreat into the security and understanding of his own group. The implication here is that the immigrant's resistance to assimilation is itself often a result of the dominant native group's resistance to him. This suggests that assimilation can best be achieved not by trying to force immigrants to adopt American ways but by accepting them as social equals and encouraging their active participation in American society.

If we accept the principle that the assimilation of immigrants into American society is something to be encouraged, the problem becomes one of educating the American public to accept immigrants as equals. Fifty to sixty years ago, when massive European immigration was at its height, a great many Americans were not willing to do this. Today the recent relaxation of our immigration laws suggests that this earlier resistance has undergone substantial reduction (this does not, unfortunately, apply as far as some native groups—notably Negroes and Puerto Ricans—are concerned). In part, the immigrants have themselves to thank for this: despite barriers and the hostility they frequently encountered, the immigrants have succeeded in becoming "Americanized," thus demonstrating to the native population that many of their earlier fears were groundless. In this respect, it may be suggested that the "fears" that motivate discrimination against ethnic minorities such as Negroes and Spanish-speaking groups in the nation today may be equally groundless. The higher incidence among these groups of such phenomena as drug addiction, unemployment, illegitimacy, and juvenile delinquency does not reflect such traits as loose morals or laziness. Rather, it reflects economic and social frustration and a resentment against being treated as second-class citizens. This suggests that a more equitable treatment of these minorities would lead to a substantial modification of the deviant behavior patterns that the bigots of our society so righteously point to in justifying their discriminatory practices.

(5) *Summary.* Many volumes, a few of which are cited at the end of this chapter, have been written on the consequences of immigration for the growth and development of the American nation. In this section we have indicated very briefly what some of the major consequences of this immigration have been. It is difficult to visualize an America as rich and as powerful as it is today without the immigration of past years. Moreover, there is no reason to anticipate any reduction in the significance of the contributions that will be made by immigrants of future years. Perhaps this knowledge will help promote a greater tolerance among the American population for groups of people whose language sounds strange to our ears, whose customs seem a little unorthodox, or whose skin is of a different color. A greater tolerance for such differences will greatly reduce the unfavorable consequences of immigration and very likely speed up the realization of positive contributions.

Migration is a long-established tradition in the United States. Even though the volume of foreign immigration has been greatly reduced since the 1920's, internal movement is continually modifying the distribution of the population within the United States. Each new year sees the center of population move farther westward as the people became more evenly dispersed throughout the land, and each new year sees an increase in the proportion of the population living in or near large urban areas of the country. Within the urban areas, migration trends recently have brought about a shift in the balance of the population from the older central cities to the newly developing suburban fringe areas.

The extent to which Americans are mobile is well illustrated by this fact: slightly more than half of the persons five years old and over living in the United States at the time of the 1960 census were living in a different house from the one they lived in five years earlier. Other estimates indicate that approximately one out of every five persons in this country move from one house or apartment to another every year, and about one in twenty move from one county to another. Not more than 2 or 3 per cent of the adult population spend their entire lives in the same house or apartment, and perhaps not more than 10 to 15 per cent live their entire lives within the same county. Few if any populations in the world today are so mobile. In the remainder of this section, further consideration will be given to the extent to which Americans are mobile, with particular emphasis on the differences in mobility levels of the major subgroups in the population. Before discussing general mobility trends and differentials, however, it is necessary to become acquainted with the basic mobility concepts currently in use in the United States.

(1) *Mobility concepts defined.* Because residential mobility is one of the fundamental mechanisms of population change, a knowl-

edge of the extent to which people are moving, the characteristics of movers, and their respective areas of origin and destination is necessary for an adequate understanding of the developments that are taking place in any population. For this reason the United States Bureau of the Census periodically collects information designed to measure population mobility. One question on the 1960 decennial census schedule asked for usual place of residence on April 1, 1955, of persons who were five years old or over on April 1, 1960. The extent of mobility in the population was then determined by comparing the answers to this question to usual place of residence at the time of the census.

In classifying the population according to mobility status, the Bureau of the Census distinguishes these three main categories:

(a) *Nonmobile Persons* (nonmovers). This category includes all persons five years old and over reported living in the same house in both 1955 and 1960.

(b) *Mobile Persons* (movers). This category consists of all persons who were living in a "different house in the United States" in 1955 from the one they occupied in 1960. All mobile persons were further subdivided into two main groups: *Intracounty movers,* or persons who lived in a different house in 1960 than in 1955, but whose place of residence at the two dates was in the same county; and *intercounty movers,* or *migrants*—persons who not only moved between 1955 and 1960, but whose place of residence in 1960 was located in a "different county" than in 1955. This migrant category was further subdivided into *intrastate migrants* (persons who moved to a different county within the "same state"), and *interstate migrants* (persons who moved to a different county in a "different state").

(c) *Persons Living Abroad.* This group consists of persons, either citizens or aliens, living in this country in 1960, whose place of residence in 1955 was outside the United States. This group includes persons who were living either in an outlying area under the jurisdiction of the United States or in a foreign country. These persons are distinguished from the general category of movers who moved from one place to another within the United States.

Finally, there is a *not reported* category that includes persons five years old and over who had changed their place of residence during the five years preceding the census, but for whom sufficient information regarding 1955 place of residence was lacking.

(2) *Mobility status of the American population.* The mobility status of the United States population as of April 1, 1960, is depicted in Table IV-3. Of the nearly 160 million persons five years old and over living in the nation at that time, slightly more than 79 million (50 per cent) were living in the same house as the one they lived in five years earlier. During the same period (1955–1960), 47 million persons had changed their place of residence within a single county (roughly 30 per cent of the population), and another 28 million persons (17 per cent of the population) had moved across county boundaries. This migration was fairly evenly divided between intrastate and interstate moves, with a slight majority (14 million, or 9 per cent of the total population age five and over) moving between states. About 2 million of those persons five years and over had been living outside the boundaries of the United States, and an additional 25 million had moved, but their place of residence in 1955 was not reported. In all, roughly half of the nation's population age five and over in 1960 were living in a different house from the one they had lived in on April 1, 1955.

Statistics on "year moved into present house" (see Table IV-4 below) shed additional light on the extent of mobility in the population. Of the 180-odd million people in the United States on April 1, 1960, roughly one-fourth had moved into their house sometime after December 31, 1958. This means that approximately one out of every four persons in the nation had been living in the same house for less than two years. Nearly 19 million persons (11 per cent) had moved during 1958, and another 15 million (8 per cent) had moved in 1957. At the other extreme, 11.3 million per-

Table IV-3: Per cent distribution of the population by residence 5 years prior to the census date, by sex, color, and residence, United States, 1960.

Residence 5 years prior to census date	United States total	White	Nonwhite	Male	Female	Urban	Rural nonfarm	Rural farm
Total age 5 and over								
Number	159,003,807	141,742,113	17,531,694	77,963,696	81,040,097	111,221,500	35,670,194	12,112,113
Per cent	100.0	100.0	100.0	100.00	100.0	100.0	100.0	100.0
Same house	49.9	50.1	48.0	49.1	50.6	47.9	48.7	71.4
Different house in U.S.	47.3	47.2	48.4	47.6	47.0	48.9	49.0	28.0
Same county	29.8	28.9	37.6	29.5	30.1	31.3	29.0	19.2
Different county	17.4	18.3	10.7	18.1	16.9	17.6	20.0	8.8
Same state	8.5	9.0	4.7	8.7	8.5	8.1	10.7	5.9
Different state	8.9	9.2	6.1	9.4	8.4	9.4	9.3	2.8
Abroad	1.3	1.3	1.0	1.5	1.1	1.5	1.0	0.2
Not reported	1.6	1.4	2.7	1.8	1.3	1.7	1.4	0.4

SOURCE: U.S. Bureau of the Census, United States Census of Population: 1960, Final Report PC(1)-1C, General Social and Economic Characteristics: United States Summary, Washington, D.C., 1962; and Final Report PC(1)-1D, Detailed Characteristics: United States Summary, Washington, D.C., 1963.

Table IV-4: Per cent distribution of the population by year moved into present house, for the United States, urban and rural, 1960.

Year moved into present house	United States total	Urban	Rural nonfarm	Rural farm
Total population				
Number	179,325,671	125,283,783	40,596,790	13,444,898
Per cent	100.0	100.0	100.0	100.0
1959 to 1960	25.4	26.1	27.1	14.1
1958	10.5	10.8	10.8	6.7
1957	8.2	8.5	8.2	5.7
1954 to 1956	17.0	17.8	15.9	13.1
1950 to 1953	12.8	13.0	11.9	13.3
1940 to 1949	13.3	12.6	13.1	20.3
1939 or earlier	6.5	6.2	5.8	12.0
Always lived in this house	6.3	5.1	7.1	14.8

SOURCE: U.S. Bureau of the Census, *United States Census of Population: 1960*, Final Report PC(1)-1C, *General Social and Economic Characteristics: United States Summary*, Washington, D.C., 1962.

sons, or 6 per cent of the population, had always lived in the same house, and another 11.7 million (7 per cent) had lived a minimum of twenty years in the house in which they were living at the time of the census.

Due to changes in both data collection and tabulation procedures, fully comparable data on population mobility are not available for decennial censuses before 1960. The data available, however, suggest that the overall mobility of the American population has remained relatively consistent at least since the end of the Second World War. To illustrate, according to a sample survey conducted by the Census Bureau in the spring of 1948, 19.9 per cent of the population had moved during the preceding twelve-month period. For an approximately comparable period ten years later, the proportion of movers was 19.8 per cent; and according to a survey conducted in the spring of 1965, 20.1 per cent of the population had changed residence during the preceding year.[6] Clearly, the relatively high mobility characteristic of the United States population has not shown any signs of declining.

(3) *Differential mobility in the United States*. Although Americans in general are very mobile, not all segments of the population are characterized by the same mobility patterns. According to data collected in the 1960 census, for example, nonwhites are slightly more mobile than the white population; males are more mobile than females; and nonfarm residents are more mobile than the farm population. In 1960, only 48 per cent of the nonwhites in the United States were living in the same house as they lived in five years earlier. By contrast, slightly more than half of the white population was classified as nonmobile. Although they were slightly more mobile in general, nonwhites tended to travel shorter distances than whites (for example, the proportion of movers who remained within the confines of the same county was well over three-fourths for nonwhites as compared to less than two-thirds for whites). On the one hand, the greater overall mobility of the nonwhite population in the United States probably reflects the increasing tendency, during the postwar decades, for southern Negroes to migrate to the larger cities of the North in search of economic opportunity. On the other hand, the greater short-distance movement among nonwhites reflects both the greater instability characteristic of the urban nonwhite family, and particularly the many inequalities in American society that make it necessary for nonwhites to move around more in search of a better job, new and improved housing conditions, and so on.

American males tend to be more mobile than females. Although the overall differential is a small one, it has been observed consistently in this country; moreover, it is a difference that becomes more pronounced as the distance covered by a move increases. Among short-distance movers (i.e., within the same county) females have a slight edge; but among the longer intercounty and interstate movers males clearly predominate. This higher rate of mobility among males is easy to explain. For one thing, it is influenced by the fairly large proportion of males in the armed forces (1.7 million in 1960). For another thing, the cultural role of the male as the family "breadwinner" makes it likely that men will move around more in search of better job opportunities. Males also have a greater tendency to attend college (especially at longer distances from home). Finally, men in our Western culture have always enjoyed a greater freedom to travel than women. Given all these factors, it is surprising that the sex mobility differential is as small as it is. One reason why it is not larger is that when men move they frequently take their families with them, and these wives and children also show up as movers in the mobility statistics. To illustrate, a survey conducted by the Bureau of the Census at the end of World War II disclosed that roughly three-fourths of the female migrants had moved because the head of their family had moved, whereas only a third of the males had moved for such a reason.[7] Further evidence in support of this explanation for the low sex mobility differential is the pronounced widening of the differential when the influence of family relationships is removed. According to the 1960 census, for example, the migration rate for all males was 7 per cent greater than for the total female population. Among unmarried persons age fourteen and over, however, the corresponding male excess was 35 per cent.[8] Clearly, American males are much more mobile than American females.

Rural farm residents were by far the least mobile of any residence group in the population. Nearly three-fourths of the 1960 farm population of the United States was living in the same house in 1955. In sharp contrast, less than half of the rural nonfarm and urban populations were nonmovers. The relative immobility of farm dwellers compared to other groups in the population is further revealed by the fact that less than one in ten of the rural farm population age five and over in 1960 was living in a different county than in 1955, compared with roughly two in ten for both the urban and rural nonfarm residence groups.

The statistics in Table IV-4 on year moved into present house further confirm the relative immobility of farm people. Slightly more than one-fourth of the urban and the rural nonfarm population had moved during the fifteen months preceding the 1960 census, but only 14 per cent of the farm population had moved into their house during that most recent period. On the other hand, roughly one-fourth of the rural farm population had lived twenty years or longer in the same house, compared with only about 10 per cent for the urban and the rural nonfarm population.

With regard to this residential differential, the low farm mobility rate masks the fact that there continues to be a great deal of migration *out* of rural farm areas to rural nonfarm and especially urban areas. These persons, who are in fact mobile farm residents, are counted as mobile persons at their area of destination only. That is, the characteristically low rural farm mobility rate merely indicates that there is relatively little mobility *within* farm areas. Farm dwellers either do not move, or, if they do, they tend to move out of their farm environment entirely.

Another important variable according to which mobility rates differ is *age* (see Table IV-5). The young adult population is by far the most mobile age group in the United States. More than seven out of ten persons twenty to twenty-nine years of age in 1960 had changed their place of residence sometime during the five-year period preceding the census. As age increased beyond thirty years, the percentage of movers decreased. Slightly more than six out of ten persons thirty to thirty-four years of age were living in a different house in 1960 than they had lived in five years earlier. At age forty to forty-four this figure decreased to roughly four out of ten. At ages fifty to fifty-four it was slightly more than three in ten, and from sixty to eighty-four somewhat less than three in ten had changed their place of residence between 1955 and 1960. From seventy-five on, the proportion of movers increased slightly with age, once again reaching three in ten at ages eighty-five and over. At the other end of the life cycle, slightly more than half of the children five to nine years of age had moved

Table IV-5: Selected mobility characteristics of the population age 5 and over, by age, United States, 1960.

Age	Number of people	Per cent who are:		
		Movers	Intercounty migrants	Interstate migrants
Total, 5 and over	159,003,793	47.3	17.5	8.9
5-9	18,659,141	55.0	19.7	9.9
10-14	16,815,965	45.5	15.3	7.5
15-19	13,287,434	47.7	19.7	9.8
20-24	10,803,165	72.6	34.9	19.2
25-29	10,870,386	72.3	31.2	17.5
30-34	11,951,709	61.3	23.3	12.0
35-39	12,508,316	50.9	18.4	9.4
40-44	11,567,216	42.8	14.3	7.1
45-49	10,928,878	37.4	11.5	5.4
50-54	9,696,502	33.7	10.1	4.6
55-59	8,595,947	31.1	9.1	4.1
60-64	7,111,897	28.8	8.6	4.0
65-69	6,186,763	28.4	9.2	4.5
70-74	4,661,136	27.4	8.5	4.0
75-79	2,977,347	27.2	8.1	3.4
80-84	1,518,206	28.6	8.7	3.4
85 and over	863,785	31.0	9.4	4.0

SOURCE: U.S. Bureau of the Census, *United States Census of Population: 1960*, Final Report PC(1)-1D, *Detailed Characteristics: United States Summary*, Washington, D.C., 1963.

during the five years preceding 1960, and about 45 per cent of the children age ten to nineteen had changed their place of residence between 1955 and 1960.

The general pattern described above is fairly consistent for all moves, whether they occurred within the same county, between counties in the same state, or between states. Mobility rates reach a peak during the twenties, subsequently decline with age up to age seventy-five, and then increase slightly at the older ages. The high rate of mobility among persons in their twenties very likely results from this being the age when young people leave the paternal home, marry, and establish homes of their own. The decline in mobility at succeeding ages reflects a trend toward greater stability as persons develop strengthening social and economic ties to a particular job or community. Naturally, there are exceptions to these rules. Not all young people leave home when they mature; some persons never achieve a stable relationship in a community; and some jobs entail a higher degree of mobility than others. For the majority of persons, however, this general pattern applies. Finally, the slight tendency for mobility to increase at the oldest ages is due in part to the breakup of families upon the death of a spouse, and in part to persons moving upon retirement from active participation in the labor force. The mobility rate of children, on the other hand, coincides with that of their parents.

There is also some evidence to suggest that migration is more frequent among the higher *socioeconomic status* groups in the population. For example, a recent survey by the Bureau of the Census revealed that 22 per cent of the mobile population had completed one or more years of college as compared to only 18 per cent among nonmovers. Similarly, professional and technical persons accounted for 15 per cent of the mobile male population but only 12 per cent of the non-mobile group.[9] Although these differences are small, they do suggest that areas of out-migration might be experiencing a qualitative as well as a simple quantitative loss. One instance where this is in fact the case, and where the pattern of out-migration is contributing to a lowering of the overall socioeconomic composition of the population, is in the current suburbanization trend. The implications of this situation will be discussed more fully in a subsequent section (see Chapter 7 below).

(4) *Problems relating to population mobility.* The various problems associated with the mobility of the American population are much more complex than the clear-cut inequalities that exist with regard to mortality levels or accessibility to birth control information. Because of their variety and complexity, a detailed discussion of mobility problems is beyond the scope of this book.

Instead, we can attempt to outline broad problem areas and cite a few specific examples to indicate the kinds of problems that may arise as a consequence of population mobility. The various mobility-related problems may be grouped into three broad categories: (a) those that relate to the generally *high degree of mobility* in the population as a whole; (b) those that relate to the impact of mobility on the *individuals* involved; and (c) those that relate to the impact of mobility on the *communities* involved.

To begin with, it has been noted that, with roughly 20 per cent of the population moving each year, Americans are among the most highly mobile people in the world. Historically this has proven to be a definite economic advantage in that it has helped to balance the distribution of numbers in relation to available resources as the nation has grown and expanded. By dispersing people from each section of the country to all other sections, it has also helped to create a relatively homogeneous society. On the other hand, this relatively high degree of mobility creates numerous problems. The basic problem is the difficulty in preparing and maintaining adequate estimates of the population of local areas, and this seriously impedes the effectiveness of a wide variety of local, state, regional, and national planning organizations. For example, it hampers the effective operation of various health control programs wherein efforts are made to keep track of persons afflicted with particular diseases (such as tuberculosis patients and typhoid carriers).

To take another example, the high degree of population mobility makes it difficult for civil defense organizations to devise plans for sheltering the population in the event of attack. A similar dilemma faces the various groups whose task it is to: (a) plan for the utilization and conservation of local natural resources (such as land and water); (b) evaluate the adequacy of existing schools, hospitals, and other community services; (c) provide for the housing and other needs of older persons; and so forth. In short: persons or groups who want to know something about the size and composition of local populations in order to have a sound basis for devising programs have their efforts severely complicated by the high mobility of the American population.

Such problems are minimal at the time of decennial censuses, and their existence during interim periods is mainly due to the absence of a systematic program of data collection. Until current mobility data become more readily available for local areas in this country, problems of high mobility such as those cited above will continue to exist.

From a more purely sociological perspective, interest focuses on the effects of mobility on the individuals who move and on the communities between which they move. In part, the problems here are similar to the problems foreign immigrants had to face (cultural shock, assimilating to a new environment, marginality, ethnic ghettos, and so on). Considering the *individual* level first: since people often cite some sort of economic reason for moving (take a new job, obtain better housing), migration frequently results in an improvement in one's economic situation. But this is not always the case, as is clearly revealed by the experience of migrant farm workers, and by the growing concern over problems of poverty in the rapidly expanding ethnic ghettos of many of our large urban centers. Moreover, discounting the economic impact, a number of other frequent corollaries of population mobility may be noted. For one thing, the incidence of personal and social disorganization (for example, crime, divorce, prostitution, drug addiction, illegitimacy, alchoholism) is higher among mobile persons than among the more sedentary segments of the population. One such area that has been studied quite extensively in recent years is mental health, and the results of these investigations clearly show that the incidence of mental disorders is substantially higher among migrants than among nonmovers.[10] This is not meant to imply that mobility is necessarily a pathological process or that it generally leads to an increase in personal or group tensions. Rather, the intent is merely to call attention to the existence of such mobility relationships. As a matter of fact, a related problem that may be cited here concerns the need for contemporary migration research to focus more attention on the "chicken or the egg" questions to which such observed relationships give rise. For example, is the migration/mental disease relationship due to a greater propensity to move among persons who are mentally unstable to begin with? Or does the relationship mean that mobility actually is a pathological process in some respects, and that the loss of old and familiar surroundings after a change of residence so unsettles people that they become more susceptible to mental illness than nonmovers? There are now no satisfactory answers to such questions; and this lack of information may be regarded as a major mobility-related problem in the United States today.

Migration (particularly group differences in migration) may also indicate other social and economic problems in the nation. The greater mobility of nonwhites, for example, is a sign of greater instability among that segment of the American population—as reflected in the greater incidence of mental disorders among non-whites.[11] This greater instability is in turn the result of ethnic discrimination which has historically made it necessary for nonwhites to move around more in order to find a good job, decent housing, and so forth. In fact, if there was no ethnic discrimination in this country the color mobility differential would probably be much smaller, and a narrowing of this differential (if and when it occurs) may be regarded as a sign that the socioeconomic opportunities open to nonwhites are approximating more closely those available to the white population. Similarly, the farm-to-city movement reflects the availability of fewer economic opportunities in rural areas. One can also cite here the cases of particular groups, such as migrant workers, whose need for access to health, education, and other welfare services is particularly acute.

Turning to a consideration of the impact of mobility on the *community,* the most general observation is that heavy in-migration is often an indicator of economic growth and development, whereas heavy out-migration more commonly signifies a decaying socio-economic environment. With regard to the community of *destination,* the in-migration can also create problems. It may cause a housing shortage, for example; overcrowding in the schools; or a widening gap between various public service needs (police and fire protection, hospital facilities, public utilities) and the services actually provided. For the most part, the nature of mobility-related problems in any community reflects the particular characteristics of the in-migrants. Conflict of one degree or another often results when the new arrivals differ sharply from the old residents (vis-à-vis the contrast between foreign immigrants and the native population, or the white-nonwhite color differences). But even such less obvious variations as difference in age or in the stage of family cycle can lead to conflict concerning such things as the need for new schools, hospitals, old-age and other welfare programs, and so forth.

For example, if the in-migrants are young married couples, the receiving community must provide adequate housing and educational facilities. Many are the settled rural communities in the United States that have had their traditional social organization drastically upset during the 1950's and 1960's by the influx of large numbers of ex-urbanites with their demands for new and improved schools, better roads, and increased public services. The in-migration of older persons, on the other hand, increases the need for specialized housing and for expanded health and welfare programs. When there is a heavy influx of Negroes (or some other ethnic minority group), the receiving community must contend with a wide variety of social problems resulting not only from the "cultural shock" entailed by migration but also from the discriminatory treatment frequently meted out by the dominant group. Such problems are reflected most vividly in the widespread poverty and higher incidence of various forms of personal and social disorganization in the ethnic ghettos of our larger cities. The seriousness of such problems in contemporary urban America cannot be overemphasized. To appreciate the need for drastic reforms one has only to reflect on the increasing frequency of violent outbreaks in these ethnic conclaves as the American Negro has become more and more dissatisfied with the second-class status allotted to him, and as he has become more and more militant in his efforts to right the wrongs resulting from over a century of prejudice and discrimination. To cite only a few specific instances, racial violence erupted during the mid-1960's in New York City; in Atlanta, Georgia; in Cleveland and Dayton, Ohio; in Chicago and neighboring Cicero, Illinois; and in the now famous Watts section of Los Angeles.

As far as communities of *origin* are concerned, the impact of migration is often the converse of the impact on the communities of destination. If young people are moving out, for example, the need for school facilities is reduced at the same time that the size of the tax base is decreased for the support of other basic community services. When a particular area is losing population, it may frequently be regarded as a reflection of a pathological situation and a sure indication that some problem needs attention. The large-scale movement of Negroes out of the South into northern cities not only creates problems in the receiving areas but also reflects the pronounced lack of economic opportunities for nonwhites in the South—particularly in the *rural* South. Similarly, the more recent suburbanization movement of middle-class Americans is not only due to the "pull" of the aesthetic features of a non-urban environment but is also a reflection of a very strong "push" out of the crowded, dirty, and noisy cities—many of which are well on their way to becoming large urban slums. The extent to which urban decay is becoming recognized as a major problem in the United States is clearly indicated by the rapid growth in recent years of urban renewal and redevelopment programs in many cities, and by the creation in the mid-1960's of a special cabinet post, Housing and Urban Development (HUD), to try to contend with the problems of contemporary urban America. Clearly, to say that mobility has no significant impact other than to redistribute people in relation to resources is naive. Mobility creates problems and continues to play a pervasive role in the growth and development of American society.

REFERENCES AND SUGGESTIONS FOR FURTHER READING

Donald J. Bogue, *The Population of the United States,* Glencoe, Ill., Chapters 14 and 15.

Oscar Handlin, *The Uprooted,* New York, 1951.

Oscar Handlin, ed., *Immigration as a Factor in American History,* Englewood Cliffs, 1959.

E. P. Hutchinson, *Immigrants and Their Children: 1850-1950,* New York, 1956.

William Petersen, *Population,* New York, 1961, Chapters 5–7.

President's Commission on Immigration and Naturalization, *Whom We Shall Welcome,* Washington, D.C., 1953.

Henry S. Shryock, *Population Mobility Within the United States,* Chicago, 1964.

Conrad and Irene B. Taeuber, *The Changing Population of the United States,* New York, 1958, Chapters 3–5.

Dorothy S. Thomas, *Research Memorandum on Migration Differentials,* Social Science Research Council Bulletin 43, New York, 1938.

Ralph Thomlinson, *Population Dynamics,* New York, 1965, Chapters 11–12.

U.S. Bureau of the Census, *United States Census of Population: 1960,* Final Reports PC(2)-1A, *Nativity and Parentage,* Washington, D.C., 1965; PC(2)-2B, *Mobility for States and State Economic Areas,* Washington, D.C., 1963; PC(2)-2C, *Mobility for Metropolitan Areas,* Washington, D.C., 1963; and PC(2)-2D, *Lifetime and Recent Migration,* Washington, D.C., 1963.

5

Population size and growth

In the relatively short period of his known history, man has passed through a series of major cultural epochs, each of which raised him to a higher level of civilization. With every advance in culture came an increase in man's ability to control his physical environment, and with this greater environmental control came an increase in the potentialities of human population growth. Today we live in a world where population is growing at a rate never before equaled in human history—and the rate has been accelerating rapidly in recent years. At the end of World War II the world population growth rate was estimated to be about 1 per cent per year; it was about 1.5 per cent in the mid-1950's, and it is now growing at a rate approaching 2 per cent per year.

Many of the problems confronting mankind today are intimately associated with the explosive nature of current population trends. In order to fully understand these problems, so that rational and intelligent solutions may be worked out for them, we must know the basic facts of population growth. This chapter, therefore, will highlight some of these facts—in the world as a whole, and particularly in the United States—and indicate briefly the nature of some of the problems that must be faced in the years ahead.

WORLD POPULATION GROWTH TRENDS

Estimates prepared by the Statistical Office of the United Nations indicate that the number of people living on earth at mid-twentieth century was approximately 2.5 billion. By 1965 the inhabitants of this planet numbered approximately 3.3 billion. This is a far cry from the 500 million or so persons who were living on earth at the beginning of the modern era (generally taken to be about 1650), and it represents more than a sixfold increase in numbers since that time (see Table V-1).

Table V-1: Size and growth of world population since 1650.

Year	Population in millions	Average annual rate of increase (per cent) between dates
1650	545	......
1750	728	0.3
1800	906	0.5
1850	1,171	0.6
1900	1,608	0.7
1920	1,810	0.6
1930	2,013	1.1
1940	2,246	1.2
1950	2,495	1.1
1960	2,990	2.0
1965	3,308	2.1

SOURCE: United Nations, *The Determinants and Consequences of Population Trends* (ST/SOA/A-17), New York, 1953; United Nations, *1964 Demographic Yearbook;* and Population Reference Bureau, "World Population Data Sheet," Washington, D.C., December 1965.

The magnitude of the increase in population in the modern era can be more readily appreciated by a compression of the time dimension. If the length of time that man has existed on earth is compressed into a single day, then this modern era represents less than one minute; yet this briefest period of human existence has witnessed the greatest increase in numbers. It took hundreds of thousands of years for the population of the world to reach its half-billion level at the beginning of the modern era. It took less than two hundred years for the next half-billion to be added, and less than fifty years for the next half-billion after that. At the present rate of growth, however, it will take only seven years for the world's population to increase by another half-billion persons!

Considered somewhat differently, the population of this planet doubled between 1650 and 1850, a period of two hundred years. It doubled again between 1850 and 1930, a period of eighty years; and if it keeps going at its present rate, the third doubling of world population in the modern era will take place in less than thirty-five years.

Viewed in the long run (see Figure 1), the growth of the world's population can be likened to a long, thin powder fuse that burned slowly and haltingly through centuries of human existence until it reached the charge and exploded in the modern era.[1] Before the advent of the modern era, the number of people on earth increased with infinitesimal slowness—at rates substantially below half of 1 per cent per year. But since that time the rate of increase has risen steadily; the annual average rate of increase exceeded half of 1 per cent throughout the nineteenth century and has been greater than 1 per cent ever since 1920. In the most recent period, world population has been growing at the unprecedented rate of 2.1 per cent per year.[2] As a consequence of these developments in the modern era, such terms as the "population bomb" and the "population explosion" have become part of our everyday vocabulary.

(1) *The demographic transition.* What has caused this tremendous spurt of growth in the modern era? To answer this question, it is necessary to understand the concept of "demographic transition." Demographically speaking, world population growth

Figure 1: Graphic representation of world population growth from the beginning of the Christian era to the middle of the twentieth century

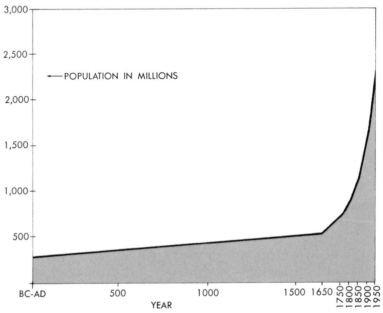

is determined by only two factors—fertility and mortality; population grows according to the extent that the number of people born each year exceed the number who die. Thus, the first step in attempting to explain the unprecedented growth of modern times is to ascertain the relative importance of these two variables.

Throughout the thousands of centuries that preceded the modern era, the brutally harsh conditions of life made human survival an extremely touch-and-go affair. Although population data before the modern era are very scanty for all parts of the world, the evidence that can be gleaned from various anthropological and archaeological sources indicates that the death rate of primitive man was very high. A newborn infant had only about a fifty-fifty chance of surviving to adulthood, and the average length of life could not have been much more than twenty to twenty-five years. In the face of such high death rates, a high fertility level was a necessary condition for the survival of the species, and birth rates often approached their biological maximum. As human culture developed over the ages, however, the chances of survival improved. The first great advancement came with the neolithic cultural achievements of agriculture and the domestication of animals, roughly six to eight thousand years ago. With a more stable food supply, the base was laid for a larger population. But widespread disease resulting from the extremely unsanitary conditions of life continued to keep death rates high, and although population began to increase, it grew so slowly and gradually as to appear almost stationary by modern standards.

It was not until the advent of the Industrial Revolution—the latest stage in man's cultural progress—that the first real burst of population growth came. The Industrial Revolution brought with it the emergence and advancement of modern science; and with this development, the mortality pattern of a million years was broken. The discovery of vaccination for smallpox by Edward Jenner in 1796 was the first in a long line of discoveries and inventions destined to improve substantially the chances of survival, particularly among infants and young children (see Chapter 2). This and other applications of the scientific method to biology and medicine, with continued improvements in agricultural technology, the development of better means of transportation and communication, and all the social, economic, and psychological changes that accompanied the emergence of an urban-industrial civilization, combined to set in motion forces which dramatically lowered death rates and substantially increased human reproductive efficiency.

Although death rates began to fall fairly rapidly, the birth rate was not at first affected by these developments, and fertility remained at high levels for several generations. This widening spread between levels of fertility and mortality (which meant that an increasingly larger proportion of births survived through adulthood), is commonly referred to as the "demographic gap," and it was the creation of this gap that produced the mushrooming of population growth in the modern era.

Eventually, as social and cultural values shifted from an emphasis on the group to an emphasis on the welfare and development of the individual, and as continued technological progress provided the means for controlling fertility, the birth rate began to catch up with the earlier decline in the death rate. A new demographic balance between low birth and death rates was achieved, and the rate of population growth—at least in the industrial nations of the Western world—slowed down considerably (see Figure 2). This shift from the old balance of high birth and death rates, through a period of sustained growth as a declining death rate created an imbalance between fertility and mortality, to a new balance of low birth and death rates, is called the "demographic transition." The completion of this transition marks the end of rapid population growth.

(2) *The problem today.* The problem of increasing numbers we face today derives from the fact that less than half of the world's population has completed this transition. The majority of people in the world today have just entered the initial phase of rapid population growth; in the years ahead, the numbers contributed by these people will considerably dwarf any previous growth the world has ever known. Two facts stand out to reinforce the expectation of explosive growth in the years ahead. In the first place, the base population today is much larger than it was when the Western nations began their transition, and even a moderate rate of growth will, when applied to a larger population base, yield substantial numerical increases. In the second place, because the underdeveloped countries can make immediate use of modern techniques for postponing death—techniques that the West developed only after many years—the decline of mortality in the underdeveloped countries of the world today is taking place much more

Figure 2: Graphic illustration of the demographic transition

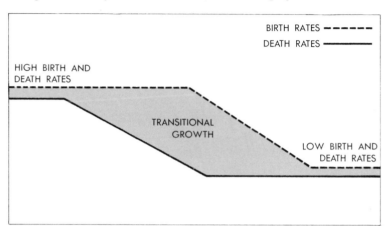

rapidly than it did in the West. The extent to which this is so is brought out quite dramatically by Figure 3, which compares birth and death rate trends in Ceylon and Sweden: whereas it took 140 years for the Swedish death rate to decline from an annual level of 25 to 10 per 1,000, Ceylon has experienced a comparable reduction in only thirty years. Fertility levels in the newly emerging nations, however, have shown very little sign of declining. Furthermore, given the economic and cultural conditions in which fertility is embedded in these countries, it is unrealistic to look for any substantial decline in the birth rate in the immediate future.

The unlikelihood of any immediate fertility decline, coupled with the more drastic mortality reductions possible today, assures us of continued rapid world population growth. In no country of the Western world was the fertility decline sharp enough to close the demographic gap in less than a hundred years. While it may not take this long for the non-Western world to bring its fertility under control and complete its transition, it is certainly not going

Figure 3: Birth and death rate trends in Sweden (1820–1960) and Ceylon (1900–1960)

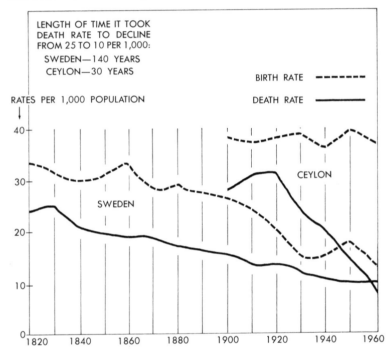

SOURCES: Warren S. Thompson, *Population Problems*, New York, 1953, pp. 162 and 236. Data for 1960 were obtained from United Nations, *Population and Vital Statistics Reports*, Statistical Papers, Series A, 13:2 (April 2,1961.)

to take place overnight. As long as the gap between fertility and mortality persists among most of the world's people—and it is likely to persist for some time to come—we cannot expect any respite from the problem of extremely rapid world population growth.

POPULATION GROWTH IN THE UNITED STATES

When the modern population explosion first began in the middle of the seventeenth century, the area which today comprises the United States of America was virtually uninhabited. At that time it is estimated that the population of the entire North American continent numbered no more than a few hundred thousand aborigines and a handful of European colonists scattered along the eastern seaboard and in Mexico; not until midway through the eighteenth century did the first million people of European descent accumulate in this country. Since then, however, the population has doubled and redoubled at a rate astounding to all who reflect upon it. During the late colonial and early national period, the population of the United States increased at an average rate of 3 per cent a year—a rate which doubled the population every twenty-five years. Numbers more than quadrupled between 1800 and 1850, more than trebled from 1850 to 1900, and nearly doubled from 1900 to 1950. Throughout the 1950's and early 1960's the population increased by an average of nearly 3 million persons per year, or by an annual rate of nearly 2 per cent.

When the first federal census was taken in 1790, the population of the United States numbered less than 4 million (see Table V-2); it was nearly 180 million in 1960, and by the middle of the 1960 decade there were approximately 195 million people living in this country. In the relatively short time since its formation as a nation, the United States has grown from a population of a few million to one of several hundred million. Today it is the fourth most populous nation in the world.[3] The entire history of mankind records no other population as having grown to such a size, and at such a rate, over a comparable span of time.

There are only two ways in which the population of an area can change: through reproduction (the balance between births and deaths) and through migration (the movement of people into or

Table V-2: Size and growth of the United States population since 1790.

Year	Population	Average annual rate of increase (per cent) between dates
1790	3,929,214	......
1800	5,308,483	3.5
1810	7,239,881	3.6
1820	9,638,453	3.3
1830	12,866,020	3.4
1840	17,069,453	3.3
1850	23,191,876	3.6
1860	31,443,321	3.6
1870	38,558,371	2.7
1880	50,189,209	2.6
1890	62,979,766	2.6
1900	76,212,168	2.1
1910	92,228,496	2.1
1920	106,021,537	1.5
1930	123,202,624	1.6
1940	132,164,569	0.7
1950	151,325,798	1.5
1960	179,323,175	1.9
1965	194,583,000	1.7
1975 (low)	214,100,000	1.0
1975 (high)	227,474,000	1.7

SOURCE: U.S. Bureau of the Census, *U.S. Census of Population: 1960*, PC(1)-1A, *Number of Inhabitants: United States Summary*, Washington, D.C., 1961; and "Revised Projections of the Population of the United States by Age and Sex to 1985," *Current Population Reports*, P-25:329, Washington, D.C., March 10, 1966.

out of an area). In discussing the trend of world population size and growth, one need only consider the reproductive component of change. Below the world level, however, one must consider the effect of both reproduction and migration. This is particularly true in the case of the United States where, beginning with its initial settlement by the wandering nomadic bands who crossed over the Bering Strait land bridge thousands of years ago, and lasting well into the twentieth century, population growth has been significantly influenced by human migration.

Reproduction and migration have exerted different influences at different times in this country; thus an adequate understanding of United States population trends can best be obtained by considering its growth in terms of distinct phases or time periods. In general, it can be said that the nation has passed through five distinct phases of population growth and is currently in the midst of a sixth.

(1) *Colonial growth phase*. The first phase is the colonial phase and covers the period from the initial settlement of the United States until about 1820. This phase was characterized by high rates of both natural increase and net immigration from abroad. The early settlers married at a younger age than their European contemporaries, which meant that each married couple was exposed for a longer time to the likelihood of bearing children. The longer exposure to the risk of childbearing, coupled with the fact that large families were considered an asset in conquering the wilderness, meant that birth rates were very high and often approached the maximum of which the human race is biologically capable. The high birth rates, combined with a steady stream of immigration from Europe, resulted in extremely rapid rates of population growth. While America was in this phase of her growth, it is estimated that her population increased, on the average, by a rate of 3.5 per cent a year.

(2) *Frontier growth phase*. Growth continued to be rapid during the second or frontier phase of American growth. During this period, lasting from about 1820 until the end of the nineteenth century, reproduction rates were high but declining as a falling birth rate began to narrow the "demographic gap." At the same time, however, immigration from abroad swelled to tremendous proportions. Rapid population growth on the other side of the Atlantic, agricultural advances which displaced large segments of the rural population, and an expanding frontier with seemingly limitless opportunities in this country, all combined to bring about one of the greatest population transfers in history: between 1820 and the end of the nineteenth century it is estimated that close to 20 million people entered this country from Europe. In all, this period saw the population of the United States grow from slightly less than 10 million to over 75 million—more than a sevenfold increase during a scant eighty years.

(3) *Early twentieth century growth phase*. During the third phase, lasting roughly from 1900 to 1925, the rapid rates of growth that had characterized the nineteenth century began to decline. The reproduction increase began to level off as fertility continued to decline and the United States neared the completion of its demographic transition; and, due both to the disruptive effects of World War I in Europe and to increased agitation for restrictive legislation here at home, the volume of European immigration declined until it was about a third of what it had been previously. Growth rates during this period amounted to only 2 per cent a year, compared with average annual growth rates in excess of 3 per cent throughout most of the nineteenth century.

(4) *Interwar growth phase*. The following phase, lasting from about 1925 until America's entry into the Second World War, saw growth rates continue to decline—only now the decline was much more rapid than before. The Immigration and Nationality Act of 1924 sharply curtailed immigration from abroad, and as the country slid into a severe economic depression, the birth rate fell to an unprecedented low level. During the years immediately preceding World War II, the population of the United States increased at a rate of less than 1 per cent a year, and it appeared that the era of rapid population growth had come to an end.

(5) *Baby boom growth phase*. Beginning in the mid-1940's it became apparent that the United States had entered another phase of fairly rapid population growth. Although the volume of immigration remained a mere fraction of its former size, the historical decline in fertility underwent an unexpected and substantial re-

versal. From an all-time low level of about 18 live births per 1,000 population during the 1930's, the birth rate rose to a level of 26.2 per 1,000 in 1947 and remained at about 24 to 25 per 1,000 until the late 1950's. This unexpected phenomenon, popularly known as the "baby boom," caused the rate of population growth to increase from less than 1 per cent a year during the 1930's to nearly 2 per cent a year during the 1950's. Although the growth rates that prevailed during the postwar decade were much lower than those experienced during the nineteenth century, their application to a larger population base brought about some really dramatic numerical increases. The number of people added to the population between 1940 and 1960, for example, accounts for nearly half of the total population gain of the entire twentieth century.

(6) *Growth trends since 1960.* The late 1950's were characterized by two major developments with regard to fertility and mortality trends in the United States (see Chapters 2 and 3). On the one hand, the long-term decline in mortality came to a halt and the death rate became more or less stabilized. On the other hand, the postwar baby boom came to an end and the birth rate began to decline. The combined effect of these two developments has been a steady and fairly pronounced decline in the *crude rate of natural increase.* (This rate is computed simply as the difference between the crude birth and death rates, and is defined as the net number of people added to the size of a population each year for every 1,000 members of that population.) During the 1950's the impact of the postwar baby boom resulted in natural increase rates of 14 to 15 per 1,000 per year, but by 1965 this rate had fallen to a level of 10 per 1,000—a level it had not occupied since the early years of World War II (see Table V-3). Since the impact of foreign immigration is still negligible (i.e., during the early 1960's the number of immigrants to the United States averaged only about 275,000 per year), this decline in the crude rate of natural increase has meant a corresponding decline in the overall

Table V-3: *Crude rates of birth, death, and natural increase in the United States, selected years, 1900–1965.*

Year	Crude birth rate	Crude death rate	Crude rate of natural increase
1900	32.3	17.2	15.1
1910	30.1	14.7	15.4
1920	27.7	13.0	14.7
1930	21.3	11.3	10.0
1935	18.7	10.9	7.8
1940	19.4	10.8	8.6
1945	20.4	10.6	9.8
1950	24.1	9.6	14.5
1955	25.0	9.3	15.7
1960	23.7	9.5	14.2
1961	23.3	9.3	14.0
1962	22.4	9.5	12.9
1963	21.7	9.6	12.1
1964	21.0	9.4	11.6
1965	19.4	9.4	10.0

SOURCE: See Tables II-1 and III-1.

rate of population growth. Between 1960 and 1965 the population of the United States increased by only 8.5 per cent—or by an average rate of 1.7 per cent per year, compared with an annual average growth rate of 1.9 per cent between 1950 and 1960. Moreover, unless there is an end to the downward trend of fertility, the 1970 decade could have even lower annual rates of population increase.

In discussing the declining rate of population growth in the United States during the 1960 decade, there is one very important consideration to keep in mind: a rate is a relative number, and although the *rate* of growth declined, it was applied to an increasingly larger population base; therefore, *numerical* increases continued to be substantial. Thus, although the annual growth rate between 1960 and 1965 (1.7 per cent) was slightly less than the 1950–1960 annual rate (1.9 per cent), it was still sufficient to add more than 15 million persons to the population. This represents an average annual addition of just over 3 million people—nearly 10 per cent greater than the average of 2.8 million per year added to the population between 1950 and 1960! Moreover, there is every indication that numerical increases in the size of the American population will continue to be fairly substantial throughout the 1970's. This is because the oldest of the larger birth cohorts born during the postwar decade have aged; during the late 1960's and early 1970's these infants of yesterday will be attaining adulthood, marrying, and having babies of their own. Even if the fertility of these baby boom cohorts does not rise above the level of the mid-1960's, there would still be close to 2 million people added to the population each year between 1965 and 1975 (see Table V-2; "low" projection of the Bureau of the Census). At the other extreme, should the baby boom babies decide to have as many children as their mothers were having during the early 1950's, the 1965–1975 numerical gains would exceed 3 million per year ("high" projection of the Bureau of the Census). What all this means is that although the postwar baby boom was clearly over by 1965, the full effects of this boom had not been felt. These effects will not become fully apparent until all the larger birth cohorts of the late 1940's and early 1950's have entered the reproductive ages and started having babies of their own, and this will not be until after 1980.

It is impossible for anyone to say for certain what the population of the United States will be at any particular time in the future. Nevertheless, unless the fertility level declines to a level substantially below that of 1965, or unless it undergoes another reversal and rises to a level exceeding even that of the baby boom era, then the population of the United States in 1975 will probably fall somewhere between 215 million and 230 million. In other words, there is little doubt that the people of this country can look forward to a continued increase in their numbers for a long time to come.

The high birth rates that once performed such a positive function have persisted in many parts of the world and have led to such rapid and tremendous numerical increases that the human race may well be in danger of breeding itself out of existence. Be that as it may, it is a fact that developments since the 1940's have created (or intensified) a number of problems that man must face up to if he expects to make the world a safe, healthy, and happy place for *all* of its inhabitants. In the remainder of this chapter, we shall focus on some of the more significant problems (in the world in general and in the United States in particular) that have been generated by the population explosion of the mid-twentieth century.

(1) *Population growth and economic development.*[4] One of the major problems confronting mankind today is the fact that two-thirds to three-fourths of the world's population lives in countries characterized by extremely low levels of economic and social well-being. To take a specific illustration, in contrast to an annual per capita income of roughly $1,900 in the United States at mid-century, almost 70 per cent of the countries of the world had annual per capita incomes of less than $400. Furthermore, in most of these countries the persistence of high birth rates in the presence of falling death rates were (and are) resulting in extensive population increases. In fact, the greatest numerical growth since the war has occurred in those underdeveloped nations in Asia, Africa, and Latin America that could least afford it. Moreover, the persistence of rapid population growth in these countries has been a major impediment to efforts to raise low standards of living and has imposed a real barrier to sustained economic development. As one author noted: "If an economy is growing but the population remains unchanged in size, then any increase in goods and services, minus that needed for reinvestment purposes, is available for

improving the level of living of the people. . . . On the other hand, if there is any amount of population growth, then the increase in goods and services minus that needed for reinvestment, when divided amongst a larger population, will result in smaller gains per capita in the level of living." [5]

There is a very real basis for challenging the universal validity of this proposition. In the United States, for example, rather than being harmful, the rapid rate of population growth during the nineteenth century played a key role in stimulating tremendous economic advance. The situation in the underdeveloped nations in the middle of the twentieth century, however, is markedly different from that of the United States one hundred years ago; and for these underdeveloped countries the proposition does appear to be valid.

The extent to which rapid population growth acts as a deterrent to economic development today can be demonstrated quite easily. The economic development of any country is a process which involves changes in nearly every aspect of economic and social life. Although there are many and varied indicators of this process, the trend of per capita real income is perhaps most significant. The movement of per capita income is highly correlated with other changes in the social and economic welfare of a society, and the direction and speed of this movement is a rough but reliable indicator of the extent to which a society is becoming better or worse off. Thus, by considering the relationship between annual rates of population growth in underdeveloped countries and corresponding annual rates of increase in per capita income, it is possible to illustrate the adverse effects of rapid population growth on economic progress in the so-called "have not" countries of the world. The opportunity for such a consideration is afforded by the data in Table V-4, which shows recent population and income growth rates for selected low-income countries (i.e., all had per capita annual incomes of less than $400 in 1955).

Although a complete account of the relationship between popu-

Table V-4: Annual rates of increase in population and per capita income in selected low-income countries, 1952–1958.

Country	Annual per cent increase in:	
	Population size	Per capita income
Austria	0.2	7.2
Italy	0.5	5.8
Portugal	0.9	3.1
Greece	0.9	7.5
South Korea	1.0	3.0
Burma	1.2	2.9
India	1.4	1.6
Pakistan	1.4	0.9
Cyprus	1.7	2.9
Belgian Congo	1.9	2.8
Argentina	2.0	1.7
Chile	2.6	1.2
Philippines	2.7	3.6
Turkey	2.8	2.8
Honduras	2.8	0.3
Ecuador	3.2	0.8

SOURCE: Edward G. Stockwell, "The Relationship Between Population Growth and Economic Development," American Sociological Review (April 1962).

lation growth and economic development would consider both the effect of income changes on population growth and the effect of population growth on the movement of per capita income, attention here is focused solely on the latter effect. If one equates economic development with an increase in per capita real income, it is clearly apparent that a rapidly increasing population can seriously impede the economic progress of low-income countries. With only a few exceptions, the data show that those countries that experienced the highest annual rates of population growth during the 1950's also realized the smallest gains in per capita income. For those countries that grew at a rate of less than 1 per cent per year, the annual rate of increase in per capita income ranged from 3.1 per cent to 7.5 per cent, with an overall average of roughly 6 per cent a year. In contrast, the average annual rate of per capita income increase was only 2.5 per cent for countries whose annual rate of population growth fell between 1 and 2 per cent; and among countries where population growth rates exceeded 2 per cent a year, per capita income increased at an average annual rate of substantially less than 2 per cent. Furthermore, among the countries in this latter group the annual rate of population growth was, with the exception of the Philippines, as great as or greater than the corresponding rate of increase in per capita income.

Although the data here are confined to only a few selected low-income countries, they clearly demonstrate a negative relationship between changes in economic status and the rate of population growth. All of the countries examined had extremely low levels of per capita income, but all of them had been experiencing increases in per capita income. Since economic development has been equated with an increase in per capita real income, it is apparent that all of the countries were undergoing some degree of economic development. At the same time, however, this economic growth was most pronounced among those countries with low or moderate rates of population growth. This evidence strongly suggests that economic progress would have been greater if their populations were not growing so fast. The implication here is clear: the rate at which the poverty-stricken nations of the world improve their level of social and economic well-being (in fact, whether or not they are able to improve it at all—or even forestall further deterioration) will depend largely on how successful they are in curbing rapid rates of population growth. This in turn means that the future well-being of these underdeveloped countries (and of the entire world, for that matter) will be largely determined by the speed with which the diffusion and acceptance of effective methods of birth control bring about substantial reductions in fertility.

(2) *The food crisis.* A major problem intimately associated with

population growth and the socioeconomic well-being of the people in the world relates to *food*. Writing in England at the close of the eighteenth century, the Reverend Thomas Robert Malthus made two salient observations: (1) man cannot live without food; and (2) the human sex drive is very powerful—so powerful, in fact, that man would constantly be in danger of increasing his numbers at a faster rate than he was able to increase his food supply. In Malthus' words, ". . . the power of population is infinitely greater than the power in the earth to produce subsistence for man. Population, when unchecked, increases in a geometrical ratio. Subsistence increases only in an arithmetic ratio. A slight acquaintance with numbers will show the immensity of the first power in comparison with the second." [6] In order to keep population within the limits set by man's ability to produce food, Malthus believed that some check to population growth would always be necessary. He recognized two such checks: *positive checks* (by which he meant such things as war, famine, and disease) which held population size down by keeping death rates high; and *preventive checks* (by which he meant moral restraint or the postponement of marriage and abstinence within marriage) which controlled population size by keeping birth rates down. But because he regarded the human sex drive as so powerful that man would be unlikely to exercise moral restraint, Malthus foresaw a world where war, disease, and periodic famine would always be with man to curb his tendency to increase population up to (and beyond) the maximum number that could be supported by available means of subsistence.

Needless to say, the Malthusian "principle of population" was not received with open arms when it first appeared in print in 1798. The late eighteenth century was a period of widespread optimism concerning man's future, and philosophers and social critics were coming to believe that man was perfectible and easily capable of creating a better world. Into this atmosphere, the virtually unmitigated pessimism of "Parson Malthus" was decidedly unwelcome; and its advent generated a literary controversy that carried over into the field of economics and lasted well into the nineteenth century. During the late nineteenth century, however, a declining mortality and resulting rapid rates of population growth were accompanied by tremendous social and economic advances which contributed to substantial increases in the level of living. In light of these developments there seemed little basis for bothering with the "silly notions of an eccentric English clergyman," and the world appeared more or less to forget Malthus. But developments during the years since World War II have reawakened concern over the old Malthusian hypothesis that the human race was doomed to a miserable existence because of the ever-present tendency for population to outstrip the food supply.

On a global level, there may not appear to be much of a problem—*at first glance.* As of the late 1950's, for example, world population was growing at a rate of about 2 per cent per year, whereas the world's food supply was increasing by nearly 3 per cent per year.[7] The problem, however, derives from the fact that rates of increase in population and food are not distributed evenly over the face of the earth. In Africa, for example, the food supply was increasing less than 1.5 per cent per year, compared with an annual population growth rate of about 2.5 per cent. Similarly, although food production was increasing at a rate of 2.5 per cent in Latin America, population was growing at a rate of nearly 3 per cent per year. In marked contrast, food production was increasing at an annual rate of between 3.5 and 4 per cent in the economically developed nations of western Europe and North America, whereas population was growing at an overall average rate of only 1.5 per cent per year. As a result of such disparate growth rates, a majority of the people living on the earth at midcentury were not getting enough to eat. Moreover, the situation in many areas appeared to be getting worse instead of better. In the Far East, for example, the average number of calories consumed per person per day was 2,120 before World War II (substantially less than the 3,000 generally recommended as adequate); more recently this figure has been estimated at only 2,070—indicating approximately a 2.5 per cent decline in the level of food consumption since the prewar period.

Before World War II many of the countries that fall into the "underdeveloped" class were exporters of food; but since the war the growing pressures of population at home have ended this, and they are now importers. To illustrate, data published in the *Statistical Yearbook of the United Nations (1965)* indicate that food exports from underdeveloped countries declined by approximately 12 per cent between 1958 and 1965. Further, the extent to which many of these countries have become food importers is indicated by recent declines in the proportion of the food supply produced domestically. Between the mid-1950's and the mid-1960's, for example, the proportion of the total grain supply domestically produced declined from 97 per cent to 94 per cent in India, and from 96 per cent to 92 per cent in Pakistan.

The seriousness of the situation in India is particularly pronounced—the more so since close to 500 million people live in that country (roughly one-sixth of the world's population). In 1966, when a severe drought resulted in even more striking food shortages than usual, India had to import roughly a million tons of grain per month (mostly from the United States) in order to avoid an extremely severe famine that would probably have resulted in millions of people starving to death. But this sort of help cannot go on indefinitely. For one reason, the major export countries like the United States have reached the point where "vast food surpluses" are pretty much a thing of the past (for example, the United States wheat surplus declined from 1.4 billion bushels in 1961 to less than 600 million bushels in 1966). Moreover, even though the United States could, by putting idle lands to use and producing to capacity, provide the developing nations with needed food supplies through 1970, the situation thereafter looks pretty bleak. The problem is not helped by the fact that the number of people that need to be fed is continuing to increase rapidly at the same time available surpluses are diminishing. As the needs of hungry nations continue to rise, the demand will ultimately exceed our capacity to produce, and by 1985 it is estimated that our domestic grain production will be 12 million tons below what we would need for ourselves and for the underdeveloped countries. This prospect led Secretary of Agriculture Orville Freeman to warn in 1966 that "Unless the developing nations learn to feed themselves, there will be world famine."

Unless the rate of expansion in food production is greatly accelerated, it is extremely doubtful if the world's hunger will be assuaged within the coming decades. Although there are many possibilities for increasing food production (increasing the amount of acreage under cultivation, increasing per-acre yields through the use of hybrid seed, development of new foods such as algae derivatives, and so on), it is unlikely that such measures alone can alleviate the world food crisis. According to the earlier cited United Nations report, it is very doubtful if agricultural output will be able to keep up with present population growth trends. Given the rate at which population was increasing during the mid-1960's, it was estimated that an annual increase in the world's food supply of 3.5 per cent would be required to meet the needs of the population by 1980. This is a higher rate of increase than the underdeveloped countries have so far been able to achieve, and it is unlikely that many of them are in a position to attain *and maintain* such a rate through the 1970's.

Another difficulty is that the potential consumers of projected food increases are already alive. Since the majority of the world's people are already living at bare subsistence levels, any increases in food production are quickly absorbed by the already existing surplus population. Moreover, as population continues to grow— and such growth is facilitated, ironically, by mortality reductions that generally accompany increases in the quantity and quality of the food supply—the level of consumption in the underdeveloped world could fall even lower. These facts clearly emphasize the need for some sort of check on population growth. If they are to be of any value in reducing world hunger, anticipated increases in food production must be accompanied by declines in the rate of population growth (i.e., by declines in fertility).

In a nutshell, then, the major problem is to prevent population from increasing at a faster rate than the anticipated rate of increase in food production; and this will entail a reduction in fertility through a wider adoption of modern birth control techniques. The alternative is a continuation, perhaps even an intensification, of the poverty, misery, and hunger characterizing the lives of nearly three-fourths of the world's population. As the United Nations has noted in its recent report: "In terms of simple arithmetic, it seems evident that the problem of achieving the needed increases in food production during the next decades would be made easier, and the risk of failures would be diminished, if the population were to increase less than is indicated by the projections of present trends for the economically less developed regions of the world. . . . With few exceptions, the experts who have studied this question agree that the outlook would be far more favorable if the present rates of population increase in the underdeveloped countries could be slowed down by moderation of birth rates. In fact, some experts hold that *unless the growth of population becomes slower in the near future, there is little hope of improving the conditions of life in many of these countries, and even to hold the present low levels of living may prove to be difficult"* [8] (italics added). As long as the tendency persists for population to grow more rapidly than the means of subsistence, all the talk about using the wonders of science to increase food production and raise standards of living in the underdeveloped countries is sheer fantasy.

(3) *Implications for world peace.* There is one final point regarding the food problem, and that concerns its implications for the maintenance of world peace. A hungry man is a dissatisfied man, and in the past it has not been unusual for such people to

attack their neighbor and confiscate his food for themselves. On a national level, what can happen when a country becomes too dissatisfied with its share of the world's wealth was illustrated all too clearly by Japanese imperial expansion during the 1930's and 1940's. More recently, dissatisfaction within "have not" nations has been demonstrated by the border disputes between India and Pakistan and India and Red China; and the crisis stirred up by Indonesian objections to the establishment of Malaysia. Over and above all of these altercations has been the constant menace of Red China—a menace that becomes even more threatening as that nation develops nuclear power.

Famine was not a major threat to *world* peace in the pre-industrial world; but today, when hungry peoples have or are trying to develop industrial power, food shortages could become a real threat to peace. In the underdeveloped countries of Africa, Asia, and Latin America, large segments of the population already live very close to the subsistence level. Moreover, population is growing so rapidly in these areas that any increases in food production serve mainly to permit a greater number of people to subsist at the same low level. Should this situation continue, particularly if it gets worse (as it very well might), it could act as a potent force against world peace. This is not meant to imply that an imbalance between numbers and the available food supply is a necessary cause of war. Such an imbalance did not lead India to start a war in 1966 (although who is to say it would not have happened if other nations with food surpluses had not been ready and willing to help?). Neither is overpopulation a sufficient cause for war. A starving people who do not possess the industrial and military wherewithal to carry on modern warfare are not likely to start World War III. But hunger has been a *contributing* cause to war in the past and could become even more so during the coming years—particularly as hungry nations such as Red China (or India, Indonesia, Egypt, Pakistan, and others) continue to develop industrially (and militarily).

One can conclude that the problem of feeding the hungry

people of the world is not one to be solved simply for humane reasons. Nor should we do everything we can because of some moral or ethical obligation to help our fellow man. Rather, the solution of this food problem should be regarded as a fundamental precondition for the very survival of the world as we know it.

NATIONAL POPULATION PROBLEMS

Whether or not a given area is "underpopulated" or "overpopulated" does not depend solely on the absolute number of people living in the area but upon the balance between numbers and resources in relation to existing technology. That is, population problems are determined by the relationship between population size, available resources, and the level of technology. With these considerations in mind, it may seem somewhat paradoxical to think of the United States as having a "problem" in so far as the size and growth of the population is concerned. After all, the nation as a whole is the wealthiest in the world, technological progress has been and continues to be rapid, and our people are living at a level of material comfort and well-being never before experienced by man—and not now experienced by anyone else. Nevertheless, although the overall population picture in the United States may indeed appear rosy in contrast with the depressing situation faced throughout much of the rest of the world, it could be very dangerous to our national welfare if we let complacency or naive optimism obscure the potential crises facing the nation.

(1) *Population and resources.* Although the people of the United States have the fullest bellies in the world and need not live with chronic food shortages and the constant threat of famine, the recent "grain drain" in our efforts to help feed the hungry millions in the world's underdeveloped areas has virtually eliminated the huge surpluses that resulted from the once perennial problem of overproduction. The nation still has (and will continue to have for a long time to come) an abundance of food of every kind; but

the shift from surplus to scarcity has caused increases in domestic prices and a corresponding rise in the cost of living. Are we to achieve a higher level of living only to discover that many Americans cannot afford it? Writing in the late 1950's, Frederick Osborn warned that agricultural efficiency could not continue to increase indefinitely and that our food surpluses were in danger of disappearing: "With continued growth of population in the United States and a diminishing proportion of land to people, there will come a point when the trend will change and food costs will go up." [9] It would appear that day has arrived.

What's more, food is not the only resource, and the United States has long consumed much more than its "fair share" of the world's raw materials. At the turn of the century the United States was producing substantially more non-food raw materials than it was consuming, but since the end of the Second World War the country has been consuming more than it has produced. To illustrate, available data show that in 1960 domestic consumption exceeded domestic production by roughly 2.5 per cent for natural gas, 5 per cent for steel, and 25 per cent for crude petroleum. [10] Today the United States must import a substantial portion of the raw materials it uses, and the volume of imports has grown steadily as rapid industrial growth has continually increased the demand for raw materials. In 1960, for example, this country imported some 400 million barrels of crude petroleum; this compares with only 174 million barrels imported in 1950 and represents an increase during the decade of about 130 per cent. Even more striking, the 1950 decade was characterized by roughly a fourfold increase in the volume of imports for both bauxite (an aluminum compound) and iron ore.

Although no difficulties have yet been encountered in the supply of raw materials, there are two important points to keep in mind. First, the domestic production of many industrial raw materials has been declining in recent years. Between 1940 and 1960, for example, total coal production fell by some 15 per cent. Similarly, the late 1950's saw various declines in the domestic production of copper and sulfur (1 per cent); crude petroleum (2 per cent); zinc, silver, and usable iron ore (roughly 20 per cent); and manganese (slightly more than 75 per cent). In many cases, however, patterns of consumption are on the increase. For example, although the late 1950's was characterized by a 2 per cent decline in the domestic production of crude petroleum, domestic consumption during the period increased by 7 per cent.

The second point is that many of the countries from which the United States imports raw materials are themselves in the process of industrial expansion. As this process continues, their own domestic needs for raw materials will increase, thus reducing the amounts available for exports. This tendency can be illustrated by considering the import-export relationship between the United States and the still developing nations of South America: in 1950 the value of imports from South America to this country exceeded the value of exports by 42 per cent, but by 1960 this difference was down to 16 per cent.

To sum up: the demand for both food and nonfood resources increases steadily as the population grows. Although the United States is certainly not on the verge of becoming one of the hungry nations of the world, and although the raw materials situation is not likely to become critical for some time to come, recent years have clearly been characterized by a steadily increasing pressure of numbers on resources. In many cases, domestic production has not been able to keep up with increasing demands for resources, and the United States has had to rely more and more heavily on imports.

(2) *The quality of American life.* Although we cannot afford to close our eyes to severe hunger and poverty in many parts of the underdeveloped world, the United States clearly does not face a similar crisis in the foreseeable future as a result of population growth. Rather than threatening life itself, population growth in the United States has its greatest impact on the quality of life. As one American couple has recently noted, the most significant con-

sequence of excessive population growth in the more affluent nations such as ours is that it acts "as a depressant on certain of the personal freedoms and pleasures achieved by mankind upon liberation from extreme want. It is not that we are threatened by a condition of standing room only. . . . What we stand to lose—and what to some extent we have already lost—is to be reckoned essentially in *qualitative* terms." [11] In other words, continued population increase in the United States could well mean that we shall be unable to enjoy many of the aesthetic rewards that should go along with the increasing affluence of our society.

One of the most obvious problems that comes to mind here relates to *space*—particularly space for recreation. Although a walk along the littered shore of a public beach on Monday morning after a hot summer weekend may cause the cynic to wonder just how much we really appreciate the beauty of our natural resources, the fact is that Americans have long been lovers of the "great outdoors." Our appreciation of natural beauty and the need to preserve it is attested to by the vast amounts of public lands set aside for parks and other recreational purposes. The problem today is that the amount of available land is finite; yet the continued growth of population (not to mention the trend toward shorter working hours and increased leisure time) is constantly increasing the need for parks, beaches, picnic grounds, and camping areas—not to mention just plain wilderness. In the areas outside larger American cities, once empty meadows and rolling green hills have been bulldozed away to make room for Levittown-type residential areas and blacktop parking lots for sprawling suburban shopping centers. Nowhere is this more apparent than in the great urban sprawl of the Northeast. This "megalopolis," forming a triangle with Portland, Maine in the north, Chicago in the west, and Washington, D.C., in the south, was home for some 80 million Americans in 1960 (roughly 40 to 45 per cent of the total population). For these people, a Sunday afternoon drive in the "country" has become a virtual impossibility.

Although the efforts of some farsighted individuals and groups have ensured that some open spaces still exist, they are woefully inadequate to meet the aesthetic and psychological needs of the population—and they are becoming more so as numbers continue to increase. Everywhere in the mid-1960's Americans were leaving overcrowded cities to spend their vacations at similarly over-crowded beaches, at overcrowded picnic areas, at overcrowded lake and mountain resorts, and at overcrowded camping areas (if they were lucky enough to get in). If one visited scenic Yosemite National Park during the summer of 1966 and climbed to a mountainous vantage point overlooking the valley, one beheld a magnificent panoramic view of a veritable sea of tents and trailers. "The damp night air, heavy with a pall of eye-watering smoke, is cut by the blare of transistor radios, the clatter of pots and pans, the roar of a motorcycle, and the squeals of teen-agers. Except for hundreds of shiny aluminum trailers and multi-colored tents squeezed into camping areas, this might be any city after dark. . . . At dawn and dusk even fresh air is a rare commodity in these crowded campgrounds. Then, when the air is still, smoke from thousands of cooking fires hangs over these areas; . . . and the heavy wood smoke brings tears to the visitors' eyes." [12] This is living?

Yosemite is not likely to get any larger, but each year more and more Americans—with more money and more leisure time—will want to visit it (and other national parks and vacation areas as well). Rapid population growth during the postwar decade of rising prosperity has greatly increased the need for readily available space and recreational facilities; at the same time, the finite nature of land resources makes these needs even more difficult to fill. The problem will not recede as (if?) population growth, with its attendant increase in density, continues during the coming decades.

Accompanying the increased demand for space and all the other features of "good living" has been an *increase in costs*. What most Americans today regard as necessary to meet the minimum standards for "the good life"—garbage collection, air and water purification, traffic control, police and fire protection, schools, libraries, hospitals and roads, not to mention the myriad of other public-supported social services—today cost more and more merely to maintain, let alone improve. Moreover, when one considers such things as the increasing pollution of many of our major waterways, the problem of maintenance gives way to the problem of re-creating what has already been lost. Fresh air is already a thing of the past for many American cities that today are surrounded by a haze of polluted air. Roadways are already overtaxed by an ever-increasing number of automobiles and motorists. Many municipal hospitals are experiencing shortages of beds and other facilities. Schools and colleges are overcrowded and understaffed; housing needs have increased faster than the supply, with the result that building costs have soared; public health and welfare agencies have too few workers and inadequate budgets to cope efficiently with the rising problems of our burgeoning urban centers; the shortage of physicians and other trained professionals (nurses, teachers, physical therapists, social workers, and so forth) is daily becoming more acute; . . . and so on *ad infinitum.* The sad truth of the matter is that in many areas—not only recreation, but also in more vital areas such as health, education, and welfare—the quality of American life already shows signs of deteriorating. Continued increases in the size of the population will make it increasingly necessary to spend more and more on every conceivable kind of public service; and as maintenance costs rise, it will become less and less possible to achieve further progress in raising the standard of living. The ultimate outcome of this, unfortunately, could very easily be a pronounced speeding up of the already visible deterioration in the quality of American life.

(3) *The problem of individual freedom.* Nowhere is the threat to the quality of American life more serious than in the area of individual freedom. Americans have long cherished their privacy—as witness the western pioneer who decided it was time to move

when the smoke from his neighbor's fire became visible. And our love of the basic democratic freedoms (freedom of speech, thought, assembly, travel, and so on) is well attested to by the wars we have fought (in other countries as well as our own) to protect them. But today we stand in real danger of losing this cherished freedom and privacy.

The democratic institutions which we know and love so well are today being challenged from two directions—both intimately related to the numerical increase of population. On the one hand, we are challenged from without by the ever-present danger of an "explosion" among the seething masses in the world's under-developed areas. On the other hand, we are challenged from within by the growth of formal organization and bureaucracy with its emphasis on conformity and its de-emphasis of the individual and individuality.

The implication of the present population crisis for world peace has already been discussed in an earlier section of this chapter; nevertheless, the problem is sufficiently serious to merit further attention. To begin with, the tensions and political instabilities generated by explosive population growth in the economically underdeveloped nations have a very special significance in the contemporary world. This is because the split between the "have" and "have not" nations cuts across the cleavage between communist and non-communist nations of the Western world. Many of the underdeveloped countries that are today trying to raise their standards of living are as yet uncommitted in the East-West power struggle that has emerged since the end of the Second World War.[13] In their efforts to generate sustained economic growth, these poorer nations of Africa, Asia, and Latin America are faced with the problem of choosing between the Western *evolutionary* way or the communist *revolutionary* program. The most significant "race for development" in the world today is the race between democratic-oriented India and communist-oriented China. Many of the new uncommitted, neutral nations of the underdeveloped world are watching this race very closely; and its outcome, by influencing which side the uncommitted nations will take, will be extremely significant for the balance of world power. If the underdeveloped communist nations demonstrate that they can achieve more rapid economic progress than the underdeveloped free nations (i.e., if the communist world wins the race toward economic development), then the way of life cherished by peoples of the Western world will be seriously threatened. It is not sufficient for people in the West to sit complacently by, comforting themselves with the belief that the communist approach is doomed to failure (a belief that is not necessarily true). The struggling nations must be offered all the help possible. In particular, we must help them reduce their birth rates and thereby their rate of population growth. Success or failure in the East-West struggle may well hinge on the ability of the nations involved to control their rate of population growth; and in order to preserve our freedom from the threat of communism, it behooves us to do everything in our power to aid the democratic progress of the underdeveloped countries.

The second threat to individual freedom in the United States (the threat from within) is less dramatic—and consequently all the more insidious—than the threat posed by the potential expansion of communism. This threat arises from the simple fact that societal life necessarily becomes more complex as numbers increase. For one thing, an increase in numbers creates the need for more organization which means, in effect, the further enhancement of group or societal values rather than individual values. The trend toward increasing complexity of organization has been pronounced in the United States during the postwar period, and a continuation of this tendency could, it has been suggested, "result in such a diminution of personal freedom as to approximate the condition of totalitarianism." [14]

As numbers increase, so does the need for police and fire protection, educational facilities, sanitation control, health and welfare programs, and so on. Such services are not as important to the smooth functioning of smaller groups, and where they are necessary they can generally be handled on an individual level. As the population grows, however, the task of providing such services becomes too large to be carried out on an individual basis, and collective action becomes more and more necessary; and as collectivities increase in importance, the freedom of the individual declines proportionately.

The impact of population growth on greater control of the individual (and consequent loss of individual freedom) can be seen in a number of ways. The more numbers increase, the greater the need for formalized laws to regulate more and more aspects of human behavior. Our behavior is already controlled in many ways: traffic speed laws, stop signs and stoplights; requirements for a license to marry, drive a car, hunt, fish, and so on. Such seemingly incidental control measures could become considerably more widespread if the population grows much larger. Many communities throughout the nation, for example, have suddenly found themselves faced with numerous problems resulting from haphazard land development; and they have recently established planning and zoning commissions as well as created legislation (building codes, zoning restrictions) in an effort to achieve more orderly development. The controls adopted could become even more stringent if population continues to increase. In this respect, the years ahead could see the use of privately owned land (if land is allowed to remain privately owned!) becoming further and further circumscribed. "Eventually, there could be no such thing as a 'family farm' or a 'place in the country'—or, under still greater pressure of numbers, even a backyard—whose owner could be allowed the luxury of determining for himself how he wanted to use it, whether to use it for growing flowers instead of for the production of food or minerals. In these more extreme conditions, the right of eminent domain would become little more than a museum piece; the idea that a man's home was his castle, something of a wry joke." [15]

The increasing control over the individual is also felt in the need for greater centralization. As numbers continue to swell, and particularly as density continues to increase, the autonomy that many local communities now cherish will have to be sacrificed to the dictates of regional needs. In the urban sprawl of the northeastern metropolitan belt, where localities run into and overlap each other in what is fast becoming a virtually uninterrupted chain across the entire length of the Atlantic Coast, the idea that one community can exist and function independently of its neighbors begins to sound ridiculous. Given this situation, the persistence of autonomous communities acting independently of one another is virtually impossible, and it is readily apparent that some sort of new governmental unit is needed, with sufficient powers to plan and administer over a wider geographical area. (This issue will be discussed more fully in Chapter 7.)

Still another indication of the deleterious impact of population growth on individual freedom is the widening gulf between the individual and the various groups controlling his destiny. Such groups are not limited to those governmental bodies that "run" the country but also include the "managing elite" of labor unions, educational institutions, religious bodies, and corporations. When Andrew Jackson was President, any American could call at the White House and expect to be received cordially; but the idea of a President today trying to welcome every complainant or well-wisher is horrendous to contemplate. Similarly, a generation ago it was not infrequent for college professors to entertain their classes at home; today's student is likely to wait in line for long periods of time just to obtain his grade from a graduate assistant. Both of these illustrations reflect the impact of simple increases in sheer numbers. This gap between the individual and members of formal organizations with which he is associated does not necessarily damage the operation of the organizations concerned. But it does mean that the individual has progressively less influence on decisions concerning his welfare.

It should now be clear that with a large and increasing population the individual is not only more and more constrained to follow the dictates of the group, but he also has less and less of a say in determining those dictates. Population growth is admittedly not the only cause of the de-emphasis of the individual in the modern era; but it is a major trend in that coalition of forces which has transformed society from one in which individual values are paramount to one in which the group dominates. "The urbanization of society, the collectivization of economic activity into huge corporate concentrates with the accompanying trade unions, the change in nature of government from the 'Nightwatchman State' to the 'Security State,' the rapid depletion of natural resources, the dangers from hostile ideologies and national power centers, the rise of mass democracy and the trend toward equality—all of these and more merge into an unmistakable movement away from individualism to a new type of society, one in which the person qua individual tends to be submerged into a congeries of collectivities." [16] There is little doubt that population growth is a major cause of all of these trends, and as long as it persists it will continue to help toward the further depersonalization of the individual.

As long as population continues to grow we can anticipate increasing control over individual actions—principally through the expansion of government programs and activities. But even though greater control is inevitable, the magnitude and severity of the increase is still an open question: just how stringent this control will be depends on how soon the population of the United States becomes stable. The more people there are when the population becomes stabilized (as eventually it must, given the finite qualities of the earth), the greater will be the control exercised over individual activities. Thus it would be to our advantage to adopt and adhere to a positive population policy that aims for a population sufficiently small so that it "would be reasonably likely to produce the conditions (economic, political, and social) enabling the maintenance of a society in which democratic values are maximized." [17] The desired numerical stability must come soon in the United

States if we are to maintain (let alone extend) many of the traditional high qualities of our "American way of life." Greater control may be inevitable, but the smaller the ultimate population the less stringent (and therefore less "painful") the controls will be.

PROBLEMS OF POPULATION SIZE AND GROWTH: AN OVERVIEW

It is abundantly clear that our planet is currently in the midst of a tremendous population explosion—an explosion that has as yet shown no signs of subsiding. Regardless of whether or not the "population bomb" represents a greater threat to the peace and security of mankind than the hydrogen bomb (as at least one recent writer has asserted), [18] the fact remains that the accelerating rate of population growth during recent years has created an extremely serious situation throughout many parts of the world. Too many people today avoid the simple yet inescapable facts of population growth. But the present vast, world-wide problems relating to it, and the probability of even greater ones ahead, require that all people acquaint themselves with the basic facts of population growth—not only on the world level but on the national level as well. The task of this chapter has been to highlight a few of the more significant aspects of past and present population growth trends.

Ironically, the greatest numerical growth today occurs within those economically underdeveloped countries of the world that can least afford it. These nations have only recently emerged from a primitive stage of social and economic development and are just now starting out on the long, hard road to modernization. To the extent that their population growth continues to be rapid, it will act as a major obstacle to economic development and will seriously retard efforts to improve the lot of the underprivileged millions now living in Asia, Africa, and Latin America. Since the end of the Second World War, it has become more and more apparent that population control is a "must" issue today. Unless there is a substantial reduction in conceptions and births it is not inconceivable that the Malthusian prediction will come true in many parts of the world, and that famine, malnutrition, and the associated low resistance to disease will bring an increase in the death rate.

In recent years the magnitude of the world population crisis has been dramatized by a rash of newspaper editorials, television programs, and magazine articles. But scant attention has been given to the fact that one of the greatest population explosions during the postwar period has occurred right here in the United States. At first glance it may seem absurd for people in this country to be concerned with rapid population growth—especially since our population is living at a level of comfort and well-being unknown anywhere else in the world, and since one of our major problems has long been how to handle and dispose of vast surpluses of food. But many of our food surpluses have been seriously depleted in recent years, and food is not the only consideration. There are also such issues as adequate school and college facilities, recreation, housing, public utilities, employment opportunities, hospitals, and a myriad of other services; and the rapid rate of population growth since the end of World War II has put more and more pressure on the ability of such services to meet the needs of the people.

Although we do not yet face the problem of hungry millions within our own borders, this does not mean that the United States is free from a population problem. Moreover, the prospect of continued growth in the size of the American population means that present problems are likely to become intensified. Even at the relatively low rate of about 1 per cent a year being approximated in the middle of the 1960's, the year 2000 would see roughly two Americans for every one alive at mid-century; and one hundred years from now there could be as many as four Americans for every one in 1950. Whether or not this situation actually develops will depend entirely on the American people themselves. We possess the technological means for controlling our growth, and all that we need do now is utilize them properly. Admittedly this will require some sacrifice on the part of many Americans. In order to avoid the "people, people everywhere" type of existence immanent in continued unrestrained growth, many Americans will have to do without as many children as they might like. Of course, increased control of fertility must come about *voluntarily;* if it comes about any other way (for example, through state regulations of a *Brave New World* kind), it would mean not only a degradation of parenthood but also a loss of one of the most cherished qualities of American life—the loss of individual freedom of choice. The decisions of present and future generations of American couples will in large measure determine the well-being of the world in which our children and our children's children will have to live. We can only hope that the decisions will be the right ones, that they will be made voluntarily, and that they will be made soon enough to achieve population stability and thereby avert the dangers inherent in continued numerical expansion. As the experts have noted: "If we are to retain for ourselves and our posterity much of what is valuable in the American way of life, we must bring our population growth to a halt—and we must do so soon. If we are to emphasize democratic and not totalitarian values, this cessation must be achieved by individual couples acting without coercion. If we are to emphasize the value of parenthood and the dignity and worth of the individual, there must be no greater restriction on the proportion who become parents than there is now.

"In short, what we must have . . . is a society in which: (1) no unwanted child is born; (2) the decision to bear or not to bear a child is made solely by the potential parents; and (3) most important of all for the goal of a stable population, this decision is made in a social and cultural context in which a family of three children is considered large." [19]

REFERENCES AND SUGGESTIONS FOR FURTHER READING

Donald J. Bogue, *The Population of the United States,* Glencoe, Ill., 1959, Chapters 1 and 26.

Lincoln H. and Alice T. Day, *Too Many Americans,* Boston, 1964.

Philip M. Hauser, ed., *Population and World Politics,* Glencoe, Ill., 1958.

Philip M. Hauser, ed., *The Population Dilemma,* Englewood Cliffs, 1963.

Fairfield Osborn, ed., *Our Crowded Planet,* New York, 1962.

Frederick Osborn, *Population: An International Dilemma,* New York, 1958.

William and Paul Paddock, *Hungry Nations,* Boston, 1964.

Conrad and Irene B. Taeuber, *The Changing Population of the United States,* New York, 1958, Chapters 1 and 15.

Ralph Thomlinson, *Population Dynamics,* New York, 1965, Chapters 2, 4, 14, 16, and 22.

Warren S. Thompson and David T. Lewis, *Population Problems,* New York, 1965, Chapters 2, 14–17, and 19.

United Nations, *The Future Growth of World Population* (ST/SOA/Series A/28), New York, 1958.

U.S. Bureau of the Census, *United States Census of Population: 1960,* Final Report PC(1)-1A, *Number of Inhabitants: United States Summary,* Washington, D.C., 1961.

6

Population composition

Composition involves the characteristics and traits of a population that can be observed and measured at any moment (the number and per cent of persons age sixty-five and over, the number of children enrolled in high school, the per cent of adults who are college graduates, the number of families with income below $3,000 a year, the number and per cent of men and women who are married, nonwhite, foreign born, unemployed, and so on). These static characteristics differ from the more dynamic features of a population—such as birth and death rates—in that the latter can be observed and measured only by collecting data over an extended period of time.

Broadly speaking, there is no limit to the number of characteristics that can be used to classify the members of a population. They would include the basic characteristics of *population structure* (age and sex); *ethnic characteristics* (race, nativity, mother tongue); *social and economic characteristics* (marital and family status, education, religion, criminal record, employment status, occupation, income); *physiological characteristics* (height, weight, blood pressure, fecundity, morbidity status); and *psychological characteristics* (temperament, degree of achievement orientation, conservative-radical attitudes, various neurotic disorders). In actual practice, however, interest in population composition is generally confined to a relatively few characteristics. Specifically, interest usually is concentrated on clearly recognizable characteristics that can be measured fairly easily and inexpensively. For example, although it would be useful to know the fecundity status of populations in comparative fertility analyses, such information is not readily available and would be difficult and expensive to collect. First of all, then, when we refer to the composition of a population we mean those characteristics and traits of the individual members that are easily observed and measured.

The ease of observation and measurement is not, however, the only criterion for determining what characteristics are of interest to students of population composition. Height, weight, and eye color, for example, are easy to observe and measure, but a knowledge of these traits would not contribute anything to our understanding of the structure and organization of society. There are thus two criteria—ease of observation and measurement *and* sociodemographic relevance— that define the limits of the various characteristics that are of primary concern in analyzing population composition. Even within these narrow limits, a wide variety of characteristics may be of interest to demographers or sociologists. Although it is not possible to consider all such characteristics in the short space of a single chapter, we can discuss briefly some of the most important features of population composition—especially those features likely to be significant from a social problems point of view. For convenience, the many relevant characteristics are here grouped into two broad classes: demographic characteristics and socioeconomic characteristics. Of the many specific variables that could be placed under these two broad headings, the ones selected here as most relevant are: age, sex, marital status, color, and nativity (*demographic characteristics*); and education, income, labor force participation, employment status, and occupation (*socioeconomic characteristics*). These several characteristics, as well as their importance for understanding and coping with the various problems of contemporary American society, are discussed in the following sections.

DEMOGRAPHIC CHARACTERISTICS

This discussion of the demographic structure of the United States population is divided into three sections: (1) age and sex, (2) marital status, and (3) color and nativity. In each of these sections attention will be focused on (a) the sociological significance of the characteristic in question, (b) a discussion of historical trends leading up to the present situation in the United States, and (c) a discussion of some of the consequences (problems) of the prevailing situation for the well-being of the society as a whole.

(1) *Age and sex.* The most fundamental feature of any population is the distribution of its members according to age and sex. Almost any aspect of human behavior, from subjective attitudes and physiological capabilities to objective characteristics such as income, labor force participation, occupation, or group membership, will vary with age and sex. In addition, the specific needs of a given society, both now and in the future, will in large part be determined by the age-sex structure of its population. Women differ from men in the kinds of jobs they hold, the length of time they remain in the labor force, the income they earn, their consumption patterns, and their attitudes toward various social and economic issues. Similarly, a population composed mainly of young people will differ from one with a high proportion of older members in its productive capacity, in its needs and problems, and in its outlook and mode of life. The measurement of labor force efficiency and the determination of productive capacity are based upon the number of persons within the active adult ages, compared with the number of persons outside these ages, both young and old.

The adequacy of facilities such as housing, schools, and convalescent hospitals depends, respectively, on the number of young people who are marrying and starting families, the number of children at school and pre-school ages, and the number of older persons. Since women have a lower death rate than men, and since only women at certain ages can bear children, the levels of fertility and mortality and the rate of natural increase in any population are directly related to its age and sex composition. The number of elderly people in a society has important implications for problems of old-age security, such as jobs for older workers, medical and health benefits, and pensions for the aged. For these reasons, as well as for many others that could be cited, a knowledge of the current age-sex structure, how it came into being, and what consequences it is likely to have for future population trends is essential—not only as a basis for determining present needs but for future planning.

The data in Table VI-1 highlight the major trends in the age and sex composition of the United States population during the

Table VI-1: Selected age and sex characteristics of the population of the United States, 1900–1965.

Year	Median age	Per cent in broad age groups:			Males per 100 females
		Under 20	20-64	65 and over	
1900	22.9	44.3	51.6	4.1	104.4
1910	24.1	41.9	53.8	4.3	106.0
1920	25.3	40.8	54.5	4.7	104.0
1930	26.4	38.8	55.8	5.4	102.5
1940	29.0	34.4	58.8	6.8	100.7
1950	30.2	34.0	57.9	8.1	98.6
1960	29.5	38.5	52.3	9.2	97.0
1965	28.0	39.6	51.0	9.4	96.4

SOURCES: U.S. Bureau of the Census, *U.S. Census of Population: 1960*, Final Report PC(1)-1B, *General Population Characteristics: United States Summary*, Washington, D.C., 1961; and "Estimate of the Population of the United States, by Age, Color, and Sex: July 1, 1960 to 1965," *Current Population Reports*, P-25:321, Washington, D.C., November 30, 1965.

twentieth century. Considering *age* first, the most convenient measure for determining quickly whether a population is "young" or "old" and how its age composition has been changing is the *median age* (i.e., that age which divides a distribution into two equal parts, half of the cases falling below this value and half of the cases exceeding it). According to the medians presented in Table VI-1, the major trend prior to 1950 was for the population to become older. Between 1900 and 1950, median age in the United States increased from 22.9 to 30.2, or by 7.3 years (nearly one and one-half years per decade). Party because of the reduction of foreign immigration after the adoption of federal restrictive legislation, but mostly as a result of the cumulative effects of the historical decline in fertility, the rise in the median age was most pronounced after 1920. The marked increase of 2.6 years between 1930 and 1940 reflects the particularly low birth rate of the depression decade, while the substantially smaller increase between 1940 and 1950 reflects the initial impact of the postwar fertility revival.

During the most recent period, the upward movement in the median age of the population has been halted; the median age in 1960 (29.5 years) was seven-tenths of a year lower than it was ten years earlier, while that of 1965 (28.0 years) was more than two years below the 1950 level. This reversal of a trend can only be explained by referring to the end of the long-time fertility decline during World War II, and its subsequent rise and continuation at fairly high levels throughout the 1950 decade. This postwar baby boom resulted in substantial increases in both the number and proportion of youth in the population and, consequently, reduced the median age. Although the more recent revival of the downward fertility trend may, if it continues, bring back the earlier aging trend, the population of the United States at mid-century was clearing becoming younger.

Although the median is a useful measure for providing a general indication of the age composition of a population, it is of limited value in more detailed analyses. The procedure commonly used for greater precision is to examine the proportion of the population falling into particular age groups. In this respect, it is useful to designate three broad age groups which correspond roughly to the three major phases of the life cycle: *youth* (under twenty years of age); *adulthood* (twenty to sixty-four years); and *old age* (sixty-five years and over). Looking at the percentage of the population in these three broad age groups at various periods since 1900 clearly reveals the major changes that have occurred in each stage of the life cycle. Before the 1940's, a major trend was a consistent decline in the proportion of the population under twenty years of age. In 1900 slightly more than four out of every ten Americans fell into this age group; by 1940, after several decades of declining birth rates, this ratio had fallen to three in ten. Since that time the reversal of the long-time fertility decline has led to an increase in the per cent of the total population represented by this youthful segment, and by 1965 the number of persons under twenty years of age in the nation was once again nearly four out of ten.

Concomitant with the fall in the proportion of youth during the years of fertility decline, the proportion of the population twenty to sixty-four years of age increased—from 52 per cent in 1900 to nearly 60 per cent in 1940. Thereafter, as a consequence of the postwar baby boom and continued high levels of fertility, the per cent of the population falling into these active adult ages declined, and by 1965 it was lower than it had been at the beginning of the century. At that time, only 51 per cent of the population of the United States was between the ages of twenty and sixty-four.

The major difference between the population of the 1960's and the population at the turn of the century is found in the proportion of elderly persons. In 1965 the proportion age sixty-five and over was more than twice as great as it had been in 1900 (8.4 per cent as opposed to only 4.1 per cent at the turn of the century). In terms of absolute numbers the change has been even more striking. In 1900 there were slightly more than 3 million persons age sixty-five and over in the United States; by 1965 this number had swelled to more than 18 million, representing a sixfold increase in the number of older people in the population during the first sixty-five years of the twentieth century.

In spite of this continued increase in the number and proportion of elderly people, the major trend in recent years has been the marked increase in the number and proportion of young people in the United States. This development has curtailed sharply the historical trend toward an aging population, and it marks the emergence of a new trend toward a younger population. Whether or not this rejuvenating process continues will naturally depend on the future course of the birth rate: a continuation of the present downward trend in fertility will eventually bring back the earlier aging tendency; but if the present trend should reverse itself, it would reinforce the tendency toward a younger population.

Regardless of what the future may bring, it is clear that the increase in young people since the end of World War II has had a pronounced effect on contemporary American society: rock 'n' roll music fills the air as everyone tries to learn the latest teen-age dance craze; juvenile delinquency is making more headlines than ever before, whereas teen-age marriages and divorces are no longer news; schools, theatres, colleges, and recreation areas are everywhere overcrowded; the views and opinions of young people on a variety of social, economic, and political issues are continuously finding their way into print; and youth groups are more and more coming to play a leading role in dealing with social problems such as racial discrimination. Clearly, we live in a society in which the dominant sound is the sound of youth.

Perhaps the greatest impact of the young is in the area of education. Because of the declining birth rate and the decreasing number of young children, the adequacy of educational facilities was not a matter of serious concern in the years preceding the Second World War. Since that time, however, as school authorities are quick to attest, the situation has changed radically. Between 1940 and 1960 the number of youth under twenty years of age in the United States increased from approximately 46 million to just over 69 million, and today this number is estimated at close to 77 million. During the 1950's the elementary schools bore the burden of this increase, but by 1960 greatly swollen student bodies had burst the grammar schools and were beginning to flood the high schools. By 1965 the colleges (which until then had been drawing largely on the smaller birth cohorts of the late 1930's and early 1940's) were having their turn; and college administrators were everywhere finding themselves hard pressed to meet the educational needs of a greatly expanded college-age population. No matter how one looks at it, the substantial increase in the younger population since 1940 has created serious problems for our schools and colleges, and the implications for the future are that these problems will persist, perhaps becoming even more acute.

Turning to the other end of the life cycle, because of the continued effect of past fertility declines and the anticipated reduction of death rates at the older ages, the proportion of persons sixty-five years of age and over is likely to continue to expand. But even if the proportion of elderly people in the population were to remain the same, their numbers would continue to increase, thus maintaining the need for efficient programs (such as Medicare, inaugurated in the mid-1960's) to deal with problems concerning such things as medical and health plans for the aged, social welfare benefits, jobs for older workers, and the development of post-retirement activities and interests.

Turning now to a consideration of the *sex composition* of the American population, the most pertinent observation based on the data in Table VI-1 is that the United States is more and more becoming a female-dominated society. The sex composition of a population is commonly measured by the *sex ratio,* which is defined as the number of males per 100 females. Reflecting the heavy volume of immigration (especially male immigration) during the late nineteenth and early twentieth centuries, the sex ratio of the United States was on the rise until 1910: at that time there were 106 males for every 100 females in the population. Since then the sex ratio has declined consistently, and by 1965 there were only 96.4 males for every 100 females in the United States.

A number of factors have combined to bring about the recent and current reduction in the sex ratio. Part of the decline can be attributed to such things as the losses incurred in two world wars and the stationing of armed forces overseas. But the major factors have been reductions in both foreign immigration and mortality. On the one hand, the decline in immigration during recent decades has been accompanied by a shift in the composition of the new arrivals: what was once a large male-dominated stream is now a small trickle with a slight female majority. On the other hand, the marked declines in mortality during the present century have been more pronounced for women than for men, and this has reduced the relative number of males in the population. Should the present situation continue with regard to the composition of immigrants and the sex mortality differential, there is little prospect for any increase in the sex ratio in the future. On the contrary, it appears that women will continue to outnumber men in the years ahead and, in all likelihood, will do so to an even greater degree than now.

Because of migration selectivity, the magnitude of the sex ratio varies markedly among the various sections of the country. The general rural-to-urban migration trend, for example, has involved more females than males, with the results that rural areas (1960 sex ratio: 104) are still characterized by a preponderance of males; the female excess is much more pronounced in urban areas (1960 sex ratio: 94) than in the nation as a whole. There is, however, a great deal of intercity variation. In Washington, D.C., for example, where there are unusually heavy employment opportunities for women, the sex ratio in 1960 was only 88. This contrasts sharply with cities characterized by large military populations or heavy industry bases. In these cities the sex ratio generally shows a preponderance of males. To illustrate: in 1960 males outnumbered females by a ratio of 112 to 100 in San Diego, California, and by a ratio of 107 to 100 in East Lansing, Michigan.

When there is a particularly pronounced imbalance between the sexes it may indicate other social problems. *Prostitution,* for example, often flourishes where there is a heavy preponderance of males (as in the frontier towns and mining camps of the "Old West"). On the other hand, a preponderance of females is often accompanied by a higher rate of *illegitimacy* (as in many of our larger cities today). In either case, the sex imbalance can represent a major threat to traditional patterns of family living.

The potential impact of an imbalance between the sexes is strikingly illustrated by the marked increase in *homosexuality* where sex segregation is complete (in prisons, for example). Sex segregation is certainly not the only cause of homosexuality. According to the Kinsey Report, from 25 to 30 per cent of all prison inmates have had homosexual experiences before being admitted to prison.[1] Nevertheless, evidence indicates that the segregation of the sexes and the impersonalization of social relationships in prisons does contribute to a higher incidence of homosexuality. This gives rise to the current debate in some circles as to whether or not some system of "conjugal rights" could be worked out for prison inmates.

The sex ratio bears an interesting relationship to age, and in the United States today there is at least one problem relating to age variations in sex composition. For some unknown biological reason, more boys are born than girls. Thus there is a preponderance of males in the population at the younger ages. From the very first moment of life, however, death takes a greater toll among men than women. Thus the initially high sex ratio is gradually decreased by mortality as the older ages are approached. To illustrate, in 1960 the sex ratio of persons under five years of age in the United States was approximately 103. At the younger adult ages (roughly fifteen to twenty-four) the two sexes were fairly evenly balanced, but thereafter there was an ever-increasing preponderance of females in the population: the sex ratio was 95 at ages thirty-five to thirty-nine; by ages sixty-five to sixty-nine it had fallen to about 88; and among persons eighty-five and older there were only 64 males for every 100 females in the United States.

A major implication of this situation relates to the care of older persons. In an earlier era when the American family was more multi-functional than it is today, the care of the elderly was not a matter for public concern. As the role of the family has become more centered around bio-affectional functions, however, its earlier broad functions concerning such matters as education, protection, welfare, and so on, have been transferred to outside agencies in the community. One corollary of this development has been an increase in welfare programs and legislation for the elderly. Given the pronounced sex imbalance at the older ages, it is clear that contemporary problems of caring for the elderly are primarily problems of caring for *elderly women*—a significant fact to bear in mind in planning for the types of nursing homes, housing projects, medical care programs, and recreational facilities needed.

(2) *Marital status*. The distribution of a population according to marital status has both socioeconomic and demographic significance. On the socioeconomic side, marital status composition will influence the nature of housing needs in a community, the type of consumer goods purchased, the adequacy of existing recreational facilities, and so on. As far as individuals are concerned, marital status is an important determinant of such things as where a person lives, whether or not he (she) works, the kinds of groups one belongs to, and what one does during leisure hours. Marital status is also known to be related to various forms of deviant social behavior: in general, the incidence of crime, suicide, mental illness, and automobile accidents is lower for married than for unmarried persons. On the demographic side, married persons have lower death rates than the unmarried, and birth rates tend to increase as the proportion who are married rises. One of the major

reasons underlying the postwar baby boom, for example, was a substantial rise in the marriage rate during the late 1940's and early 1950's. Also, married persons are more prone to settle down than unmarried persons; hence one might expect the rate of residential mobility to be greater in communities having a large proportion of unattached persons. Thus, like age and sex, marital status is intimately associated with a great many aspects of human behavior.

Trends in the marital status composition of the American population since 1920 are depicted in Table VI-2. According to these data, the most notable development has taken place since 1940 and relates to the proportion married. Until that time, the proportion of persons who were married had remained relatively stable at about six out of ten. At the close of the Second World War,

Table VI-2: Per cent distribution of the population age 14 and over, by marital status, for males and females, United States, 1920–1960.

Sex and year	Per cent (standardized for age) who are:			
	Single	Married	Widowed	Divorced
MALE				
January 1920	31.8	61.3	6.1	0.7
April 1930	30.9	62.1	5.6	1.2
April 1940	31.1	62.8	4.8	1.3
March 1950	26.2	68.0	4.2	1.7
March 1960	24.8	70.0	3.3	1.8
FEMALE				
January 1920	24.1	60.4	14.6	0.8
April 1930	23.7	61.2	13.7	1.3
April 1940	24.3	61.0	12.9	1.7
March 1950	19.6	66.1	12.2	2.2
March 1960	18.4	67.8	11.1	2.7

SOURCE: U.S. Bureau of the Census, *Historical Statistics of the United States: Colonial Times to 1957.* Washington, D.C., 1960; and *Historical Statistics of the United States: Continuation to 1962 and Revisions,* Washington, D.C., 1965.

however, there was a rush to "make up" marriages that had been postponed earlier due to depression and war. The postwar prosperity also encouraged a "moving ahead" of marriages that would otherwise have occurred at a later time. This latter trend is indicated by a steady decline in the average age at marriage between 1940 and 1950. As a result of these trends the proportion of the population that is married rose from roughly six out of ten during the years preceding World War II to aproximately seven out of ten in 1960. By then, however, it was apparent that the "marriage boom" was running out of steam (i.e., the 1950–1960 increase was much less than that of the 1940 decade). There are a number of reasons for this letup—the continued pressure for young people to attain a higher education, and the increasing participation of women in the labor force, to name just two. But the decline should not obscure the fact that the increase in the proportion married has had a pronounced impact on American society. As already noted, the marriage boom was a major factor underlying the postwar fertility increase; hence, all of the problems generated by the baby boom (such as the increased pressure on available school and college facilities) are in part traceable to the increased propensity to marry. The demand for housing and associated services has risen; and there has also been a marked increase in family-oriented recreational facilities (witness the growing popularity of camping in recent years, not to mention the enhanced "respectability" of drive-in movie theatres). All of the problems arising out of the postwar marriage and fertility booms, it is worth stressing, could very easily be repeated during the 1970's (only on a vaster scale) as the children of the 1950's reach adulthood and start to marry and have children of their own.

Another corollary of the marriage boom can be seen in the slight decline in widowhood. Between 1940 and 1960 the proportion of the population fourteen years old and over that was widowed fell from roughly 5 to 3 per cent for males and from 13 to 11 per cent for females. In part this decline is due to greater longevity, but mostly it is because widowed persons are more inclined to remarry than they formerly were. But again the sex differential accounts for at least one major problem associated with widowhood. As indicated in the preceding section, the higher male death rate leads to an even greater disparity between the numbers of men and women as age increases. Among other things, this results in the proportion of widowed females being approximately four times as great as the proportion of widowed males. As indicated earlier, this means that many of the problems relating to older persons in the United States today are primarily problems of elderly women. Moreover, as long as the sex mortality differential prevails, this situation and its associated problems will persist.

The data in Table VI-2 reveal that there has also been a notable increase in the incidence of divorce in the United States. This suggests that although marriage may be more popular, it has not become more durable. On the contrary, the rise in divorce is an indication of growing family instability. This, in turn, is due to such other developments as the emancipation of women, the increasing emphasis on romantic love, a decline in the importance of the family as a major production as well as consumption unit, and, say some, a relaxation of fundamental moral principles. Although there is room for debate about the various causal factors, there is no doubt that the broken home is a major source of many of the ills of contemporary American society. Broken families, for example, are characteristically associated with a greater incidence of such things as crime and mental illness. Since a large proportion of divorces involve children, the harmful effects of marital dissolution are not limited to the contending adults. Thus, juvenile delinquency is much higher among children of divorced parents than among children of more stable families. Although part of this relationship may be due to divorce and delinquency having the same underlying causes (for example, poverty),[2] there is also evidence suggesting that the children of divorced parents are more likely to experience feelings of insecurity, and that this enhances truancy, runaways, and other forms of deviant social behavior.[3]

Although there is some reason to expect that the propensity to marry is not likely to increase much further, there is no evidence to suggest that the prevalence of divorce has reached a peak. On the contrary, many of the developments cited as being causally related to the rise in divorce (such as the emancipation of women and the decline in the economic importance of the family) seem likely to become even more pronounced in the years ahead. Thus it is quite possible that the proportion of the population that is divorced will continue to rise, and this could lead to a corresponding increase in the various social problems associated with broken homes.

(3) *Color and nativity.* Like age, sex, and marital status, the color-nativity composition of a population has a significance for a great many aspects of human social life. Although the deterministic aspect of inherent ethnic characteristics may be minimal, the fact remains that these two characteristics exhibit a marked relationship to a number of socioeconomic and demographic variables. Color and nativity have been extremely important factors in determining where persons have been allowed to live, where they have been permitted to attend school, the type of job skills they could acquire, the kinds of jobs available, the amount of money that could be earned, and so forth. No one can deny the inferior treatment meted out to Negroes and nonwhite ethnic groups in our own time. These inequalities, in turn, have led to other group differences—in intelligence, prevalence of deviant behavior, and levels of fertility and mortality, among others. That is, the observable racial and ethnic differences in prostitution, illegitimacy, crime, mental health, birth and death rates, and so on, are not due *directly* to differences in color and nativity. Instead, they are due to differences in the nature and availability of opportunities to participate in the mainstream of American life. Many of

the social problems that have arisen at various periods of American history have, in fact, been directly traceable to the kind of treatment the dominant native white group has meted out to different ethnic minorities.

No attempt will here be made to discuss in detail the various problems associated with the ethnic composition of the population. Race relations and minority group problems are themselves major fields of study and have been the subject of a great many scholarly books. And many of the problems associated with color and nativity are discussed elsewhere in this book (see especially the sections on fertility and mortality differentials, on the consequences of foreign immigration, and the following section on socioeconomic characteristics). But since color and nativity are so closely associated with many contemporary social problems, we should at least consider the major trends in the ethnic composition of the American population.

Table VI-3: Per cent nonwhite and foreign born in the United States, 1900–1960.

Year	Per cent nonwhite	Per cent foreign born
1900	12.1	13.7
1910	11.1	14.8
1920	10.3	13.2
1930	10.2	11.6
1940	10.2	8.8
1950	10.5	6.9
1960	11.2	5.4

SOURCE: U.S. Bureau of the Census, *United States Census of Population: 1960,* Final Report PC(1)-1B, *General Population Characteristics: United States Summary,* Washington, D.C., 1961; and *General Social and Economic Characteristics: United States Summary,* Washington, D.C., 1962.

When the first federal census was taken in 1790, nonwhites accounted for roughly one-fifth of the American population. Thereafter, this proportion declined consistently until it reached a low of 10 per cent during the early years of the twentieth century.

This decline occurred in spite of the fact that the nonwhite rate of natural increase has generally been much higher than the corresponding white rate, and it can only be explained by reference to migration trends. On the one hand, the end of the slave trade during the early nineteenth century put a stop to the "immigration" of Negroes. On the other hand, the nineteenth century was characterized by a steady rise in the volume of free immigration from Europe. These two developments meant that the nonwhite population grew almost entirely through natural increase, whereas the white population increased by both natural increase and immigration. This explanation is further supported by recent developments: ever since federal legislation drastically curtailed immigration during the 1920's, the proportion of foreign born in the population has undergone a sharp decline (i.e., the low volume of immigration has meant that the older foreign born have not been replaced when they died). Conversely, the proportion of nonwhites in the population has increased slightly. These two opposing trends have not affected the existence of ethnic group problems, but they have altered their nature somewhat. During the early days of the twentieth century it was the foreign born group that was most intimately associated with prevailing social problems; today it is the nonwhite group, especially the American Negro, that is most characteristically associated with slum ghettos and the higher incidence of prostitution, illegitimacy, crime, divorce and desertion, and so forth. Again it must be stressed that the higher incidence of such deviant behavior does not reflect any inherent biological differences between whites and nonwhites. Rather, it reflects the great disparity in socioeconomic status of the two color groups. These differences will be considered more fully in the following section.

SOCIOECONOMIC CHARACTERISTICS

This section will be concerned with the (1) educational and (2) income status of the American population, and (3) the characteristics of the labor force. As in the preceding section, we shall focus on the sociological significance of particular characteristics, historical trends, and the major implications of the prevailing situation.

(1) *Education.* The educational status of the population as reflected in (a) the number and proportion of young persons currently enrolled in school at various levels; and (b) the number of years of schooling completed by persons who have finished their formal education, is a vitally important feature of any modern society. In the first place, it indicates the extent to which the labor force is getting the more highly trained technicians it needs to carry out the increasingly complex tasks of an expanding industrial society. For example, labor force experts designate those persons who have not completed at least five years of elementary school as *functionally illiterate;* that is, they are not equipped to perform anything but the most menial tasks that require little or no technical skill. Moreover, since only literate persons with some background in history, government, and other related subjects can clearly understand the issues at stake and can vote intelligently, the situation with regard to school enrollment and the level of educational attainment also indicates how well we have prepared our young people to participate in the political life of a democratic society. The educational level of a community is closely related to its economic and political attitudes, its consumer buying habits, its social status relative to that of other population groups, and its attitudes and opinions covering a wide range of human social life. On the other hand, the trend in school enrollment is a measure of the adequacy of educational facilities, and points out where expansions are desirable—or necessary. Finally, patterns of school

enrollment and the differential levels of educational attainment of various subgroups within the population point out the degree to which the opportunities and advantages of education are being shared equally by all members of the society.

Table VI-4: School enrollment of the population 5 to 24 years old, by broad age groups, United States, 1940–1960.

Year and age	Total number of persons	Enrolled in school	
		Number	Per cent
1940			
Total, 5-24	46,351,915	26,759,099	57.7
5-13	20,024,827	16,839,906	84.1
14-17	9,720.419	7,708,871	79.3
18-24	16,606,669	2,210,322	13.3
1950			
Total, 5-24	46,532,055	29,085,685	62.5
5-13	22,304,760	19,136,400	85.8
14-17	8,442,875	7,067,840	83.7
18-24	15,784,420	2,881,445	18.3
1960			
Total, 5-24	59,235,784	42,502,299	71.8
5-13	32,558,772	29,139,918	89.5
14-17	11,203,808	9,792,045	87.4
18-24	15,473,204	3,570,336	23.1

SOURCE: U.S. Bureau of the Census, *U.S. Census of Population: 1960*, Final Report PC(1)-1C, *General Social and Economic Characteristics: United States Summary*, Washington, D.C., 1962.

Considering school enrollment first, the data in Table VI-4 show that the size of the school population in the United States has risen substantially in recent years. In 1960 there were roughly 42.5 million persons between the ages of five and twenty-four years enrolled in school, or about 60 per cent more than there were in 1940. This enrollment increase is due not only to the growth of the total population at these ages (which increased from 46 to 59 million between 1940 and 1960, or by 28 per cent); it is also due to an increase in *school enrollment rates* (i.e., the per cent of persons of school age who are enrolled in school). In 1960, 72 per cent of the five- to twenty-four-year-olds were enrolled in school. This compares to a national enrollment rate of 63 per cent in 1950 and 58 per cent in 1940, and it represents an increase of 24 per cent in school enrollment rates during that twenty-year period.

The significance of rising enrollment rates can be seen most clearly by comparing the above figures on the 1940–1960 increase in the total population five to twenty-four years old (28 per cent), and the increase in the number actually enrolled in school at these ages (59 per cent).

The increase in school enrollment during the past two decades has not been uniform for all ages and levels of enrollment. The greatest numerical increase is in the group five to thirteen years of age (roughly equivalent to the elementary school-age population), where the number of students increased from roughly 17 million in 1940 to 29 million in 1960, or by 73 per cent. The college-age category (eighteen to twenty-four years), with an increase from 2.2 million to 3.6 million (62 per cent), ranked second, while the number enrolled at ages fourteen to seventeen (the high school-age group) increased from 7.7 to 9.8 million during the same period, or by 27 per cent.

Changes in the size of the school-age population and in enrollment rates played noticeably different roles in affecting the size of the enrolled population. At ages five to thirteen, where enrollment rates increased by only 6 per cent between 1940 and 1960, the increase in the number of persons enrolled was brought about largely by increases in the number of persons at these ages (an increase resulting from the postwar baby boom and the continuation of relatively high levels of fertility throughout the 1950 decade). At the high school ages, population growth accounted for about 60 per cent of the enrollment increase; whereas it was a pronounced increase in the enrollment rate that swelled the ranks of the college-age students. In 1940, 13 per cent of the eighteen- to twenty-four-year-olds in the United States were enrolled in school, but by 1960 this figure had risen to 23 per cent, representing a near doubling during the intervening twenty years. The influence of rising enrollment rates on the number of eighteen- to twenty-four-year-olds enrolled in school is revealed most dramatically when considered in relation to the population changes that have taken place. Specifically, the number of eighteen- to twenty-four-year-olds enrolled in school increased by 62 per cent during a period when the total population at these ages actually *declined* by 7 per cent! The decline in the number of persons at these main college ages reflects the smaller number of annual births during the depression years of the late 1930's and early 1940's. When this trend toward rising college enrollment is viewed in conjunction with the substantial numerical increases that we can expect during the late 1960's and early 1970's as a consequence of the continued aging of postwar babies, it becomes abundantly clear that the nation's colleges and universities face a very real problem. Its magnitude can be appreciated more readily when we realize that in the fall of 1965 the number of eighteen- to twenty-four-year-olds enrolled in school was fully 67 per cent greater than it had been five years earlier.[4]

A more detailed discussion of this topic would note that the pattern of school enrollment is not the same for all segments of the American population. Enrollment rates tend to be highest for men, whites, and urban dwellers, and lowest for women, nonwhites, and rural residents. As will be seen in the following paragraphs, however, the significance of these and other enrollment differentials (which largely reflect variations in the tendency to drop out of school prematurely) lies in the associated differences in levels of educational attainment.

Table VI-5: Educational attainment of the population 25 years old and over, 1940–1965; and educational attainment differentials for specific age, sex, color, and residence groups, United States, 1960.

Year and selected demographic characteristics	Median school years completed by persons age 25 years and over	Per cent with specified levels of educational attainment		
		Less than 5 years of elementary school	High school graduates	College graduates
1940	8.6	13.7	24.2	4.6
1950	9.3	11.1	34.2	6.2
1960	10.6	8.4	41.1	7.7
1965	11.2	7.1	44.8	8.8
1960 DIFFERENTIALS				
25-29	12.3	2.8	60.6	11.0
30-34	12.2	3.3	55.8	10.9
35-39	12.1	3.9	54.6	9.5
40-44	11.8	4.7	48.4	8.1
45-49	10.6	6.0	40.7	7.4
50-54	9.7	7.6	34.8	7.3
55-59	8.8	10.4	28.5	6.2
60-64	8.6	13.3	24.5	5.0
65-69	8.4	18.2	20.7	4.1
70-74	8.3	20.9	18.7	3.7
75 and over	8.2	22.8	17.6	3.2
Male	10.3	9.4	39.5	9.7
Female	10.9	7.4	42.6	5.8
White	10.9	6.7	43.2	8.1
Nonwhite	8.2	23.4	21.7	3.5
Urban	11.1	7.3	44.3	8.9
Rural nonfarm	9.5	10.9	34.4	5.3
Rural farm	8.8	11.3	29.5	2.8

SOURCES: U.S. Bureau of the Census, *U.S. Census of Population: 1960*, Final Report PC(1)-1C, *General Social and Economic Characteristics: United States Summary*, Washington, D.C., 1962. Final Report PC(1)-1D, *Detailed Characteristics: United States Summary*, Washington, D.C., 1963; and "Projections of Educational Attainment in the United States: 1965–1985," *Current Population Reports*, P-25:305, Washington, D.C., April 14, 1965.

Data in Table VI-5 reveal that the educational level of the American population as a whole has risen markedly since 1940. As of 1965 the median number of years of school completed by persons twenty-five years old and over in the United States was 11.2, or approximately 30 per cent higher than the 8.6 years that had prevailed twenty-five years earlier.[5] The proportion of adults who had completed high school (including those who went on to college) rose from slightly less than one-fourth in 1940 to nearly 45 per cent in 1965, while the proportion who had completed four or more years of college rose from 5 to 9 per cent. At the other end of the scale, the proportion of functional illiterates (i.e., persons who had completed less than five years of elementary school) had been cut nearly in half. In 1940, 14 per cent of the population twenty-five and over was in this functionally illiterate group, but by 1965 only 7 per cent of the adult population had completed less than five years of elementary school. This latter trend in part reflects the dying off of foreign-born persons who immigrated to this country during the late nineteenth and early twentieth centuries. On the other hand, the increase in the proportion of high school and college graduates reflects the growing tendency during the postwar era for more and more people to stay in school beyond the ages of compulsory attendance. Together, these two facts have combined to cause a substantial rise in the overall level of educational attainment in the United States.

The rise in the educational status of the population over time can be viewed more clearly by examining current differences by age. To illustrate: among persons seventy-five years old and over in 1960 (i.e., persons who attended school a few generations ago), only 18 per cent were high school graduates. For ages sixty to sixty-four (persons who were educated about two generations ago), 25 per cent had finished high school; and at ages forty to forty-four (persons whose schooling was completed roughly one generation ago), the figure for high school graduates was 48 per cent. For the youngest age group, twenty-five to twenty-nine years, most of whom have only just passed through the educational system, 61 per cent had completed a minimum of four years of high school.

In spite of the overall improvement in the level of educational attainment in the United States, marked differences still characterize many of the various subgroups in the population. For example, American women have a slightly higher level of educational attainment than men: in 1960 the median number of school years completed was 10.9 for females as opposed to 10.3 for males. There were also notable differences in the educational distributions of men and women. The proportion of functional illiterates, for example, was higher for men (9 per cent) than for women (7 per cent); and the proportion who had completed high school was greater for females (43 per cent) than for males (40 per cent). At the highest level of educational attainment, however, the men clearly predominate: in 1960, 10 per cent of the adult male population—as opposed to only 6 per cent of adult females—had completed four or more years of college.

The educational attainment of nonwhites in the United States is substantially lower than that of the white population. In 1960 the median number of school years completed by the latter group (10.7) was more than two and a half years above that of the former (8.2). Similarly, the proportion of functional illiterates was nearly four times as great for nonwhites as for whites, and the proportion of high school graduates was over twice as high among whites. Finally, 8 per cent of the white population of the United States had graduated from college as of 1960, as opposed to only 3.5 per cent of nonwhites.

Among residence groups, the highest educational level was found in the urban areas, whereas the lowest educational level characterized the rural farm population. The median number of school years completed in 1960, for example, was 11.1 for urbanites, 9.5 for rural nonfarm dwellers, and 8.8 for persons living in rural farm areas. This same general pattern of differences among residence groups held for the proportion of persons having completed less than five years of elementary school (lowest for urban, highest for rural farm), and for the proportion who had graduated from high school or college (highest for urban, lowest for rural farm).

Our system of free public education, at the elementary level first and later at the high school level, continues to be a major strength of the United States. Coupled with this has been the emergence and expansion of the land-grant college system which has provided low-cost higher education to qualified youth. The aim of these institutions has been twofold: (1) to provide an opportunity for education to young people who otherwise—because of economic status, ethnic background, or social class—might have been forced to live out their lives in obscure mediocrity; and (2) to provide the society with the more highly trained workers necessary for continued rapid scientific and technological progress. That these institutions have been successful in increasing school enrollment and raising the overall level of educational attainment in the United States has been amply demonstrated in the preceding discussion. Moreover, the steady increase in school enrollment rates throughout the postwar period indicates that the upward trend in the educational level of the population will continue. To illustrate, it has been estimated that by 1985 the proportion of functional illiterates in the United States could be as low as 2.5 per cent of those aged twenty-five and over, whereas the proportion of high school graduates could be as high as 60 per cent or more.[6]

But in spite of the past and the projected increase in the educational achievement of the population, several differences still characterize various subgroups within the United States. Thus, while there is indeed reason to be proud of past accomplishments, there is still ample room for improvement before all members of the society can enjoy equally the many opportunities and advantages to be gained through education. Although variations in individual ability and incentive make it unlikely that the day will ever come when all persons graduate from college, it does seem realistic to aim for such goals as the elimination of functional illiteracy or universal high school graduation.

(2) *Income.* Money income is an extremely sensitive index of the economic well-being of a population. To the extent that income levels are rising (or declining), we can assume that the overall standard of living of a population is also rising (or declining). Moreover, income differences among members of a population indicate many other basic differences (in educational attainment, technical skills, physical and mental abilities, discriminatory wage scales, and so forth). Such income differentials are also major determinants of still other differences that relate to such things as the quantity and quality of food consumed, place of residence and condition of housing, family size and living arrangements, use of leisure time, and levels of morbidity and mortality. Because of this pervasive influence, a knowledge of the income characteristics of a population—and especially of existing differentials with regard to the ability to purchase needed goods and services—is particularly essential for an adequate understanding of our society and its problems.

The income status of the American population has both positive and negative aspects. On the positive side, the years since the end of the Second World War have seen a marked increase in income levels, and more families are earning more money today than ever before. To illustrate, between 1950 and 1960 the median income of families in the United States increased from $3,083 to $5,657, or by 83 per cent (see Table VI-6). By the middle of the 1960 decade median family income was up to $6,569, or well over twice the level of 1950.[7] In noting these income changes, however, it is necessary to keep in mind that the cost of living has also risen fairly substantially during the postwar period; thus only part of the dollar increase represents a gain in "real income" or in the purchasing power of the dollar. When price changes are taken into

Table VI-6: Distribution of families by level of income, United States, 1950, 1960, and 1965.

Income level	Per cent of families		
	1950	1960	1965
All levels	100.0	100.0	100.0
Under $1,000	14.7	5.6	3.2
$1,000–$1,999	14.6	7.5	6.3
$2,000–$2,999	19.2	8.3	8.1
$3,000–$3,999	19.4	9.5	8.4
$4,000–$4,999	12.1	11.0	8.6
$5,000–$5,999	7.8	12.3	9.9
$6,000–$6,999	4.3	10.7	9.9
$7,000–$7,999	4.9	20.1	23.2
$10,000 and over	4.3	15.0	22.5
Median income	$3,083	$5,657	$6,659

SOURCE: U.S. Bureau of the Census, *U.S. Census of Population: 1960,* Final Report PC(1)-1C, *General Social and Economic Characteristics: United States Summary,* Washington, D.C., 1962; and "Incomes in 1964 of Families and Persons in the United States," *Current Population Reports,* P-60:47, Washington, D.C., September 24, 1965.

consideration, the magnitude of the increase in family income levels becomes noticeably less. In terms of constant (1960) dollars, for example, the increase in the median income of American families between 1950 and 1960 would have been from approximately $3,840 to $5,657—an increase of only 47 per cent.[8] While this increase in real income is only about half as great as the dollar change, it nevertheless represents a substantial increase in the buying power of the American population in recent years.

Accompanying the increase in median income since 1950 has been a major shift upward of families along the entire income scale. On the one hand, the proportion of families with annual incomes of $3,000 or less declined from very nearly one-half in 1950 (48.5 per cent) to well below one-fifth (17.6 per cent) in

1965. Families with incomes in excess of $10,000 per year, on the other hand, increased from roughly 4 per cent to 23 per cent between 1950 and 1965. Stated somewhat differently, less than one out of every ten American families had annual incomes of $7,000 or more in 1950; but by 1965 nearly five out of every ten families had annual incomes this large. Clearly, the years since 1950 have witnessed a marked improvement in the income status of the population.

The preceding discussion provides only a very general picture of the income characteristics of families in the United States, and it does not consider the substantial differences in income levels among various subgroups in the population (see Table VI-7). Such differences must be considered if one is to assess adequately the economic well-being of any population. From a social problems point of view, one of the most important income differentials in the United States is associated with color. In 1960 the median annual income of white families in the United States ($5,893) was 86 per cent greater than the corresponding median for nonwhite families ($3,161). This color differential (which probably reflects differences in educational attainment, aptitude, and technical skills, as well as ethnic discrimination in wage scales)[9] is underscored by the fact that nearly five out of every ten nonwhite families in the United States had annual incomes below $3,000 in 1960, compared with just under two out of every ten white families. At the other extreme, only 4 per cent of nonwhite families fell into the $10,000 and over income class in 1960, whereas 16 per cent of the white families had annual incomes this large.

The income characteristics of families also varied noticeably among the three basic residence areas. To illustrate, the 1960 median annual income of urban families ($6,166) was 30 per cent greater than that of rural nonfarm families ($4,750); and it was 91 per cent higher than the median income of rural farm families ($3,228). The relatively disadvantaged position of the nation's farm population is further revealed by comparing the proportion of families receiving incomes of less than $3,000 a year. Nearly five out of every ten rural farm families fell into this low-income group, compared with only three out of ten rural nonfarm families and less than two out of ten urban families. The relatively unfavorable income status of the rural farm population is due to a number of factors. Among them are (1) the generally higher proportion of elderly people in this group; (2) the lower level of education and lack of industrial skills which make it difficult for people to transfer from an agricultural to a more lucrative nonagricultural occupation; and (3) the failure to include as cash income such items as food raised for personal consumption. The relatively higher position of the two nonfarm residence groups, on the other hand, may in part be explained by such things as (1) a smaller proportion of elderly persons; (2) the greater availability of jobs for persons with limited skills; and (3) the higher salaries generally characteristic of non-agricultural occupations.

The median income of males age fourteen and over in the United States in 1960 was $4,103, compared with only $1,357 for females. That is, the average income of men was approximately three times as great as that of women. Reasons behind this differential would include (1) more part-time jobs among employed females than employed males; (2) more seasonal or part-year employment for females; (3) a not uncommon tendency for women to receive lower wages for performing the same tasks done by men at higher rates of pay; and (4) more older widows as compared with widowers who do not work and whose only income is a small pension or social security check each month.

Age, in fact, is a very important variable as far as income is concerned. The pattern of the relationship approximates a normal curve: incomes start out low at the youngest ages, increase very rapidly up to a maximum level at ages thirty-five to forty-four, and then decline with each advancing age. To illustrate, the 1960 median income of persons fourteen to nineteen years old in the United States was only $710. From there it rose sharply to $2,201 at ages twenty to twenty-four. At ages twenty-five to fifty-four median annual incomes averaged about $4,000, but they fell fairly rapidly thereafter. The 1960 median income was only $1,443 for persons sixty-five to seventy-four years of age, and for persons seventy-five and over it was only $971. This age and income relationship is relatively simple to explain. On the one hand, the middle age groups where incomes are highest represent the most productive years of a person's life—years that are usually characterized by a steady advancement in one's chosen vocation. At the younger ages, especially under twenty years, incomes are low partly because there is a great deal of part-time and seasonal employment at these ages, and partly because those persons who do hold full-time jobs have only recently entered the labor force and have not yet worked their way up the income scale. At the other extreme, incomes are lower at ages sixty-five and over because many persons at these ages have retired from active participation in the labor force and must subsist on small incomes from social security or some other pension program.

One other notable income differential merits consideration. Earlier in this chapter we noted the advantages of higher education from the point of view of the society as a whole (for example, the higher the educational level of a population, the better equipped it is to perform the increasingly complex tasks of an expanding industrial society, and the more likely it is to be able to cope with the many problems generated by rapid social change). The advantages of higher education are not limited to the society, however, but also accrue to the individual. There is in fact a pronounced direct association between individual incomes and level of educational attainment in the United States. The magnitude of this association is strikingly revealed in Table VI-7. The median annual income in 1960 of persons who had completed at least four years of college was $7,646. This was roughly one-third higher than the median income of persons whose level of educational attainment fell in the interval "high school 4 to college 3" ($5,593).

Table VI-7: Selected income characteristics of specified subgroups in the population, United States, 1960.

Population subgroups	Median annual income	Per cent with income	
		Under $3,000	$10,000 and over
FAMILIES			
All classes	$5,660	21.4	15.1
White	5,893	18.6	16.2
Nonwhite	3,161	47.9	4.2
Urban	6,166	16.4	17.7
Rural nonfarm	4,750	28.9	9.0
Rural farm	3,228	47.1	6.8
PERSONS AGE 14 +			
Total with income	$2,798		
Male	4,103		
Female	1,375		
Age 14–19	710		
20–24	2,201		
25–34	3,827		
35–44	4,249		
45–54	4,009		
55–64	3,299		
65–74	1,443		
75 and over	971		
MALES AGE 25 +			
Total with income	$4,617		
Less than 5 years of elementary school	1,745		
Elementary 5 to high school 3	3,826		
High school 4 to college 3	5,593		
College 4 or more	7,646		

SOURCE: Same as Table VI-3.

It was almost twice as high as that of persons in the "elementary 5 to high school 3" category ($3,826), and it was more than four times as high as the median income of the so-called "functional illiterates," or persons who had completed less than five years of elementary school ($1,745). Such impressive income differentials should cause young Americans to consider seriously before they drop out of high school to "make some money." While not all persons are prepared to undertake college study, most people are capable of finishing high school; and the available data strongly suggest that, in terms of subsequent financial returns, the time spent in acquiring a high school diploma is definitely time well spent.

In concluding this section it should be stressed that the increase in the income level of the population as a whole has by no means meant an end to poverty. On the contrary, fairly wide discrepancies in income status still prevail. To illustrate, for the nation as a whole roughly four out of every ten persons had annual incomes of less than $2,000 in 1960. This proportion was more than five out of ten for rural farm dwellers; it was six out of ten for nonwhites, seven out of ten for persons sixty-five years old and over, and eight out of ten for persons seventy-five and over. Among nonwhites living in rural farm areas of the United States, fully nine out of ten had annual incomes below $2,000 in 1960. Such wide discrepancies in income are very likely related to other differences in the level of living of particular groups (such as differences in both the quantity and nutritional quality of food consumed, conditions of housing, and ability to purchase medical care and other needed services); and they clearly emphasize that there are still a number of battles to be won in the "war on poverty" if all citizens are to benefit equally from living in our increasingly affluent society.

(3) *Labor force characteristics.* Labor force analysis interests a great many persons and groups for several different reasons. Educators, for example, are interested in the changing skill requirements of the labor force and whether or not the coming genera-

tion of workers is receiving the necessary training to fulfill these requirements. Sociologists, on the other hand, may look at the trend with regard to women in the labor force and investigate topics such as the effects of the working wife on fertility and family size, child rearing attitudes and practices, juvenile delinquency, and general life-style of the family. Government personnel and agencies seeking to alleviate unemployment problems need to know something about the number and distribution of unemployed persons as well as the occupational skills they possess. Similarly, the number of available workers and their occupational skills are important factors to be considered by businessmen who may be contemplating the expansion or relocation of industrial activities; by political scientists who are concerned with the balance of power in the world today; and by labor economists who may be interested in a wide variety of topics such as the relationship between residential and occupational mobility, the changing importance of particular occupations in the society, variations in the rate of retirement from one occupational group to another, and so forth.

On a more general level, the size and distribution of the labor force and the characteristics of its members can reveal a great deal of information about a given population—how it has organized itself to earn its livelihood, the social and economic well-being of its members, its potential for industrial expansion, and so forth. Moreover, changes over time in the size and composition of the labor force also reflect changes in the level of economic well-being and reveal new patterns of economic and social organization. For these and other reasons that could be cited, labor force analysis helps us to understand the organization of our society and the changes occurring therein.

In the United States the labor force is defined as all persons age fourteen years and over who are either currently working at a specific job, either full or part time (*employed*), or who—although without a job at the moment—want to work and are actively looking for some form of regular employment (*unemployed*).[10] The labor force is composed of many diverse types. It includes all persons who receive a monetary return for their labors, whether they are on a fixed salary, hourly wage workers, or self-employed professional people such as doctors, lawyers, and shopkeepers. In addition, it includes unpaid family workers who perform gainful work but who receive no money income (such as the son who helps out on the family farm or the woman who helps her husband tend the grocery store). Finally, members of the armed forces are included as part of the labor force (although this latter group is often excluded when concern is limited to an analysis of the "civilian labor force"). Not included in the labor force are (1) dependent children, (2) women who have no job other than keeping house, (3) students who are not working, (4) inmates of institutions, such as jails or hospitals, and (5) persons who are retired or who are unable to work because of ill health or for some other reason (for example, resident aliens who do not have a work permit).

A major trend in the United States in recent years has been a substantial increase in the size of the labor force (Table VI-8). As compared with 53 million workers in 1940, the 1960 labor force of the nation numbered nearly 70 million, a 32 per cent increase. This trend has continued, and it is estimated that in the spring of 1965 there were slightly more than 77 million workers in the United States, or 46 per cent more than there had been in 1940.[11] As might be expected, most of this increase is due to the overall increase in the population. To illustrate, between 1940 and 1965 the total number of people age fourteen and over in the United States increased from roughly 102 million to 136 million, or by slightly more than one-third.

Although the increase in the size of the labor force has been due largely to the growth of the population as a whole, this should not obscure the fact that there has also been some increase in the *labor force participation rate* (i.e., the per cent of the population age fourteen and over that is in the labor force). In 1940 the labor force participation rate in the United States was 52 per cent. It has increased slowly but steadily since that time, and by 1965 approximately 57 per cent of the population fourteen years of age and over was in the labor force. This slight increase in the overall rate of labor force participation is due to an expansion of employment opportunities for women and a corresponding increase in female employment. The labor force participation rate for males has actually declined (from 79 per cent in 1940 to 77 per cent in 1960), but the proportion of females in the labor force rose from roughly one-fourth in 1940 to more than one-third (35 per cent) in 1960. In 1965 the female labor force participation rate was up to 37 per cent.

The vast majority of the workers in the United States are in the civilian labor force. However, although they make up only a small fraction of the total labor force, the number and proportion of persons in the armed forces have increased substantially in recent years. In 1940 the 305,500 military personnel in the nation accounted for only six-tenths of 1 per cent of the labor force. By 1965 the size of this group had increased more than eightfold (to 2.7 million), while its proportion of the total labor force had increased sixfold. This growing importance of the armed forces in the economy is, of course, a reflection of the Cold War and the various "brush-fire" hot wars in southeast Asia and other parts of the world (Korea, Laos, the Congo, and more recently Viet Nam).

Another trend accompanying the increase in the size of the labor force has been a substantial decline in unemployment. In 1940, at a time when the nation was just beginning to emerge from severe economic depression, nearly one out of every seven workers was unemployed. By 1950, when the postwar prosperity boom was at its peak, this proportion had been reduced to less than one out of twenty; and, testifying to the continued economic growth and prosperity of the nation, it has remained close to this level ever since.

Finally, it may be noted that a substantial proportion of the population age fourteen and over is classified as "not in the labor force." As indicated earlier, these include housewives, students, inmates of resident institutions, and others who do not work for one reason or another. Although the number of such persons has increased in recent years, the proportion which they represent of the total age fourteen and over has undergone a slight decline— from 48 per cent in 1940 to 43 per cent in 1965. This decline is of course complementary to the increase in the rate of labor force participation, and like that increase it reflects the greater tendency for women to join the labor force today than a generation ago.

One of the most notable developments in recent years has been a pronounced change in the occupational structure of the American labor force. Two changes in particular stand out. First, there has been a substantial reduction in the number and proportion of farm workers in the nation. Between 1940 and 1960 the number of farmers and farm laborers declined from approximately 8.3 million (nearly one-fifth of the total employed) to less than 4 million (only about 6 per cent of the total employed). Second, among nonfarm workers there has been a marked growth in the importance of *white-collar* occupations and a corresponding decline in the significance of *blue-collar* occupations. Of the 58 million persons working at nonfarm jobs in the United States in 1960, approximately 27 million (46 per cent) were white-collar workers. This compares with roughly 15 million white-collar workers in 1940 (40 per cent of the nonfarm labor force), and represents an increase of 81 per cent during the intervening twenty years. In contrast, the number of blue-collar workers in the nation increased by about half this amount (43 per cent) between 1940 and 1960. On the one hand, these trends are due to increases in professional and technical occupations (doctors, teachers, engineers, physical scientists, and so on), and in the clerical group. On the other hand, they are the result of declines in the lesser-skilled blue-collar occupations (operatives, service workers, and especially unskilled laborers). Very slight declines have characterized managers, officials, proprietors, and sales workers, whereas skilled craftsmen account for a slightly larger proportion of the nonfarm workers than they did before World War II. Although blue-collar workers still outnumber white-collar workers, the differential growth rates

Table VI-8: Selected labor force characteristics of the population 14 years old and over, United States, 1940–1960.

Labor force characteristics	1940	1950	1960
Total 14 and over	101,457,844	112,801,417	126,276,548
In labor force	53,010,582	60,329,231	69,877,481
Per cent of total 14 and over	52.2	53.5	55.3
Armed forces	305,500	1,025,511	1,733,402
Civilian labor force	52,705,082	59,303,720	68,144,079
Employed	45,070,315	56,449,409	64,639,252
Unemployed	7,634,767	2,854,311	3,504,827
Per cent of civilian labor force	14.5	4.8	5.1
Not in labor force	48,447,262	52,472,186	56,399,067
Per cent of employed persons with farm occupations	18.6	12.1	6.4
Per cent distribution (by occupation) of nonfarm workers:			
Total nonfarm workers	100.0	100.0	100.0
White-collar workers	40.4	42.6	46.3
Professional and technical	9.8	10.1	12.6
Managers, officials, and proprietors	10.0	10.3	9.4
Clerical workers	12.1	14.2	16.2
Sales workers	8.5	8.0	8.1
Blue-collar workers	59.6	57.5	53.7
Craftsmen and foremen	14.2	16.0	15.2
Operatives	22.2	22.8	20.7
Service workers	14.6	11.7	12.5
Laborers	8.6	7.0	5.4

SOURCE: Same as Table VI-4.

of these two groups are rapidly narrowing the gap. Compared to 1940, when blue-collar workers outnumbered white-collar workers by a ratio of 3 to 2, estimates for 1965 indicate that blue-collar workers account for only 52 per cent of the nonfarm labor force, whereas the white-collar segment has increased to 48 per cent.

These two trends (the decline in the size of the farm labor force, and the shift away from the lesser-skilled nonfarm occupations) have been in evidence for several generations, and they reflect the increasing mechanization, bureaucratization, and spread of automation in a society that is daily becoming more complex. In particular, they reflect a fundamental reorganization of our mode of gaining a livelihood, necessitated by the rapid technological progress of the twentieth century. Moreover, since this process of technological change is a continuous one—in which new occupations are constantly being created while others become obsolete—it is likely that these trends will continue in the years ahead. Although one may not foresee the day when digital computers will replace farmers, there is little doubt that the role of the unskilled laborer will steadily decline while that of the skilled data-processing technician will continue to grow.

The discussion so far has not considered any of the differences in labor force characteristics among various segments of the population—differences that often reflect the existence of major social problems. For example, rates of both labor force participation and unemployment vary systematically with age: the former is distributed normally whereas the latter approximates a U-shaped curve, being especially high at the younger ages (see Table VI-9). The age differences in labor force participation are easily understandable and do not really represent a problem. At ages fourteen to nineteen, labor force participation is low because so many are still attending school. The substantial increase for the next age group (roughly two-thirds of the population at ages twenty to twenty-four was in the labor force in 1960) reflects the entrance into the work force of large numbers of young people upon the completion of their formal education. From this point on, as more and more people complete their advanced education, the rate of labor force participation rises steadily. It reaches a peak at ages forty-five to forty-nine (at which time seven out of every ten persons is in the labor force), and then begins to decline as people begin to reach retirement age: slightly less than one out of every

Table VI-9: Labor force participation and employment status of the population 14 years old and over, by age, sex, color, and residence, United States, 1960.

Age	Per cent in labor force	Per cent unemployed	Sex, color, and residence	Per cent in labor force	Per cent unemployed
14–19	31.1	10.4	All classes	55.3	5.1
20–24	65.1	7.5			
25–29	64.0	5.1	Male	77.4	5.0
30–34	65.0	4.4	Female	34.5	5.4
35–39	67.3	4.2			
40–44	69.8	4.1	White	55.2	4.7
45–49	70.6	4.2	Nonwhite	56.3	8.7
50–54	68.6	4.3			
55–59	63.1	4.5	Urban	57.0	5.1
60–64	52.4	4.8	Rural nonfarm	51.3	6.1
65 and over	19.4	5.2	Rural farm	51.5	3.0

SOURCE: Same as Table VI-3.

five Americans age sixty-five and over was in the labor force in 1960.

In contrast to labor force participation, the pattern of unemployment does indicate some specific problem areas—in particular, high unemployment among teen-agers. In 1960, one out of every ten persons fourteen to nineteen years of age was unemployed, compared with one in twenty for the labor force as a whole. This high unemployment rate in part reflects the fact that this is the age when people start to leave school and enter the labor force for the first time, and many of these fourteen- to nineteen-year-olds are probably still looking for their first full-time job. Part of this phenomenon may also be due to the failure of the economy to expand at a fast enough rate to provide jobs for the growing number of teen-agers. This is suggested by the steady increase in teen-age unemployment as the aging of the postwar baby boom cohorts has dramatically increased the size of this age group. In

April 1965, for example, slightly more than 14 per cent of the fourteen- to nineteen-year-olds in the labor force were unemployed. This is roughly half again as high as the 1960 teen-age unemployment rate and clearly indicates a trend toward a serious social problem.

Men and women differ notably with regard to labor force participation, but they have fairly similar unemployment rates. On the other hand, whites and nonwhites have fairly similar rates of labor force participation but markedly different levels of unemployment. The sex differential does not represent a serious problem and is just what one would expect to find. The reason for this is twofold. First, the role of women in our society is culturally defined as one of dependence, and for the most part they are not required to earn their own living. Second, and perhaps more important, the biological role of the female with regard to bearing children, and her related housekeeping responsibilities, have been, and will probably continue to be, major factors restricting the employment activities of many women and reinforcing the traditional cultural attitude that "women's place is in the home."

Turning to a consideration of color, the white-nonwhite unemployment differential is cause for serious concern. The fact that the nonwhite unemployment rate in 1960 (8.7 per cent) was approximately twice as high as the corresponding rate for the white population (4.7 per cent) provides a real basis for the often heard remark that the Negro is "the last to be hired and the first to be fired." This differential is in part due to racial prejudice and a resulting discrimination in hiring practices; but it is also due to other more objective characteristics of nonwhites—such as their lower level of educational attainment and their relative lack of occupational skills. Of course, these characteristics may themselves be a function of racial discrimination. For example, a low level of educational attainment is partly due to a lack of adequate educational opportunities and facilities; and this lack of a good education means that occupational skills are more difficult to acquire.

Finally, labor force participation is notably higher in urban than in either of the rural residence classes; but the rural farm population has the lowest rate of unemployment. In the first instance, the high labor force participation rate in urban areas reflects more and wider job opportunities in cities than in rural areas. But the low proportion of the farm population unemployed does *not* necessarily reflect greater economic opportunities in such areas. Rather, it is probably due to such things as the greater prevalence of self-employment on family farms: persons who live and work on farms can always find something to do and are thus likely to report themselves as employed even though they may be actively seeking full-time nonfarm work.

As with overall labor force participation and employment status, the various subgroups in the population differ notably with regard to their occupational composition. The major differences relate to sex, color, and urban-rural residence and are illustrated by the percentages shown in Table VI-10. One of the most striking differences revealed by these data concerns the proportion of employed persons with farm occupations. Among males the proportion of employed persons working at a farm occupation was nearly 8 per cent, compared with just under 1.5 per cent of female workers. Farm workers were also more common among nonwhites (slightly more than 8 per cent) than whites (nearly 6 per cent).

Of equal significance are the pronounced variations in the proportion of persons with nonfarm occupations who can be classified as white-collar or blue-collar workers. Nearly six out of every ten working women were employed in a white-collar occupation in 1960, compared with only four out of ten males. The difference was even more marked between the color groups: roughly half of the employed whites were working at white-collar jobs in 1960, compared with less than one-fifth of the nonwhite population. Finally, white-collar employment is much less characteristic of the rural population—particularly the rural farm population. Although nearly half of the employed persons in urban areas held white-collar jobs, only 37 per cent of the rural nonfarm labor force consisted of white-collar workers, and only 35 per cent of

Table VI-10: Occupational distribution of employed persons, by sex, color, and residence, United States, 1960.

Occupation	Male	Female	White	Nonwhite	Urban	Rural nonfarm	Rural farm
Total employed	100.0	100.0	100.0	100.0	100.0	100.0	100.0
Farm occupations	7.9	1.4	5.9	8.3	0.8	6.7	59.1
Nonfarm occupations	92.1	98.6	94.1	91.7	99.2	93.3	40.9
Nonfarm occupations (total)	100.0	100.0	100.0	100.0	100.0	100.0	100.0
White-collar workers	39.9	58.6	49.2	18.1	49.1	36.7	34.9
Professional and technical	11.8	14.0	13.2	6.4	13.3	10.2	10.2
Managers, officials, and proprietors	12.2	4.0	10.2	2.2	9.6	9.1	6.7
Clerical workers	8.0	32.1	17.1	7.7	17.7	10.8	11.8
Sales workers	7.9	8.5	8.7	1.9	8.5	6.6	6.3
Blue-collar workers	60.1	41.4	50.8	81.9	50.9	63.3	65.1
Craftsmen and foremen	22.4	1.3	16.0	7.7	14.5	18.1	15.0
Operatives	22.8	16.6	20.4	23.1	19.1	25.8	29.0
Service workers	7.0	23.0	9.9	36.6	12.6	11.9	12.9
Laborers	7.9	0.5	4.4	14.5	4.8	7.5	8.2

SOURCE: Same as Table VI-4.

the population employed in the rural farm areas of the United States was so classified.

Reflecting the converse of the pattern just described, males, nonwhites, and rural area residents had much greater representation among blue-collar occupations than females, whites, and urban dwellers. In concluding this section it is worth noting that the occupation differences just described are closely related to education and income differences. To be more specific: a person's income is in large part determined by the nature of his occupation; and his occupation is influenced a great deal by the amount of education he has. The implication of this interrelationship is that as long as all persons in our society do not have access to the same educational opportunities, the United States will continue to be faced with a social, cultural, and economic imbalance among large segments of the population.

REFERENCES AND SUGGESTIONS FOR FURTHER READING

Donald J. Bogue, *The Population of the United States,* Glencoe, Ill., 1959, Chapters 6–8, 11, 13, 16–20, and 23.
Herman P. Miller, *Income Distribution in the United States,* Washington, D.C., 1966.
Conrad and Irene B. Taeuber, *The Changing Population of the United States,* New York, 1958, Chapters 2 and 8–12.
Ralph Thomlinson, *Population Dynamics,* New York, 1965, Chapters 19 and 20.
Warren S. Thompson and David T. Lewis, *Population Problems,* New York, 1965, Chapters 4–5, 7, and 8.
U.S. Bureau of the Census, *United States Census of Population: 1960,* Final Reports PC(1)-1B, *General Population Characteristics,* Washington, D.C., 1961; PC(1)-1C, *General Social and Economic Characteristics,* Washington, D.C., 1962; PC(1)-1D, *Detailed Characteristics,* Washington, D.C., 1963; PC(2)-1A, *Nativity and Parentage,* Washington, D.C., 1965; PC(2)-1C, *Nonwhite Population by Race,* Washington, D.C., 1963; PC(2)-4C, *Sources and Structure of Family Income,* Washington, D.C., 1964; PC(2)-5A, *School Enrollment,* Washington, D.C., 1964; PC(2)-5B, *Educational Attainment,* Washington, D.C., 1963; PC(2)-6A, *Employment Status and Work Experience,* Washington, D.C., 1963; and PC(2)-7A, *Occupational Characteristics,* Washington, D.C., 1963.

7

Population distribution

On a world level the most pertinent fact about population distribution is its unevenness in relation to the distribution of land and other natural resources. In Asia, for example, the number of people per square mile of land area is roughly 63, compared with about 19 per square mile in the United States and only 2 per square mile in Oceania (Australia, New Zealand, and the other island nations of the South Pacific). As indicated in Chapter 5, one of the most serious problems facing mankind today is that numbers of people and population growth rates are greatest in those regions of the world where the level of social and economic development can least afford it. The population is already so large in many low-income countries that even without additional growth it would be very difficult to achieve significant improvements in the level of socioeconomic well-being. In these already over-crowded countries, the persistence of rapid rates of population growth does not merely intensify the difficulty of generating sustained economic development. Rather, it makes it difficult to forestall even further declines in an already marginal level of living! Although the United States may not have to contend with such acute problems as threatened starvation and economic chaos, we are not entirely free of distribution-related problems. In this chapter we shall focus on (1) a brief description of the basic trends and changes in the distribution of the American population; and (2) a discussion of some of the major problems related to the pattern of human settlement in the United States today.

POPULATION DISTRIBUTION TRENDS IN THE UNITED STATES

When the first federal census was taken in 1790 there were roughly 4 million people in the United States. Virtually all of them lived on a relatively narrow strip of land running north and south along the eastern seaboard, and nearly all of them (95 per cent) lived in small rural communities. This is radically different from the situation in 1960. At the time of the most recent census, only 55 per cent of the population was living in the eastern part of the country, and some seven out of every ten Americans were living in large urban areas. *These fundamental changes in the pattern of settlement could only have been effected through migration.* Although differences in the rate of natural increase have always existed among the various areas of the nation, such differences have never been great enough to bring about changes in population distribution as substantial as those just described. In essence, then, when one talks about trends and changes in the spatial distribution of the American population one is talking primarily about trends in the volume of human migration between geographic areas.

Of the many streams of migration that have prevailed (and still prevail) between various areas in the United States, four stand out as having exerted a particularly profound influence on the distribution of the population over the land area. These four migration streams and the associated shifts in the spatial distribution of the population may be identified as follows: (1) the east-west trend, (2) the Negro exodus from the South, (3) the rural-urban trend, and (4) the suburbanization trend.

(1) *The east-west trend.* One of the most significant migratory trends in this country has been the east-to-west dispersion of the population. The initial settlement of the nation was largely confined to the Atlantic coastal belt; but from the time the nation achieved its independence it has been characterized by a continuous

Table VII-1: Regional distribution of the population of the United States, 1790–1960.

Year	Per cent of total population living in:			
	Northeast	North central	South	West
1790	50.1	......	49.9	......
1800	49.6	1.0	49.4	......
1810	48.2	4.0	47.8	......
1820	45.2	8.9	45.9	......
1830	43.1	12.5	44.4	......
1840	39.6	19.6	40.7	......
1850	37.2	23.3	38.7	0.8
1860	33.7	28.9	35.4	2.0
1870	31.9	33.7	31.9	2.6
1880	28.9	34.6	32.9	3.6
1890	27.6	35.6	31.8	5.0
1900	27.6	34.6	32.2	5.7
1910	28.0	32.4	31.9	7.7
1920	28.0	32.1	31.2	8.7
1930	27.9	31.3	30.7	10.0
1940	27.2	30.4	31.5	10.9
1950	26.1	29.4	31.2	13.3
1960	24.9	28.8	30.7	15.6
Per cent change, 1950–60	13.2	16.1	16.5	38.9
Population per square mile (1960)	273	68	63	16

SOURCE: U.S. Bureau of the Census, *U.S. Census of Population: 1960,* Final Report PC(1)-1A, *Number of Inhabitants: United States Summary,* Washington, D.C., 1961.

westward expansion. The nature of this east-to-west redistribution of the population is clearly revealed by the statistics in Table VII-1 and Figure 4, showing the percentage of the population living in each of four broad regions at every census since 1790. The states and geographic divisions comprising these four broad regions are shown in Figure 5.

For about two hundred years after initial colonization early in the seventeenth century, there were no major shifts in the distribution of the American population. At the time of the first census in 1790, the entire European population was settled along the Atlantic coast, more or less evenly divided between the Northeast and the South. But after 1800 the increasing congestion in what was still largely an agrarian society began to encourage westward migration, and each subsequent decade has seen a smaller and smaller proportion of the population living in these two eastern regions.

When this westward movement first began it was not a movement to the far West. Instead, it was largely a settling of the central part of the nation. Not until after the Civil War was there any sizable settlement on the West Coast. At this time the impetus to westward migration provided by the completion of the transcontinental railroad was reinforced by the passage of the Homestead Laws. These laws, the first of which was enacted in 1862, provided large tracts of farm land at relatively little cost to persons who agreed to occupy, cultivate, or otherwise improve the land within a specified period of time. The purpose of these acts was to encourage the settlement of the whole country as well as to increase food production to enhance the strength of the nation. Their success is attested to not only by the rapid westward expansion of the population during the late nineteenth and early twentieth centuries, but also by the United States' rapid growth as the wealthiest and one of the most powerful nations in the world.

The spreading out of the population from the area of initial settlement toward the West is still taking place today. During the most recent intercensal decade, for example, the population of

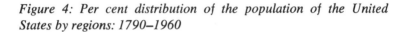

Figure 4: Per cent distribution of the population of the United States by regions: 1790–1960

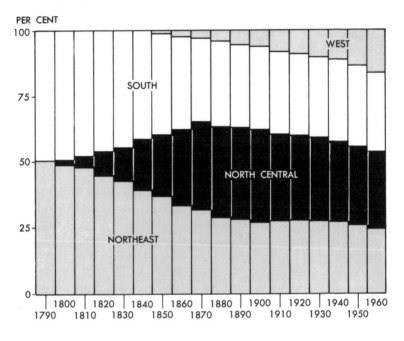

the West increased by approximately 39 per cent—well over twice the increase recorded in either the South (17 per cent) or the North Central region (16 per cent), and roughly three times that of the Northeast (13 per cent).

Although the West may be the fastest growing region, the fact that it was so late in getting started (compared to other regions) means that it is still the least populated section of the country. In 1960 the West accounted for only 16 per cent of the total national population, and it had a density of only 16 persons per square mile. The South had the largest share of the population in 1960 (31 per cent), but it was followed closely by the North

Central (29 per cent). In spite of having the largest share of the nation's population, both of these regions had relatively low man-land ratios. In 1960 the number of people per square mile was only 68 in the North Central and only 63 in the South. In the North Central this is partly a reflection of later settlement; in the South it is partly a reflection of the earlier emphasis on plantation agriculture and thus a delayed industrial growth.

In marked contrast to the other three regions, the Northeast (wherein lived one-fourth of the American population) had a population density of 273 persons per square mile. This clearly reflects not only the earlier settlement of this part of the country but also the fact that American industrial development began in this region; hence it was the first to experience large-scale urban growth and expansion. The point is that westward expansion has obviously not been accompanied by any thinning out of the eastern population. Furthermore, given the concentration of large industrial complexes in the Northeast, it is highly unlikely that the continuation of the westward migration will lead to any significant thinning out in the years to come. What can be expected, rather, is a further spreading out of the area of concentration. Under present trends (and there appears to be little likelihood that these will change in the near future), this expansion will have its greatest impact in the West, and the years ahead will witness a steady increase in the size and density of the population in this youngest region of the country.

(2) *The Negro exodus from the South.* The Negro population of the United States has always been concentrated in the South. This of course reflects the historical development of a plantation slave economy in that region. To illustrate, in 1790 there were roughly 757,000 Negroes in the United States, of whom well over 90 per cent were slaves and living in the South.[1] In recent years, however, there has been a pronounced tendency for the Negro population to become more evenly dispersed throughout the nation. Although Negro migration out of the South began almost immediately after the Civil War, it was not a large movement at

Figure 5: Regions and geographic divisions of the United States

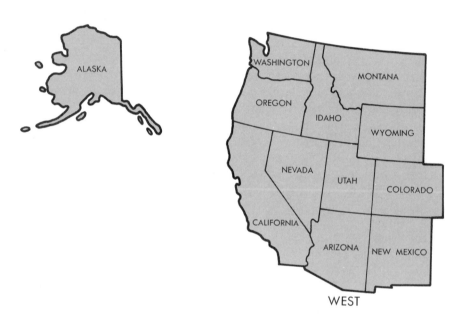

WEST

NORTH CENTRAL

NORTH DAKOTA
MINNESOTA
SOUTH DAKOTA
WISCONSIN
MICHIGAN
NEBRASKA
IOWA
ILLINOIS
INDIANA
OHIO
KANSAS
MISSOURI

NORTHEAST

NEW HAMPSHIRE
VERMONT
MAINE
MASSACHUSETTS
NEW YORK
RHODE ISLAND
CONNECTICUT
PENNSYLVANIA
NEW JERSEY

SOUTH

MARYLAND
DELAWARE
WEST VIRGINIA
VIRGINIA
KENTUCKY
NORTH CAROLINA
TENNESSEE
OKLAHOMA
ARKANSAS
SOUTH CAROLINA
GEORGIA
TEXAS
ALABAMA
FLORIDA
MISSISSIPPI
LOUISIANA

first. This was partly because of good agricultural employment opportunities in the South, and partly because the heavy foreign immigration to northern industrial centers during the latter part of the nineteenth century meant greater competition there for non-agricultural employment. That is, during the late nineteenth century there was neither a very strong "push" out of the South nor a significant "pull" to northern industrial centers.

But shortly after World War I the situation began to change. On the "push" side, continued technological progress made agricultural employment opportunities more and more scarce. On the "pull" side, restrictive legislation adopted during the early 1920's brought a sudden and drastic fall in the volume of foreign immigration, thus increasing the availability of unskilled and semiskilled industrial jobs in northern cities—jobs for which southern Negroes were actively recruited. As a result, Negro migration out of the South began to gain momentum (see Table VII-2). In

Table VII-2: Distribution of the Negro population by major regions in the United States, 1860–1960.

Year	Total Negro population	Per cent living in:			
		Northeast	North central	South	West
1860	4,441,830	3.5	4.1	92.2	0.1
1870	4,880,019	3.7	5.6	90.6	0.1
1880	6,580,793	3.5	5.9	90.5	0.2
1890	7,488,676	3.6	5.8	90.3	0.3
1900	8,833,994	4.4	5.6	89.7	0.3
1910	9,827,763	4.9	5.5	89.0	0.5
1920	10,463,131	6.5	7.6	85.2	0.7
1930	11,891,143	9.6	10.6	78.7	1.0
1940	12,865,518	10.6	11.0	77.0	1.3
1950	15,042,286	13.4	14.8	68.0	3.8
1960	18,860,117	16.1	18.3	60.0	5.7

SOURCE: U.S. Bureau of the Census, *Historical Statistics of the United States: Colonial Times to 1957*, Washington, D.C., 1960; and *Historical Statistics of the United States: Continuation to 1962 and Revisions*, Washington, D.C., 1965.

1930 the proportion of Negroes living in the South had declined to less than 80 per cent. This figure was below 70 per cent in 1950, and by 1960 the South contained only 60 per cent of the total Negro population. The increasing momentum of the Negro exodus from the South is further revealed by the growing proportion of southern-born Negroes living in other parts of the country. In 1930 only 17 per cent of the Negro population born in the South was living in some other section of the country, but in 1960 nearly one-fourth (23 per cent) of all southern-born Negroes were living in other regions.[2]

(3) *The rural-urban trend.* A third major trend in the growth and development of the United States has been the shift in the distribution of the population from rural to urban areas. This urbanization trend is revealed in two basic ways: (a) by an increase in the number and size of urban places, and (b) by an increase in the number and proportion of the population living in urban places. According to the first federal census there were only twenty-four urban places in the United States in 1790, and they contained only 5 per cent of the population. Since that time there has been a continuous increase in the number of urban places and a continuous shift in the distribution of the population away from rural areas to the emerging cities (see Table VII-3 and Figure 6). Based on the current definition, roughly seven out of every ten Americans in 1960 lived in one of more than six thousand urban places.[3]

Another indication of pronounced urbanization is the changes in the *size* of urban places. In 1790 only five of the twenty-four urban places had populations of ten thousand or more, while none had as many as fifty thousand inhabitants. In 1960, however, there were approximately 1,900 places with ten thousand or more inhabitants, and there were 332 places whose population exceeded fifty thousand. In 1960 there were also five cities with over a million inhabitants.

The pervasive significance of the rural-to-urban migration trend is further revealed by the fact that it has cut across other major

Table VII-3: Urbanization trends in the United States, 1790–1960.

Year	Number of urban places	Per cent of population living in urban places	Number of urban places with population over:	
			10,000	50,000
1790	24	5.1	5	0
1800	33	6.1	6	1
1810	46	7.3	11	2
1820	61	7.2	13	3
1830	90	8.8	23	4
1840	131	10.8	37	5
1850	236	15.3	62	10
1860	392	19.8	93	16
1870	663	25.7	168	25
1880	939	28.2	223	35
1890	1,348	35.1	354	58
1900	1,737	39.7	440	78
1910	2,262	45.7	597	109
1920	2,722	51.2	752	144
1930	3,165	56.2	982	191
1940	3,464	56.5	1,077	199
1950	4,054	59.6	1,351	237
1960	4,996	63.1	1,899	333
New definition *				
1950	4,741	64.0	1,262	232
1960	6,015	69.9	1,891	332

SOURCE: Same as Table VII-1.
* See note 3 to Chapter 7.

distribution trends. The historical westward expansion, for example, had a pronounced rural-to-urban character. In 1860 the West contained roughly 2 per cent of the American population, of which only 6 per cent was urban (compared with 20 per cent for the total United States). One hundred years later, however, this region was more urban than the nation as a whole. At the time of the 1960 census only 16 per cent of the American people were

Figure 6: Urban and rural population: 1790–1960

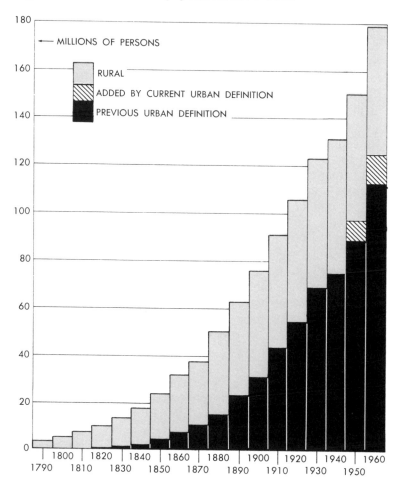

living in the West, but 78 per cent of the West's population was urban, compared with only 70 per cent for the total United States.

Like the east-to-west movement of the population as a whole, the Negro exodus from the South has also been largely rural-to-urban in character. In 1920, when the Negro migration was just beginning to gain momentum, only about a third of the Negroes in America were living in urban areas (compared with 51 per cent for the population as a whole). By 1960, however, Negroes were slightly more urbanized than the general population. At the time of the 1960 census the proportion living in urban areas was 70 per cent for the total population but as high as 73 per cent for the Negro population. The present pattern of differential distribution becomes even more striking when the South is considered apart from the remainder of the country. In 1960, 58 per cent of Negroes in the South were living in urban areas, but approximately 95 per cent of Negroes living outside the South were living in urban areas.

As will be seen more clearly in a later section, this rapid urbanization of the Negro population in recent years has had profound consequences for the socioeconomic composition of urban populations, and it represents the source of a wide range of social and economic problems prevailing in contemporary American society.

This urbanization trend is, of course, a natural accompaniment to the basic transformation of the United States from an agrarian-based economy to a highly industrialized one.[4] Although completely comparable statistics on industrial development are not available for all periods in American history, the general significance of this transformation is relatively easy to document. In 1820, for example, before the Industrial Revolution had made much headway in this country, slightly more than seven out of every ten gainful workers in the United States were employed in agricultural industries.[5] By 1870 this proportion was down to slightly more than half, and at the end of the nineteenth century only 37 per cent of the American work force was employed in agriculture. In 1940, the last year for which reasonably comparable data are available, agricultural industries accounted for only 17 per cent of the gainful workers in the United States.

When related statistics for more recent years are considered, the same general trend is apparent. To illustrate, the proportion of the economically active population represented by farmers and farm workers declined from 38 per cent in 1900 to only 12 per cent at mid-century. Conversely, the proportion represented by skilled and semi-skilled nonfarm manual workers increased from less than one-fourth in 1900 (23 per cent) to slightly more than one-third in 1950 (35 per cent). Clearly, the basic economic trend of the first two centuries of American history has been the transformation from an agrarian to an industrial society. The basic demographic trend has just as clearly been a redistribution of the population from declining rural farm areas to growing urban industrial areas.

(4) *The suburbanization trend.* The most recent migration trend to effect a basic change in the settlement pattern of the American people is "suburbanization." The term refers to the *expansion of the urban community* beyond its politically defined boundaries as a result of the movement of urbanites out of the larger cities into the surrounding suburban towns. This is a movement that began early in the twentieth century but did not gain much momentum until after the Second World War, when the automobile really came into its own as a major means of transportation. Although the "causes" of the growing suburban movement in the postwar period must be sought in such things as higher incomes, an urban housing shortage, and a desire to provide a more aesthetic environment in which to raise a family, these cannot detract from the key role played by the automobile in *facilitating* the movement. The widespread adoption of the automobile, accompanied by the construction of a vast, interconnected network of superhighways and expressways, has greatly

extended the horizons of the urban community. By permitting persons who work in cities to live at ever-increasing distances from their place of employment, the automobile has led to the emergence of a new type of community—a city-region or *metropolitan community*—in which the population is widely dispersed over a large area far beyond the boundaries of the central city.[6] This most recent trend has not meant an end to the long-term shift of the population away from rural areas, but it has modified significantly the pattern of population distribution within the built-up urban sections of the country. The nature of this shift is clearly revealed by the data in Table VII-4. In 1940, when 55 per cent of the American people were living in what the Bureau of the Census has called *standard metropolitan statistical areas* (SMSA's),[7] more

Table VII-4: Population of Standard Metropolitan Statistical Areas in the United States, 1940–1960.

SMSA Area	1940	1950	1960
SMSA total	72,834,468	89,316,903	112,885,178
In central cities	45,652,383	52,385,642	58,004,334
Outside central cities	27,182,085	36,931,261	54,880,844
Per cent of total population living in SMSA's	55.1	59.0	63.0
Per cent of SMSA population living in central cities	62.7	58.7	51.4

SOURCE: Same as Table VII-1.

than three out of every five metropolitan residents (63 per cent) were living in the large central cities. The persistence of the basic urbanization trend is revealed by the fact that the proportion of the population living in SMSA's has continued to increase. *But the significance of the suburban migration is equally apparent from the fact that the proportion of the SMSA population living in central cities has consistently declined.* By 1960, SMSA's contained 63 per cent of the total American population, but within these areas the proportion residing in the large central cities had fallen to only 51 per cent. These two somewhat opposing tendencies have continued, and by the middle of the 1960's, 64 per cent of the American people were living in SMSA's, but only 48 per cent of the metropolitan population was living in central cities.[8]

The nature and magnitude of the suburbanization trend is also revealed by the differential rates of increase within metropolitan areas. Between 1940 and 1950, for example, the total population residing in SMSA's increased by roughly one-fourth (23 per cent). Within these metropolitan areas, however, the central city population increased by only 15 per cent, compared with an increase of 36 per cent in the surrounding suburban area. During the most recent intercensal decade, the difference has been even more pronounced: between 1950 and 1960 the SMSA central-city population increased by only 11 per cent, compared with an increase of nearly 50 per cent in the size of the metropolitan population living outside central cities. In many instances this "flight to the suburbs" has been so great that central cities have experienced a decline in population size (between 1950 and 1960 population declines were recorded for 68 out of 256 central cities).[9]

One other point needs to be stressed: *suburbanization has been primarily a middle-class white phenomenon.* Between 1950 and 1960, 89 per cent of the increase in the white population of metropolitan areas occurred in the suburban ring. In sharp contrast, 84 per cent of the increase in the metropolitan nonwhite population took place in central cities.[10] The consequence of these differential patterns of growth has been to promote greater racial disparity between urban centers and their surrounding suburbs. Moreover, given the decidedly lower socioeconomic status of the nonwhite population as a whole (see Chapter 6), these trends have also widened the gap between city and suburb with regard to per capita wealth. In short, many cities in the United States today are on the verge of becoming centers of ethnic poverty: *slum cities.*[11] More than one expert has said that ". . . this growing difference in racial composition between the central cities and their rings, combined as it is with differences in education and housing, is one of the major social problems facing the United States." [12] This will become more evident in the following section.

PROBLEMS RELATED TO DISTRIBUTION TRENDS

In this section we shall identify the general *kinds* of problems associated with the spatial distribution of the American population. To be more specific, the following discussion will focus on those problems that are either caused or made worse by the long-term trend for people to move away from rural areas and become more and more concentrated in urban areas. The reason for restricting our inquiry is twofold. First, this particular trend represents the most fundamental and most pervasive change in the human settlement pattern of the nation. On the one hand, it is a reflection of basic changes in the economic organization of the society. On the other hand, as was clearly revealed in the preceding section, this urbanization trend cuts across all the other major shifts in population distribution.

The second reason for focusing on the problems of an urbanizing America is that other major shifts in population distribution (notably the east-to-west movement and the Negro exodus from the South) are not particularly troublesome for the well-being of the nation as a whole. On the contrary, these trends are more likely beneficial, for they result in a more even distribution of the population (both total and nonwhite) over the land area. Also, it may be noted that neither of these major distribution trends has been associated with significant changes in our way of life. By contrast, the population shifts that have accompanied the historical transformation from a rural-agrarian to an urban-industrial society have caused a substantial change in the American way of living. More important in the present context, these developments have created serious problems in the United States today; and these problems are daily becoming more acute as the urbanization process continues.

No attempt will be made here to discuss (or even mention) all of the problems of contemporary urban society. To do so would require an entire volume in itself. Rather, the aim is to delineate a few *general* problem areas relating to the changing pattern of human settlement in the United States today, and, within each of these broad areas, to single out a few representative problems of a more *specific* nature. To begin with, one can identify three broad problem areas relating to (1) the depopulation of rural areas; (2) the increasing concentration of population in urban areas; and (3) the recent shift of the urban population away from core cities to surrounding fringe areas. This last area can, in turn, be looked at from two points of view: (a) from the point of view of the core cities that are losing population, and (b) from the point of view of the rapidly growing suburbs. These broad problem areas will be discussed more fully in the following pages.

(1) *Problems of rural depopulation.* Historically, the movement of people from farms to cities has been regarded as a necessary accompaniment of America's continued economic growth and development. This is because this rural-to-urban migration stream has performed the dual function of (1) removing excess population from the land as agricultural technology improved, and (2) supplying the workers needed for expanding urban industries. Beyond these economic advantages, rural-to-urban migration has played a key role in promoting greater social and cultural homogeneity and greater harmony in American society. Today farmers read city newspapers and magazines, they patronize city businesses, go to city theatres, send their children to city schools, and so forth. More recently the suburbanization trend has further increased this contact between rural and urban peoples. In the words of one leading rural sociologist, this increasing interaction has been a major factor in "breaking down provincialism in both country and city and in lessening the importance of the barriers between city

and country which sometimes result in antagonism and conflict." [13] In this respect, then, the rural-to-urban migration interchange is one means of creating and promoting national unity.

The various advantages notwithstanding, there have always been some who had strong misgivings about the growing urban concentration and who especially lamented what they referred to as the "flight from the land." Such persons have generally argued that small, relatively homogeneous rural areas produce all that is good in human society (strong family ties, high moral character, firm religious convictions, industrious work habits, integrity, thrift, and so on). These critics argue that the influence of such basic values declines in the large, heterogeneous population groups of the cities; hence they would cite cityward migration as a major factor behind what they see as the moral decay of mid-twentieth-century America.

Although there are many good reasons for challenging the contention that rural areas produce only "good things" and that the growth of cities is responsible for all that is "bad" in human social life, it is a fact that the growing concentration of the population in urban areas does create certain problems. It is equally true, however, that this urbanization trend creates many problems for the rural areas from which cityward migrants are drawn.

Problems that urbanization has created for rural areas relate to changes in both the *size* and *composition* of the rural population. On the quantitative side is the simple fact that cityward migration has reduced the absolute size of the rural population to a point where many areas are no longer able to support such basic community facilities and services as hospitals, police and fire departments, shopping centers and specialty stores, public transportation systems, schools, doctors, and dentists. In other words, rural depopulation has been accompanied by a subsequent loss of those community services that many city dwellers take for granted but that cannot exist unless there is a relatively large population base to support them. The ultimate consequence of all this has been a serious deterioration in the quality of rural life in many parts of America.

The general problems relating to population loss have frequently been intensified by the selective nature of the rural-to-urban migration stream. Although there are exceptions, this stream has tended to be most selective of young people. Cities have benefited in that urban industries have been provided with a steady influx of new recruits for the work force, but rural areas have lost the most productive segment of the population. Many rural areas have found themselves populated by a disproportionately large number of older persons—those most likely to need many of the health and welfare services that can no longer be supported by their smaller populations. The seriousness of this problem for rural areas becomes more apparent when we realize the rural community bears the cost of rearing and educating these young people only to lose out on the benefits of their productive labors. There is also a potential economic loss to rural areas in that children who move to the cities not only take away whatever benefits might be gained by their labors, but by being heirs to land they do not cultivate (as well as other personal property) they exert a further influence on draining off rural wealth. Clearly, the benefits to society from the rural-to-urban population shift have not been derived without a price. As the following paragraphs reveal, not the least of this price has been (and is being) paid by the cities.

(2) *Problems of urban concentration.* Urbanization is hardly at the root of all that is bad in human society. Historically, cities have been centers of individual freedom. In small groups where everyone knows what everyone else is doing, the individual faces strong pressures to conform to group standards of behavior or get out. Where large numbers of people are concentrated in one place, however, there is a certain amount of anonymity which gives the individual greater latitude to deviate from a single set pattern of behavior. By giving the individual greater freedom to express himself and his ideas, the city has traditionally been the center of

artistic creation and cultural innovation. Cities have also been places where people from widely different backgrounds have come to live together, and out of the mingling and interstimulation of diverse attitudes, beliefs, and knowledge has come cultural progress and civilized growth. Finally, the city has played a significant role in the economic development of modern human society. Cities grew up as advances in agriculture displaced large segments of the population from the land, and the existence of such large concentrations of people (labor) greatly facilitated industrial growth and development.

But not all aspects of city growth have been positive. Just as cities have long been centers of individual and intellectual freedom and creativity, they have also been (and still are) the locus of the major social problems found in contemporary American society. Poverty, crowded living conditions, traffic congestion and noise, ethnic ghettos and *de facto* school segregation, air and water pollution, crime and vice, filth and disease, and so forth, are the unfortunate characteristics of urban society today.

As indicated earlier, it will not be possible to enumerate here all the problems facing American cities today. Rather, the best one can do is cite a few of the more significant ones attracting the most attention and concern today.

In Chapter 2 we noted that one of the major health problems in the United States today relates to the increase in mortality from chronic respiratory diseases. One reason for this may lie in the increasing *contamination of the air* we breathe. As noted, one of the city's economic advantages was that its available labor supply greatly facilitated industrial growth and development. Thus, areas of population concentration today are usually areas of industrial concentration wherein the atmosphere is daily clouded by smoke pouring from the chimneys of hundreds of factories. Large concentrations of population also mean more houses with chimneys adding their fuel to the problem; and as population increases there is a correspondingly greater need for more public incinerators to dispose of the increasing amount of waste material.

Then there is the automobile. In addition to the *traffic problem* it has created in most cities during the postwar years, the automobile has contributed substantially to the growing amount of impurities in the air. The problem had become so bad by the mid-1960's that the question of federal legislation to control automobile exhaust fumes arose, and some municipalities even began to consider banning automobiles within city limits at some point in the not too distant future. Whether or not these measures will ever be adopted remains to be seen. In the meantime, however, it is patently clear that something must be done to put an end to the steadily increasing pollution of the air we breathe.

The rapid population and industrial growth of the United States during the twentieth century has also had serious consequences for the quantity and quality of the *water* supply. On the one hand, the factory that pollutes the air often pollutes the water as well, and it has been said of Americans today that the world's cleanest people "bathe in scented fats and drink a factory's slime." [14] On the other hand, increasing population concentration means an increase in the amount of waste created every day, and many municipal sewers are today dumping waste into rivers and streams at rates far in excess of what is considered optimal to maintain pure water. The problem of increasing population concentration is further intensified by modern technology which gives today's housewife a wide variety of labor-saving devices—such as washing machines, garbage disposals, and dishwashers—that not only increase the demand for water but also contribute toward its pollution. In some areas the situation is so acute that if pollution is not more effectively controlled, existing treatment and purification facilities will soon be incapable of producing palatable water.

A particularly serious problem facing urban Americans today relates to *housing*. There are two aspects to this housing problem: a shortage of housing in general, and the deplorable condition of much of the housing available. On the one hand, the population of many of the larger cities (especially the low-income segment of the population) is increasing at a greater rate than the supply of housing. One result of this has been increasing subdivision by slum landlords to accommodate an ever-increasing number of people, and in many cities (especially in the older established cities of the Northeast) once fashionable single-family housing units have been cut up into apartments to house several families. According to the Bureau of the Census, roughly 10 per cent of all urban housing units were overcrowded in 1960 (i.e., contained one or more persons per room). This situation was substantially worse for ethnic minorities and other low-income groups. To illustrate, roughly one-fourth of all nonwhite urban housing units were overcrowded according to this definition in 1960.[15] To indicate the extent to which this overcrowding can go, the United States Civil Rights Commission has established that if all Americans lived under the density conditions found in the most heavily populated block of Harlem, the entire population could be fitted into three New York boroughs.

Not only do many urban areas face a housing shortage, but a good deal of what is available is in bad physical shape. The 1960 census, for example, revealed that roughly 15 per cent of all urban housing units could be characterized as either deteriorating or dilapidated. Once again the problem was most acute for the economically and socially disadvantaged groups such as the nonwhite. In this instance, nearly 40 per cent of nonwhite urban housing units were found to be deteriorating or dilapidated in 1960. On the basis of these data, it is clear that the solution to the housing problem in many urban areas will mean both an increase in the supply of housing units and substantial improvements in much of the housing currently available—especially what is available to the lower socioeconomic segments of the population.

According to some critics of modern urban society, the trend for more and more Americans to live in "asphalt jungles" has been accompanied by an increase in the rule of "jungle law." Certainly there has been a marked increase in the more obvious forms of *deviant behavior* in recent years. The Uniform Crime Reports of the Federal Bureau of Investigation reveal that the number of serious crimes committed each year in the United States nearly doubled between 1950 and 1960 (this compares with a total population gain of only about 20 per cent).

This increase in the incidence of deviant behavior (which is not limited to criminality but includes all forms of socially disapproved conduct) [16] is primarily an urban phenomenon. In part this is because most American people live in urban areas. For the most part, however, it reflects basic changes in the socioeconomic composition of the urban population. As indicated earlier, the selective character of recent (and current) migration streams means that cities are more and more becoming centers of economic poverty and sociocultural deprivation; and such an environment creates a greater propensity for criminal behavior and other forms of deviance such as desertion, drug addiction, and prostitution.

Many urban problems relate to the *provision of basic services,* such as adequate police and fire protection, schools, hospital facilities, garbage removal, street repairs, all manner of welfare services, and efficient governmental administration—all of which become more difficult to provide (and more costly) as population increases. These problems become especially acute where population growth does not contribute much in the way of additional wealth to the local community (as when the greatest growth characterizes the lower socioeconomic groups).

The crowding together of hundreds and thousands of individuals also results in a progressive *loss of open space.* The growing pressure of numbers on scarce land resources greatly enhances the value of whatever unused land may be available, and this makes it unlikely that sufficient land will be set aside for parks and recreational areas required to meet the needs of the growing population. Parks may be pretty and all that, but they are not very economical when one considers the potential income from rental or tax revenues if the land were opened to residential or commercial development. And parks do not help much when it comes to solving such problems as inadequate parking facilities in the downtown section of most American cities.

There are a myriad of other problems that could be cited as being caused by (or at least intensified by) the long-time population shift from scattered rural villages to compact, densely settled urban agglomerations. The tragic fact of the matter is that the present pattern of population redistribution is such that many of the larger cities in the United States are in danger of becoming massive ethnic slums in which disease, crime, and vice run wild. That the American public is becoming aware of these dangers is clearly illustrated by the increasing number of urban renewal programs, and by growing federal legislation that tries to deal with some of these problems. In addition to the establishment of the Department of Housing and Urban Development and the more recent (October 1966) Department of Transportation to deal with urban problems in general, recent years have seen a number of pieces of legislation relating to specific problems. One of the most significant of these is the 1966 Demonstration Cities and Metropolitan Development Act, which declared the need to improve the quality of urban life to be the most critical domestic problem, and which seeks to provide more federal assistance to those cities which lack adequate resources. Although such programs are positive steps in the right direction, there is still a long way to go before the many problems relating to urban concentration are solved.

(3) *Problems of metropolitan expansion.* One might logically expect that widespread suburbanization in the United States during the postwar period would offset many of the problems associated with (a) rural depopulation and (b) urban concentration. This has definitely not been the case, however. On the one hand, this most recent distribution trend in many respects represents an expansion of the urban area. This metropolitan expansion, or *urban sprawl* as it is sometimes called, results merely in the transfer of many city problems to the country (not to mention the crea-

tion of a few new problems). On the other hand, the nature of the suburbanization process is such that it does not really alleviate concentration. Rather, it merely alters the ethnic and socioeconomic composition of the central city population and gives rise to what have been referred to as *slum cities*. There are thus two sides to this problem of metropolitan expansion: (a) the socioeconomic decline of the urban centers, and (b) the mushrooming suburbs. In the following sections attention will be given to a broader discussion of the emerging "slum city problem," as well as some of the major issues confronting American society today in both the core city *and* suburban rings of our burgeoning metropolitan areas.

As indicated earlier, one of the most serious problems facing the United States today is the *economic decline of the large urban center* that has been triggered by the "flight to the suburbs" of the higher socioeconomic status groups. As a result, many cities have lost a large source of tax revenue at the same time that the cost of providing essential services (schools, roads, hospitals, and so forth) has increased. This problem is especially serious because the suburban residents continue to use many of the facilities of the city (such as roads and hospitals) even though they no longer contribute directly to their support. This *financial crisis* has been aptly described by one contemporary journalist in the following words: "The exodus to suburbs not only increases demands on the city for the provision of streets, schools, sewer and water systems, and other public amenities, but it also compounds needs in less desirable areas the affluent leave behind. The low-income families with large broods that so often take their place, many of them migrants from another part of the country or the world and therefore new to the community, magnify the load on police, education, and welfare authorities. Their neglect of property and the dangers they often introduce to recreational and other public areas spread the blight that causes remaining residents who can afford to do so to move elsewhere. Thus, at the very time its tax opportunities are shrinking, the central city's needs are rising the fast-est." [17] This problem is further aggravated by the fact that the wealthier people who leave the city to become residents (and tax-payers) in the surrounding suburban communities continue to work in the cities where they "require more roads for their com-ing and going, more downtown real estate for their parking, and the continued provision of many other city services, from police and fire protection for themselves and their business properties to libraries and other cultural amenities." [18]

The "flight to the suburbs" of the wealthier segments of the urban population also promotes economic decline by leading to a *decline in retail sales.* In many metropolitan centers the down-town retail stores find their customers located farther away from them as the higher socioeconomic groups migrate to the suburbs while the lower status groups remain in the central city. Moreover, the problem is intensified by the fact that the population shift has been accompanied by the "suburbanization" of many retail trade and service establishments which now compete with the down-town stores. The economic impact of this latter development is clearly revealed by recent trends in sales volume. According to one estimate, the volume of sales per square foot of selling space in downtown central business districts declined by slightly more than 50 per cent between the end of World War II and the most recent census.[19]

The decline in retail sales in the central business district is also accompanied by a *loss of jobs* in the downtown area. This of course intensifies the problem of finding employment for those who remain in or move into the city. The fact that many urban migrants do experience serious problems in this respect is clearly revealed by the abnormally high level of unemployment among urban ethnic minority groups; and this in turn increases the wel-fare burden of cities—the burden generally increasing fastest where economic decline is most pronounced.

The nature of the postwar suburban trend has created a number of problems that threaten to lower the *quality of public education* in the United States. This threat is prevalent in both the mushrooming suburbs as well as in the declining cities; but it is most serious in the deteriorating areas of the central city where increasing demands for educational facilities and services have been accompanied by decreasing means to meet the demands. As one recent commentator has noted, in the emerging slum city today a wide variety of welfare functions are "thrust upon school systems to meet the needs of underprivileged youngsters who must be fed before they can be taught and assured before they can be interested, of teen-agers who lack the diligence or wherewithal to acquire the learning so vital for secure employment in an increasingly automated economy, and of adults who do not themselves understand the uses of education, much less desire its assiduous acquisition by their youngsters." [20]

Bigger financial burdens and proportionately smaller budgets in the city hurt the quality of education not only by making it more difficult to build needed new schools and replace worn out equipment; the city schools are also at a distinct disadvantage in competition for teachers, and the result is a severe shortage of high-caliber staff in many urban school systems. In this environment (old, run-down school buildings and mediocre, uninspiring teachers) it is not really surprising to find a growing lack of interest in academic pursuits. The urban youngster is tempted to become one of the new breed of misfits in contemporary American society: *the high school dropout.* This problem is becoming increasingly urgent as our society becomes technologically more complex every day, thus reducing even further the employment opportunities available to persons with little formal education and few occupational skills. This is not just an economic problem for the individual. It is also a problem for the society as a whole, which must assume a large share of the responsibility for support in the form of unemployment and other welfare payments. In addition, it represents a serious sociocultural problem in the sense that overcrowded, understaffed urban schools are "more likely to serve as a pressure cooker for differences, resentments, rivalries, and intolerance than as an instrument capable of the greatest achievement in education, the sowing of respect for others, regardless of creed or color." [21] The individual is not given adequate opportunity for full self-development; he is not prepared to participate intelligently in the political life of the community; he is less likely to develop any sense of national loyalty; and he is more likely to become a public charge—either as a criminal case or a welfare client.

Although they are definitely more serious in the declining urban areas, problems relating to the quality of education in the United States today are not restricted to the core city. For one thing, the advantages that newly constructed, brightly lit, uncrowded, well-staffed suburban schls had to offer a few years ago are becoming scarcer and scarcer under the steady pressure of suburban population growth. As more and more people have moved to the suburbs it has meant, in many cases, a transplanting of many of the city ills which they sought to escape. With regard to schools, this has often led to double sessions and strained budgets to keep up with the increasing needs of a rapidly increasing population.

Suburban schools have frequently harmed the educational process inadvertently by virtue of the socioeconomic and ethnic homogeneity of the population. The nature of this problem is best expressed as follows: "By nurturing into being communities which are more homogeneous socially, economically, and racially than cities historically were before them, sprawl is exerting a settling out effect on urban development which substitutes a 'separator' action for the 'melting pot' role cities once served. 'Mixed' schools thus become less and less common, and, unless many of the greatest educators of the past are wrong, living laboratories in democracy cease to be." [22]

The invention and continued development of the automobile lessened people's dependence on earlier forms of public transportation and made it possible for people to live almost anywhere they wished. This possibility was enhanced as more and more highways were constructed, and the general star-shape patterns that cities had tended to assume became more circular as people filled in the areas between the mass transit routes. In this sense, the automobile is the mechanism through which urban sprawl has been achieved, and many of the problems relating to declining cities and expanding suburbs can ultimately be traced to the automobile. For this reason alone, any discussion of the problems arising from the shifting distribution of the American population would be incomplete without some reference to the automobile. Another reason, however, is even more relevant today: this "horseless carriage," once hailed as a major technological development in man's struggle to conquer the limiting influence of spatial distance, is today recognized as a major cause of the growing transportation crisis.

There are many aspects to the current crisis in transportation, not the least of which is the *decline in public transportation systems.* One consequence of the urban sprawl has been to spread out population to such an extent that suburban densities are too low to support rail transit systems; and more than one railroad in the United States has recently been forced (or is in imminent danger of being forced) into bankruptcy. The effect of the automobile is especially insidious in this respect, for it leads to the creation and intensification of still another problem—the problem of *traffic congestion.* The increasing use of private means of transportation puts a greater financial strain on public transport systems and forces them either to close down completely or else raise prices or reduce services (or both) in order to stay in business. In either case, one result is a greater reliance on the automobile, as suburban housewives who do not want to pay higher fares, or who are unable to get a train at the time they want one, end up purchasing a second car to add to the confusion. The process is circular: increasing reliance on automobiles leads to a decline in the availability of public transportation, and this in turn increases the need to rely on the automobile. One major end product of this circular process is an ever-larger traffic jam.

The seriousness of the traffic problem becomes most visible when it leads to an increase in the amount of time it takes to get from one place to another. In many cities today it takes longer to go a given distance by automobile than it used to take on horseback! The contrast becomes even more striking in this age of supersonic travel when we anticipate being able to fly from New York to Los Angeles in less than two hours—or in less time than it takes to drive to and from the airports.

There are many other aspects to the problem created by the increasing reliance on automobile transportation. Among them are increasing costs to the consumer in the form of higher taxes to finance highway construction and improvement, automobile maintenance and repair bills, collision and liability insurance, and so forth. Expanded highways also require greater expenditures for upkeep, traffic regulation, and law enforcement. Downtown central business districts are well aware of the role of the automobile in bringing about the decline in urban retail sales; the transformation of parks and other open spaces into huge concrete parking lots (not only in the cities but also in suburban shopping plazas) is certainly not desirable from an aesthetic point of view; and increasing motor vehicle accident fatalities cannot be regarded as anything but a tragic waste of human life. Then, too, there are more subtle consequences, such as the wear and tear on the nerves of those people who fight the daily traffic jams—not to mention the unknown damage that may be caused by the continuous inhaling of automobile exhaust fumes. Such considerations provide ample justification for suggesting that the so-called benefits man has derived from the development of motor transport are, at best, of dubious value.

It was noted earlier (see Chapter 5) that one of the more serious qualitative problems created by continuous population growth is the decline in the amount of *open space* and an ever-increasing pressure on the limited number of parks, picnic areas, camping grounds, beaches, and other recreational facilities. Nowhere is this problem of open spaces more acute than in the expanding metropolitan areas of the nation. There is certainly no lack of space in the United States as a whole, but there is a severe shortage of unused land in urban areas. More significant in the context of this chapter is the fact that the process of suburbanization—by gobbling up the surrounding countryside for highways, residential housing, shopping plazas—is making the situation worse every day. As noted earlier, the once traditional Sunday afternoon drive in the country is no longer possible for a very large segment of the American population. As the urban population continues to expand outward, open spaces for recreation will become fewer and farther removed than they are now, and will consequently become even less accessible to an increasing majority of the people.

Today's metropolitan area consists of a large central city surrounded by several dozen smaller suburban communities, most of which are independent political entities with their own laws and their own governing bodies. That is, the contemporary metropolitan community with its many common needs and problems does not have a common governmental unit to coordinate efforts, to provide essential services, and to find solutions to major social and economic ills. Instead, one too often finds wasteful duplication of local services (such as hospitals, fire protection, snow removal, and school bus transportation) and widespread conflict and confusion of efforts at solving the problems of the wider community. How can the problem of water pollution be lessened, for example, if half the towns in an area build sewage treatment plants while the other half continue to dump refuse and raw sewage into local waterways? Nor will air pollution be eliminated if only a few communities adopt remedial legislation; and no workable solution will be found for the traffic problem without the full cooperation of *all* local municipalities. No matter what the problem, an effective solution is not likely to emerge from the uncoordinated efforts of a score of independent political units.

Sad though it may be to some, the fact is that our traditional system of independent local governments is tragically out of date. What our forefathers saw as a "good thing" in the late eighteenth and early nineteenth century, today represents one of the major obstacles to the solution of many of the problems confronting the American people. It is patently clear that a change is needed. "The metropolis of today, let alone tomorrow, can no more tackle its area-wide problems on the governmental crutches of another age than it can wage war on organized crime with mounted police or fight a blaze with water buckets." [23]

(4) *The challenge of the future.* The United States began as a rural-agrarian society. It was a well-established urban-industrial society when it entered the twentieth century. Since the end of the Second World War it has rapidly become a metropolitan society dominated not by mere cities but by huge metropolitan complexes. It is becoming more and more difficult to see where the city ends and the suburb begins. Population is still growing fairly rapidly in the United States today, and by far the greatest part of this growth is occurring in the expanding metropolitan agglomerations. The nation is already at a point in its historical development when the majority of the people are born, live, work, and die in these great complexes. This majority will become larger every year, intensifying the problems of traffic congestion, air pollution, urban blight, inadequate housing, dwindling supplies of polluted water, overburdened schools, decaying transportation systems and other public services, higher rates of juvenile delinquency, mental illness, alcoholism, prostitution, divorce, illegitimacy, drug addiction, and all the other social ills that are encouraged if not caused by increasing congestion.

The adoption of significant federal legislative programs in the 1960's (the poverty program, the urban mass transportation act, the demonstration cities bill) is clear evidence of a growing awareness at the national level of the serious problems facing metropolitan America today. But national awareness is not enough. What is needed more is local awareness of the current "crisis of our cities." Still more important, there must be significant changes on the grass roots level in some of our most cherished institutions and values. There is now a serious cultural lag between the structure of the community in which most Americans live and the institutional mechanisms that have evolved to govern that community. Not the least of the needed changes relates to the traditional view that public planning is somehow undemocratic. Another concerns the outmoded political structure of loosely integrated, semi-autonomous municipalities.

The need for sound planning should be obvious—if for no other reason than that the sorry state of many of our cities shows what happens in the absence of planning. Moreover, because the well-meaning efforts of several municipalities acting independently of one another tend more to confound than to help, it is equally obvious that effective public planning must be coordinated within the metropolitan community. Unless there is much more careful and more unified planning than there has been in recent decades, the outlook for the future is far from encouraging. Just as the present is of our own creation, the future will be what we make of it. The challenge is clear. The crucial question is, will the American people rise to meet it?

REFERENCES AND SUGGESTIONS FOR FURTHER READING

Donald J. Bogue, *The Population of the United States,* Glencoe, Ill., 1959, Chapters 2–5 and 15.
Donald J. Bogue, "Population Growth in the United States," in Philip M. Hauser, ed., *The Population Dilemma,* Englewood Cliffs, 1963, pp. 70–93.
William M. Dobriner, *The Suburban Community,* New York, 1958.
Mitchell Gordon, *Sick Cities,* Baltimore, 1965.
Leo F. Schnore, *The Urban Scene,* New York, 1965.
Conrad and Irene B. Taeuber, *The Changing Population of the United States,* New York, 1958, Chapters 1, 5–7, and 15.

Ralph Thomlinson, *Population Dynamics,* New York, 1965, Chapters 11, 13, and 22.

Warren S. Thompson and David T. Lewis, *Population Problems,* New York, 1965, Chapters 6 and 18.

U.S. Bureau of the Census, *United States Census of Population: 1960,* Final Reports PC(2)-2A, *State of Birth,* Washington, D.C., 1963; PC(2)-2C, *Mobility for Metropolitan Areas,* Washington, D.C., 1963; PC(2)-6B, *Journey to Work,* Washington, D.C., 1963; and PC(3)-1D, *Standard Metropolitan Statistical Areas,* Washington, D.C., 1963.

8

Conclusions

The years since the end of the Second World War have witnessed an increasing concern over world population problems. For the most part (and with some justification) this concern has focused on problems in the so-called economically underdeveloped nations in Asia, Africa, and Latin America. Relatively little attention, however, has been given to population problems—either real or potential—in more highly developed nations such as the United States. Although there have been some efforts to remind the peoples of the developed nations that they are not immune to population problems, they have been so few and far between that their deficit is a serious gap in the overall body of demographic literature.

As we pointed out in the introduction, the primary aim of this book has been to describe the major demographic developments (past and present) in the United States, and to indicate briefly the various kinds of problems the society must face as a consequence of these developments. This has not been a definitive discussion of *the* population problems facing the United States today.

There are so many dimensions to the demographic variable, and so many different problems associated with each dimension, that it would not be possible to do justice to the topic in the pages of a single volume. And population—like many other aspects of human society—is in a constant state of change; and as a population changes, the nature and magnitude of its population problems change.

Bearing these limitations in mind, this book has utilized the framework of demography as a convenient means of identifying six broad population problem areas—three relating to the basic processes through which population change is effected (mortality, fertility, and migration), and three relating to the major demographic variables of population size, population composition, and population distribution. In each case the plan has been first to describe the major trends in the United States and the underlying determinants or "causes" of these trends; and second to identify a few of the more important problems that have arisen as a consequence of the various population trends and changes. The aim has not been to make the reader an expert in matters of population. But hopefully he may now have a better understanding and appreciation of the intimate interrelationship between population change and social change. Perhaps this awareness will make the reader better prepared to comprehend the society in which he lives and better able to cope more efficiently with its problems.

Although none of the more serious population problems has been neglected in this book, space limitations have made it difficult to discuss any one of them in great detail. For example, we noted the existence of marked differences in family income as representing a major problem in the United States today, but we did not investigate the chronic causes of low income or the many other problems that confront those who live in severe poverty in the midst of an otherwise affluent society. Some problems have been barely mentioned in passing (the casual references to higher rates of all forms of deviant social behavior in urban slums), and others have been scarcely mentioned at all (the problem of *underpopulation,* for example—not enough people to permit the optimal development of available resources). Those readers who wish to pursue particular topics in greater depth may consult the suggested references at the end of each chapter.

There has been a growing realization of the many problematic aspects of population growth and change in the United States in recent years. More significantly, this awareness has been accompanied by more remedial programs (federal, state, and local) aimed at solutions to particular problems. The outlook is encouraging, but it is still only a beginning. Many more Americans must become aware of the many subtle (and some not so subtle) ways in which various demographic trends and differences are intimately related to so many of the major social issues of the day.

Notes

CHAPTER 1: INTRODUCTION

1. Kingsley Davis, *Human Society,* New York, 1948, p. 552.

CHAPTER 2: MORTALITY

1. United Nations, Food and Agricultural Organization, *Second World Food Survey,* Rome, November 1952.
2. United Nations, *Determinants and Consequences of Population Trends* (ST/SOA/Series A/17), New York, 1953, p. 53.
3. U.S. National Center for Health Statistics, Vital and Health Statistics, Series 3, No. 4, *Infant and Perinatal Mortality in the United States,* Washington, D.C., 1965, p. 56.
4. Francis C. Madigan, "Are Sex Mortality Differentials Biologically Caused?", *Milbank Memorial Fund Quarterly* (April 1957).
5. Philip E. Enterline, "Causes of Death Responsible for Recent Increases in Sex Mortality Differentials in the United States," *Milbank Memorial Fund Quarterly* (April 1961).
6. Lillian Guralnick, "Mortality by Occupation and Industry Among Men 20 to 64 Years of Age: United States, 1950," *Vital Statistics—Special Reports,* Washington, D.C., September 1962.

7. For a discussion of the role of the socioeconomic variable in the major mortality study carried out in connection with the 1960 census of population, see Philip M. Hauser and Evelyn M. Kitagawa, "Social and Economic Mortality Differentials in the United States, 1960: Outline of a Research Project," in *Proceedings of the Social Statistics Section: 1960,* Washington, D.C., 1960.

8. U.S. National Center for Health Statistics, Vital and Health Statistics, Series 3, No. 1, *The Change in Mortality Trends in the United States,* Washington, D.C., 1964, p. 1.

9. U.S. National Center for Health Statistics, Vital and Health Statistics, Series 10, No. 24, *Disability Days: United States, July 1963–June 1964,* Washington, D.C., 1965.

CHAPTER 3: FERTILITY

1. Kingsley Davis, "Institutional Patterns Favoring High Fertility in Under-developed Areas," *Eugenics Quarterly* (March 1955).

2. United Nations, *Population and Vital Statistics Report, Statistical Papers,* Series A: XVII:4, New York, 1966.

3. Warren S. Thompson and David T. Lewis, *Population Problems,* New York, 1965, p. 319.

4. Norman E. Himes, *Medical History of Contraception,* Baltimore, 1936.

5. The Reverend John A. O'Brien. Quoted from an article by Father O'Brien in *Look,* October 10, 1961.

6. Recent debates within the Catholic Church indicate a growing desire for a more liberal stand on this issue. This trend has been occasioned in part by the concern over poverty—national as well as international —and in part by the widening gap between official Catholic dogma and the actual behavior of an increasing number of Catholics. Whether or not the Church's official position will become modified, however, is open to speculation. In the meantime there is no lack of argument by leading Catholic laymen concerning the need for such modification. See, for example, John Rock, *The Time Has Come,* New York, 1963.

7. U.S. Bureau of the Census, *Historical Statistics of the United States: Colonial Times to 1957,* Washington, D.C., 1960.

8. Christopher Tietze and Hans Lehfeldt, "Legal Abortion in Eastern Europe," *Journal of the American Medical Association* (April 1961). Data in this article indicate that in 1959 there were approximately 151,000 live births in Hungary, compared with 187,000 abortions— of which 152,000 were legal.

9. U.S. National Center for Health Statistics, "The Aftermath of the Baby Boom," *Monthly Vital Statistics Reports* (July 1965).

10. Ronald Freedman, Pascal K. Whelpton, and Arthur A. Campbell, *Family Planning, Sterility and Population Growth*, New York, 1959.

11. Statistics on white and nonwhite fertility trends from 1909 to 1963 may be found in Anders S. Lunde, "White-Nonwhite Fertility Differentials in the United States," *Health, Education and Welfare Indicators* (September 1965).

12. Arthur A. Campbell, "White-Nonwhite Differences in Family Planning in the United States," *Health, Education and Welfare Indicators* (February 1966). Per cents refer to women fifty to fifty-four years of age in 1960, or those who had most recently completed their reproductive cycle. This article is a major reference for my discussion of the color fertility differential.

13. Pascal K. Whelpton, Arthur A. Campbell, and John E. Patterson, *Fertility and Family Planning in the United States*, Princeton, 1966, p. 356.

14. Charles F. Westoff, Robert G. Potter, Philip C. Sagi, and Elliot G. Mishler, *Family Growth in Metropolitan America*, Princeton, 1961.

15. Although *occupation* of the family head is a major component of that family's socioeconomic status, it has not been considered here. This is because (1) a person's occupation is in part determined by the amount of education he has; and (2) a person's income closely reflects his occupation status. For those who may be interested in the occupation variable, however, the average number of children ever born to women age fifty and over, classified according to husband's occupation in 1960, exhibited the expected differential: 1.9 for women whose husband had a white-collar occupation; 2.6 for women whose husband had a blue-collar occupation; and 3.5 for women whose husband had a farm occupation.

16. See the source cited for Table III-6.

17. Whelpton, Campbell, and Patterson, *Fertility and Family Planning in the United States*.

CHAPTER 4: MIGRATION AND MOBILITY

1. A good part of the increase in the median age, it must be noted, is due to the decline in the birth rate during this century. But this does not alter the fact that migrants are generally younger than the overall average. To illustrate, in 1900 roughly one-third of all foreign-born persons (i.e., immigrants) were between the ages of twenty and thirty-

four years, compared with only one-fourth for the population as a whole.

2. William Petersen, "A General Typology of Migration," *American Sociological Review* (June 1958).

3. Conrad and Irene B. Taeuber, *The Changing Population of the United States,* New York, 1958, p. 52.

4. Richard Ferree Smith, "Refugees," *Annals of the American Academy of Political and Social Science* (September 1966).

5. For a more complete discussion of this subject, see John Harmon Burma, "Some Cultural Aspects of Immigration: Its Impact, Especially on Our Arts and Sciences," *Law and Contemporary Problems* (Spring 1956). This article is a major reference for my discussion of the sociocultural contributions of immigrants.

6. U.S. Bureau of the Census, "Mobility of the Population of the United States: March 1964 to March 1965," *Current Population Reports,* P-20:150, Washington, D.C., 1966.

7. U.S. Bureau of the Census, "'Postwar Migration and Its Causes in the United States: August 1945 to October 1946," *Current Population Reports,* P-20:4, Washington, D.C., 1947. For the results of a more recent survey on the reasons for moving, see U.S. Bureau of the Census, "Reasons for Moving: March 1962 to March 1963," *Current Population Reports,* P-20:154, Washington, D.C., 1966.

8. U.S. Bureau of the Census, *United States Census of Population: 1960,* Final Report PC(2)-2B, *Mobility for States and State Economic Areas,* Washington, D.C., 1963. See Table 7 of this report.

9. U.S. Bureau of the Census, "Mobility of the Population of the United States: March 1965 to March 1966," *Current Population Reports,* P-20:156, Washington, D.C., 1966.

10. For the major pioneer study of this relationship in the United States, see Benjamin Malzberg and Everett S. Lee, *Migration and Mental Disease,* New York, 1956. More recent studies which confirm the greater incidence of mental disorders among migrants are Judith Lazarus, Ben Z. Locke, and Dorothy S. Thomas, "Migration Differentials in Mental Disease," *Milbank Memorial Fund Quarterly* (January 1963); and Everett S. Lee, "Socio-Economic and Migration Differentials in Mental Disease: New York State, 1949–1951," *ibid.,* (July 1963).

11. Lazarus, Locke, and Thomas, "Migration Differentials in Mental Disease."

CHAPTER 5: POPULATION SIZE AND GROWTH

1. Kingsley Davis, "The World Demographic Transition," *Annals of the American Academy of Political and Social Science* (January 1945).
2. In discussing such small percentages, one is apt to get the impression that these changes in the annual growth rates are not very significant. This impression may be quickly dispelled if one realizes that it takes 139 years for a population to double its size at an annual increase rate of 0.5 per cent, but only half as long—seventy years—at an increase rate of 1.0 per cent. With an annual growth rate of 2.0 per cent (a rate which the world seems to be approaching), it will take only thirty-five years for the population to double in size. At this rate, the year 2000 could see close to 7 billion people living on the earth.
3. As of 1965 the most populous nation in the world was Red China, with a population of approximately 710 million. India, with a population of 482 million, ranked second, and the Soviet Union, with 234 million inhabitants, was third. Two other nations had populations in excess of 100 million in 1965—Pakistan (115 million) and Indonesia (105 million). See Population Reference Bureau, "World Population Data Sheet," Washington, D.C., December 1965.
4. This section is based in part on an earlier article by the author: Edward G. Stockwell, "The Relationship Between Population Growth and Economic Development," *American Sociological Review* (April 1962).
5. A. J. Jaffe, "Population Trends and Controls in Underdeveloped Countries," *Law and Contemporary Problems* (Summer 1960), pp. 529–530.
6. T. Robert Malthus, *An Essay on Population,* New York, 1952.
7. United Nations, *Demographic Yearbook: 1964,* and *Population and Food Supply,* New York, 1962. The latter report is a major reference for this section on the world food crisis.
8. *Ibid.* (1962), p. 43.
9. Frederick Osborn, *Population: An International Dilemma,* New York, 1958, p. 75.
10. These statistics (as well as those in the two following paragraphs) were compiled from the 1962 edition of the *Statistical Abstract of the United States,* Washington, D.C., 1962. See especially Tables 712, 925, 996, and 999.
11. Lincoln H. and Alice T. Day, *Too Many Americans,* Boston, 1964, pp. 45–46.

12. Quoted from *Wall Street Journal,* June 24, 1966.
13. For a more detailed discussion of this problem, see Kingsley Davis, "Population and Power in the Free World," in Philip M. Hauser, ed., *Population and World Politics,* Glencoe, Ill., 1958.
14. Arthur S. Miller, "Some Observations on the Political Economy of Population Growth," *Law and Contemporary Problems* (Summer 1960), p. 614.
15. Day and Day, *Too Many Americans,* p. 69.
16. Miller, "Some Observations on the Political Economy of Population Growth," p. 615.
17. *Ibid.,* p. 627.
18. William Vogt, *People,* New York, 1961.
19. Day and Day, *Too Many Americans,* p. 246.

CHAPTER 6: POPULATION COMPOSITION

1. Alfred C. Kinsey, et al., *Sexual Behavior in the Human Male,* Philadelphia, 1948, p. 664.
2. William J. Goode, *After Divorce,* Glencoe, Ill., 1956, p. 17.
3. John S. Plant, "The Psychiatrist Views Children of Divorced Parents," in Ruth Shonle Cavin, ed., *Marriage and Family in the Modern World,* New York, 1965.
4. U.S. Bureau of the Census, "Advance Data: October 1965 Survey," *Current Population Reports,* P-20:149, Washington, D.C., 1966. The Census Bureau collects data on school enrollment every October. But its fall surveys do not yield data comparable to that collected in the decennial census, because the latter refers to school enrollment as of April 1. Nevertheless, the two are sufficiently similar to reveal that the basic trends in evidence in 1960 have persisted during the postcensal years.
5. Statistics pertaining to the educational attainment of the population are generally limited to adults age twenty-five and over. The reason for this is that by the time they have attained age twenty-five, almost all persons have completed the amount of education to which they aspire, which they can afford, or which they have been required to obtain.
6. U.S. Bureau of the Census, "Projections of Educational Attainment in the United States: 1965 to 1985," *Current Population Reports,* P-25:305, Washington, D.C., 1965.
7. In the decennial censuses and the annual surveys conducted by the Census Bureau, income data refer to income during the calendar

year preceding the enumeration. Thus, although the dates cited in the present context refer to the year in which the data were collected (1950, 1960, and 1965), the statistics actually refer to annual income during the preceding calendar year (1949, 1959, and 1964).

8. This "real income" adjustment is based on the Department of Labor's Consumer Price Index which averaged 124.6 in 1959, compared with 101.8 in 1949. See U.S. Bureau of the Census, "Income of Families and Persons in the United States," *Supplementary Reports*, PC(S1)-18, Washington, D.C., 1962.

9. It should be noted here that such things as the lower educational level and the fewer technical skills of nonwhites are in large measure the results of past discrimination in educational opportunities.

10. For a more detailed discussion of labor force concepts and definitions currently in use in the United States, see U.S. Bureau of the Census, *U.S. Census of Population: 1960*, Final Report PC(1)-1C, *General Social and Economic Characteristics: United States Summary*, Washington, D.C., 1962.

11. U.S. Department of Labor, *Monthly Report of the Labor Force: April, 1965*, Washington, D.C., 1965. Unless otherwise indicated, all data on the characteristics of the labor force in 1965 are derived from this report.

CHAPTER 7: POPULATION DISTRIBUTION

1. U.S. Bureau of the Census, *Historical Statistics of the United States: Colonial Times to 1957*, Washington, D.C., 1960.

2. U.S. Bureau of the Census, *Fifteenth Census of the United States: 1930*, Volume II, Chapter 4, *State of Birth of the Native Population*, Washington, D.C., 1932; and *United States Census of Population: 1960*, Final Report PC(2)-2A, *State of Birth*, Washington, D.C., 1963.

3. As originally defined by the Bureau of the Census, the term "urban" was used to refer to all *incorporated* places of 2,500 or more inhabitants. This initial definition was based on the assumption that politically defined city limits would embrace virtually all persons who were living under conditions that may be regarded as truly urban. By the middle of the twentieth century, however, as more and more people moved out of the cities into the surrounding fringe areas, it became increasingly apparent that this assumption was untenable, and that a change in the basic definition of "urban" was needed. Accordingly, a new definition was formulated for the census of 1950, in which provision

was made to include other places that could be regarded as essentially urban in character (for example, *unincorporated* places of 2,500 or more inhabitants as well as incorporated places). The effect of this definition change was to increase both the number of urban places and the size of the urban population. For those interested in historical trends as well as the current level of urbanization, data are presented in Table VII-3 for 1950 and 1960 on the basis of both the old and the new definitions of "urban." For a more complete discussion of the development of the definition of "urban" currently in use by the Bureau of the Census, see Warren S. Thompson and David T. Lewis, *Population Problems,* New York, 1965, pp. 129–138.

4. A similar transformation is taking place in the economically under-developed countries of the non-Western world. Lately, in fact, the process of urbanization has been more rapid than in the West. During the 1950's the urban population of the developed nations increased by about 25 per cent, compared with an increase of over 50 per cent in underdeveloped countries. See Jean Bourgeois-Pichat, *Population Growth and Development,* International Conciliation No. 566, Carnegie Endowment for Industrial Peace (January 1966).

5. This discussion of historical trends in agricultural and non-agricultural employment is based on data contained in the *Historical Statistics* volume cited in note 1 above.

6. For the classic sociological treatment of this phenomenon, see Roderick D. McKenzie, *The Metropolitan Community,* New York, 1933.

7. Standard metropolitan statistical areas (SMSA's) are large urban ag-glomerations which generally include a central city or cities of fifty thousand or more, the county or counties in which the central city is located, and adjacent counties that are sufficiently integrated with the socioeconomic life of the central city to qualify as part of its area of influence. For a more explicit discussion of the SMSA concept and the criteria used to establish it, see U.S. Bureau of the Budget, *Standard Metropolitan Statistical Areas,* Washington, D.C., 1961; and U.S. Bureau of the Census, *United States Census of Population: 1960,* Final Report PC(3)-1D, *Standard Metropolitan Statistical Areas,* Washington, D.C., 1963.

8. U.S. Bureau of the Census, "Population of the United States by Metro-politan and Nonmetropolitan Residence, April 1965 and 1960," *Current Population Reports,* P-20:151, Washington, D.C., 1966.

9. U.S. Bureau of the Census, *United States Census of Population: 1960,* Final Report PC(1)-1A, *Number of Inhabitants: United States Summary,* Washington, D.C., 1961.

10. U.S. Bureau of the Census, *United States Census of Population: 1960,* Final Report PC(3)-1D, *Standard Metropolitan Statistical Areas,* Washington, D.C., 1963. The per cents cited were computed from data in Table 1 of this report.

11. In several urban centers in the northeastern United States, the concentration of nonwhites has been accompanied by substantial increases in the Puerto Rican population. This latter group—in addition to possessing low levels of education, technical skills, income, and so forth—has the added burden of overcoming a language barrier in trying to become established members of the community. Previously the Puerto Rican population was confined largely to New York City, but more recently they have been spreading out to other urban centers in Connecticut, New Jersey, and other northeastern states. See U.S. Bureau of the Census, *United States Census of Population: 1960,* Final Report PC(2)-1D, *Puerto Ricans in the United States,* Washington, D.C., 1963.

12. Thompson and Lewis, *Population Problems,* p. 162.

13. Lowry Nelson, *Rural Sociology,* New York, 1953, p. 143.

14. Mitchell Gordon, *Sick Cities,* Baltimore, 1965, p. 110. This book, a very readable account of many of the social ills facing urban America today, is a major reference for this chapter.

15. U.S. Bureau of the Census, *United States Census of Housing: 1960,* Final Report HC(1)-1, Washington, D.C., 1963.

16. To take another illustration, statistics compiled by the National Vital Statistics Division of the National Center for Health Statistics disclose a tripling of the illegitimate birth rate between 1940 and 1960. See U.S. National Center for Health Statistics, National Vital Statistics Division, *Vital Statistics of the United States: 1960,* I:1, *Natality Statistics,* Washington, D.C., 1962.

17. Gordon, *Sick Cities,* pp. 306–307.

18. *Ibid.,* p. 307.

19. George Sternlieb, "The Future of Retailing in the Downtown Core," in Tietze McKeown, ed., *The Changing Metropolis,* Boston, 1964, p. 60.

20. Gordon, *Sick Cities,* p. 220.

21. *Ibid.,* p. 231.

22. *Ibid.,* pp. 230–231.

23. *Ibid.,* p. 419.

Index

Mortality levels: and fertility, 80–81, 83; and food supply, 26–27; and physical environment, 27–28; pre-industrial, 26–29, 172–173; in underdeveloped areas, 37–38, 174–176; in the U.S. (*see* Mortality differentials; Mortality trends)

Mortality trends: outlook for the future, 74–75; postwar cessation of, 42, 43, 68–75; pre-1900, 39–40; in the twentieth century, 40–44; in underdeveloped areas, 37–38, 174–176; in the U.S., 38–44, 68–75. *See also* Mortality decline.

National Health Survey, U.S., 76

National Origins Quota System, 141–142; discriminatory basis, 141; repeal of, 144

Nativity, 223–225; and age, 60; and mortality, 58–60; social significance of, 223–224

Natural increase, rate of, 181

Nelson, Lowry, 299

Neonatal mortality, 49

"New" immigrants, 136; discrimination of, 139–142

Non-quota immigration, 142

O'Brien, Rev. John A., 292

Obesity, and mortality, 54

Occupation, 241; by color, 249; death rates by, 63, 64; and education and income, 64–65, 251; and fertility, 293; group differences, 249–251; industrialization, 246; trends, 244–246

"Old" immigrants, 136–137, 142

Open spaces, loss of, 197–199, 275–276, 282–283

Osborn, Fairfield, 208

Osborn, Frederick, 195, 208, 295

Paddock, William and Paul, 208

Parasitic disease. *See* Acute disease.

Pasteur, Louis, 34, 47

Patterson, John E., 109, 116, 124, 293

Pessary, 90

Petersen, William, 168, 294

Pills, contraceptive, 90, 99, 107, 119

Plant, John S., 296

Pollution. *See* Air pollution; Water pollution.

Population: as a problem, 4–6; as a social process, 19–21; in the U.S., 6–12. *See also* specific topics.

Population "bomb," 205

Population composition: defined, 209–211; demographic composition, 211–225; socioeconomic composition, 226–251

Population distribution: by color, 260, 264, 267; metropolitan residence, 265–268; region, 255, 257–258; role of migration, 153, 253; unevenness of, 252

Population dynamics, 13

Population growth, components of, 177–179; and economic development, 5, 184–187, 200–201, 205–206, 252–253; general trends, 169–183; historical, 169–174; recent world trends, 174–176; U.S. trends, 177–183, 255–260

Population growth, problems of, 184–208; and food crisis, 187–192; implications for peace, 192–194, 200; qualitative problems, 196–199; and resources in the U.S., 194–196; threat to freedom, 199–203

Population mobility: concepts and definitions, 153–155; problems of, 162–168; trends in the U.S., 153–162, 253–268

Population size and growth, 169–208

Population statics, 13

Population structure, 209, 211

Positive checks, 188

Post-neonatal mortality, 49

A Note on the Author

Edward G. Stockwell studied at Harvard, Connecticut, and Brown universities, and is now Professor of Rural Sociology at the University of Connecticut. Mr. Stockwell has served as a population analyst for the United States Bureau of the Census and has written more than sixty articles on population in the past decade. He lives in Storrs, Connecticut, with his wife and three children.